EUROPE AND EMPIRE

FORDHAM UNIVERSITY PRESS NEW YORK 2016

COMMONALITIES

Timothy C. Campbell, series editor

EUROPE AND EMPIRE

On the Political Forms of Globalization

MASSIMO CACCIARI

Edited by Alessandro Carrera

Translated by Massimo Verdicchio

The editor wishes to acknowledge the financial support of the Grant-in-Aid Program of the University of Houston in the publication of this book.

The translation of this work has been funded by SEPS
Segretariato Europeo per le Pubblicazioni Scientifiche

S E P S
SEGRETARIATO EUROPEO PER LE PUBBLICAZIONI SCIENTIFICHE

Via Val d'Aposa 7 - 40123 Bologna - Italy
seps@seps.it - www.seps.it

Fordham University Press has no responsibility for the persistence or accuracy of URLs for external or third-party Internet websites referred to in this publication and does not guarantee that any content on such websites is, or will remain, accurate or appropriate.

Fordham University Press also publishes its books in a variety of electronic formats. Some content that appears in print may not be available in electronic books.

Visit us online at www.fordhampress.com.

Library of Congress Cataloging-in-Publication Data

Names: Cacciari, Massimo, author. | Carrera, Alessandro, 1954– editor. | Verdicchio, Massimo, 1945– translator.
Title: Europe and empire : on the political forms of globalization / Massimo Cacciari ; edited by Alessandro Carrera ; translated by Massimo Verdicchio.
Description: First edition. | New York : Fordham University Press, [2016] | Series: Commonalities | Includes bibliographical references and index.
Identifiers: LCCN 2015017375| ISBN 9780823267163 (hardback) | ISBN 9780823267170 (paper)
Subjects: LCSH: European federation. | Europe—Politics and government. | Globalization—Europe. | European cooperation. | Europe—Ethnic relations. | Religion and state—Europe. | BISAC: POLITICAL SCIENCE / History & Theory. | POLITICAL SCIENCE / Civics & Citizenship.
Classification: LCC D1060 .C223 2016 | DDC 327.4—dc23
LC record available at http://lccn.loc.gov/2015017375

Printed in the United States of America

18 17 16   5 4 3 2 1

First edition

CONTENTS

Preface vii

Previous Publication ix

Introduction: Massimo Cacciari's Genealogy
of Europe
Alessandro Carrera 1

Part I   Thinking Europe

1 Thinking Europe 35

2 Europeanism 44

3 Two German Speeches:

  The "Second Thought" 49

  The Language of Europe 53

4 Europe or Philosophy 57

5 Europe or Christianity 69

Part II   The Idea of Empire

6 What Is Empire? 97

7 The Myth of the Growing City 101

8 Digressions on Empire
and the Three Romes 111

9 More on the Idea of Empire 133

10 Empire and *Katechon*: A Question
of Political Theology (from Paul,
2 Thessalonians 2) 145

Addenda

11 The Europe of María Zambrano 159

12 We Cannot Call Ourselves Only
Judeo-Christians: A Conversation
with Jacques Le Goff 165

Notes 173

Works Cited 187

Index of Names 197

PREFACE

With the exception of the recent chapter on the *katechon*, I have written the essays collected in this volume in years when, at least to me, it looked like Europe was getting close to embracing a political and cultural constitution that would have made the European voice *heard* in the initial stage of the global era, after the fall of the Berlin Wall and the end of *Third* World War. To me and many others it appeared that the construction of European political unity, no matter the different accents and perspectives involved, ought to be guided by an *idea* and not just by unstoppable, market-driven necessities. It seemed that the twilight of hegemonic will to power, which had been the constant trait of European history, could signal a *new beginning*—in the wake of great traditions, undoubtedly, for every true innovation is also a reformation. My attention to the idea of empire as opposed to monarchy or, worse, tyranny stemmed from a reconsideration of some key categories of Roman law, especially the concepts of republic (*res publica*) and city (*civitas*), which were the soul of the Roman system. I can say the same for my attention to the idea of a universal public authority (*publica auctoritas universalis*), today often invoked every time the economic and financial globalization, unable to follow any rule except the market law (*lex mercatoria*), unleashes a new catastrophic crisis.

An idea of Europe as a real, strong political organism made of nations (*ex nationibus*), founded on the lasting value of their languages and traditions, at the twilight of European will to power—that was the new beginning I was trying to *read*. Considering the possibility of a new start, I set out to discern a paradigm of international relations among the great areas of the planet. It was an idea of empire as the expression of a groundbreaking pact (*foedus*) among free subjects that would understand the pact's *necessity* and on this realistic basis be willing to turn it into a *destiny*. It was an idea of empire as a relation among *autonomous* realities. In other words, an idea of Europe as a political and cultural space *in between*. Because being-in-between (*Zwischen-sein*) has always been the essence of Europe: an unending translation between East and the West, Mediterranean and Romània, Romània and Germania (Tacitus!). This *destination* is the only "value" that a united Europe ought to present to the globalized world: a political entity capable of self-translation, confident among people who are truly Other, and that finds its own identity in the act of taking care of them.

History has replied harshly to all these ideas. In the last decade, after the dream of the European Constitution failed—mostly on the account of the staggering cultural and political weakness of those who were supposed to build its frame—the European Union, pushed by the great economic crisis, has exalted its technocratic-financial side while remaining conspicuously absent in all the tragedies of the recent years. (In fact, when the European Union was present, it just followed other actors, often making things worse.) Entirely oblivious to the events unfolding on the "other shore," Europe tolerated that the Mediterranean, *her* sea, would turn into a *graveyard*. As the recent elections of the European Parliament have clearly shown, the collapse of solidarity and hospitality that has tarnished Europe's image may now be irreversible, and it also threatens the entire fabric of the union.

In the end, it seems that no resurrection will follow the demise of European political and military power, sanctioned by two suicidal world wars. The end of Europe as the political center of the world will find its conclusion in the end of Europe as a cultural and religious center (recent events in Christianity seems to point in that direction). Yet, which other history can provide the fundamental principles of a dialogue among peoples and cultures, a dialogue free from the obsession of reducing everything to One (*reductio ad unum*)? Where else can we look for a *res publica* in which political participation wields true power (*potestas*) and is not limited to electoral representation? Again, which history should we look to if we don't want to restrict the political to the supposed "laws" of economy and finance, their supposed mechanisms and automatisms, and if we don't want to hand it over, in the end, to the dire consequences that the primacy of those "laws" has produced and produces? The political unity of Europe is still a necessity, even though it is less and less likely to happen.

PREVIOUS PUBLICATION

"L'Europa di María Zambrano." *Paradosso. Quadrimestrale di filosofia* 3, no. 8 (1994): 173–178.

"Il mito della *civitas augescens.*" *Il Veltro. Rivista della civiltà italiana* 41, nos. 2–4 (1997): 161–168.

"Pensare l'Europa." *MicroMega* 4 (1999): 199–207.

"Europa o Cristianità." In *Dopo 2000 anni di Cristianesimo*, ed. Servizio Nazionale della Conferenza Episcopale Italiana per il Progetto Culturale, 103–132. Milan: Mondadori, 1999.

"Due discorsi tedeschi: Il 'pensiero secondo'; Il linguaggio d'Europa." *MicroMega* 1 (2001): 165–173.

"Digressioni su impero e tre rome." *MicroMega* 5 (2001): 43–63.

"Ancora sull'idea di impero." *MicroMega* 4 (2002): 185–196.

"Le Goff–Cacciari: Non possiamo definirci soltanto giudeo-cristiani [interview]." Ed. Vittorio Borelli. *East: Europe and Asia Strategies* 1 (2004): 8–17.

"Europa o filosofia." In *Filosofia per l'Europa. Differenze in dialogo*, ed. Luigi Alici and Francesco Totaro, 21–33. Macerata: EUM, 2006.

"Europeismo." In *Enciclopedia Filosofica Bompiani*, 4:3860–3862. Milan: Bompiani, 2006.

"Impero." In *Enciclopedia Filosofica Bompiani*, 6:5569–5571. Milan: Bompiani, 2006.

"Impero e *katechon*. Un problema di teologia politica (da Paolo, Seconda Lettera ai Tessalonicesi)." 2012. Unpublished.

EUROPE AND EMPIRE

INTRODUCTION: MASSIMO CACCIARI'S GENEALOGY OF EUROPE

ALESSANDRO CARRERA

> We must ask ourselves whether history is trying to create a synthesis between two Nietzschean concepts, the good European and the last man. The result could be the last European. We are all struggling not to become last Europeans.
>
> —WALTER BENJAMIN TO STEPHAN LACKNER, MARCH 16, 1937.[1]

THE FOUNDATION COMES TO THE RESCUE

In the winter of 1942–1943, when England was under siege from Germany, the British Minister of Education convened a Conference of the Ministers of Education of eight governments that were allied to England. In February 1943, the conference appointed a Books Commission whose primary purpose was to provide a supply of English books and periodicals to the members of the conference then occupied by the enemy. The purpose was achieved, and books were delivered wherever possible and on a constant basis from 1943 to 1945. A further goal of the conference was to select a pool of scholars to produce an "objective" history of European civilization and make it available in all the member countries, and other countries as well, once the war was over (the quiet assuredness on the part of the conference that the Axis powers were not to win the war was in itself remarkable). In March 1943, the Books Commission appointed a History Committee that proceeded to draft a large work in seven chronological parts, from prehistory to the present, complete with maps, illustrations, and selected documents. The book, called *The European Inheritance*, was to be translated in all the main languages of continental Europe and directed primarily to high school seniors and students in the early years of college. It had to be the work of independent scholars invited by the editorial board of a reputed university press to guarantee the scientific quality of the project. Clarendon Press was approached, and the editorial board was chosen in March 1944. Subsequently, the Conference of Allied Ministers of Education disclaimed all responsibility for the form and substance of the volume so as to dispel the slightest doubt of political interference with the work of the scholars. The project took time, but in 1954 Clarendon Press eventually published the three volumes of *The European Inheritance*.

Even taking into account the dramatic circumstances in which the work was conceived, one cannot fail to notice its deliciously monastic, Benedictine flavor. And, if one is inclined to make the jump from the Middle Ages to science fiction, the cosmic dream of the young Isaac Asimov comes to mind, who in 1951 published the first installment of his *Foundation* trilogy. In Asimov's tale of the distant future, a group of historians facing the imminent fall of the Galactic Empire takes on the task of compiling a Galactic Encyclopedia in order to shorten the Dark Ages to come from thirty thousand to one thousand years and foster the advent of a new Empire Renaissance. Asimov's faith in history, however, was split. As the reader soon finds out, the Galactic Encyclopedia is little more than a diversion meant to hide that the real saviors of civilization are the mysterious and seemingly omnipotent "psychologists" whose Second Foundation is nowhere to be found. History is a façade; what really matters is the psychology of the Galactic man and how to keep him in check. In a similar fashion, we may wonder whether the authors of *The European Inheritance* were dealing with their continent's "objective" history or the perennial character of the European man. The Preface to the book explicitly said:

> The work is not a history of mankind. But it is, at any rate, a history of European man, and of his influence on the rest of mankind. This is not to say, for a moment, that it has a European bias, or that it attempts to vindicate a particular eminence for the continent of Europe over other continents. It would not be "objective history" if it had this bias or made

that attempt. It is just a record of Europe and the overseas growth of Europe, set down by a number of scholars of European birth or origin, with the intention of communicating to the youth of Europe, as dispassionately and as justly as possible, some sense of the inheritance of Europe and the spread and the influence of that inheritance.

(Barker et al., 1:vii)

That the point of view of the "European man" was inherently and inevitably biased is such an acquired notion today that it would be unfair to disparage the scholars involved in the Inheritance project in the terms of the criticism that Western culture has directed at itself in post–World War II years. The cultural frame of the mid twentieth century could not be free from the legacy of colonialism and the assumption of European cultural superiority, no matter how sincere the effort was. Yet the scholars could not ignore that Europe had been on the brink of self-annihilation for almost thirty years on the account of its inner demons and not because of an external, malignant force. Was the character of the "European man" inherently flawed? Or had the decadence lamented by so many strong European spirits for so many years finally taken its toll? Perhaps that matter was indeed one for the mysterious psychologists to decide (Freud? Jung? Wilhelm Reich?). The "Conclusions" at the end of the third volume, arguably written in 1952, described a Western Europe "standing at the cross-roads" not so much between capitalism and socialism (that split had been settled with the Yalta Conference and the division of Europe between the USSR and U.S. spheres of influence) but between democracy and technocracy:

Men of goodwill in the west, who devote their energy to the cause of a future Union of Europe, believe that the continent will somehow or other be one day organized, and that if this result is not achieved democratically, by a full-scale system of parliamentary institutions, it will be achieved by the technocrats—a consummation which might lead Europe into neo-fascism, or into a form of anti-Stalin communism in the style of Tito.

(Barker et al., 3:268)

The oscillation between the temptation of technocracy (a pure administrative machine free from the burden of political choices) and the uncertainty of an untested common European democracy is—still today—the mark of the European Union. It is the greatest sign of Europe's strength and the most visible signal of its weakness. The authors of *The European Inheritance* correctly pointed out that the European mind was torn between humanism and the infinite. The Ptolemaic tradition, Christianity, democratic liberalism, and even social democracy are systems based on the individuals' sense of their own values and the assumption that man is the measure of all things. But the Copernican revolution disclosed a different universe, one not adjusted to human measure and situated well beyond man's limited grasp. In this nonanthropocentric perspective, man is cast from his birth into a world of overwhelming forces that can destroy him at any moment—a world in which he can assure his survival only by increasing his powers at the expense of his fellow creatures. Nietzsche was "the first European to proclaim the contradiction between these two paths and these two different attitudes toward the Infinite" (3:269). It was perhaps no coincidence that he was a German, a citizen of the same nation that, having first reached such a crossroads, would later bring Europe close to destruction.[2]

The European middle class, so the "Conclusions" continue, still clings to the old tradition of humanism and its emphasis on personality, but the masses, engulfed by industrial mechanization and agrarian collectivism, cannot identify with the old individual values. Not only that: given their demographic increase, the masses will ultimately absorb the middle class. An unholy alliance between the proliferating multitudes and omnipotent technology is plotting to extinguish a civilization "whose pride it has been to affirm the greatness of human personality by the creation of strong aristocratic hierarchies" (269).

So much for an unbiased perspective. Still, who could argue with the plea: "At all costs the inheritance of Europe must be saved"? The "nameless catastrophe" of the masses' takeover cannot be allowed to swallow the incomparable treasures of European legacy. Must the tragedy be avoided on the account of Europe's supposed superiority or because cultural legacies, whatever they are and wherever they come from, are too precious to disappear? In other words, shall Europe be saved for the sake of history or for the sake of anthropology? The historians of the Foundation (*pardon*, of Clarendon Press) did not provide an answer. We may surmise that Nietzsche would have appreciated their reference to strong aristocratic hierarchies only to deride the self-importance of such a statement immediately after. The historians, however, were very straightforward in the cure they prescribed for Europe's malaise. The terrified middle class of postwar Europe had to be reassured that a "synthesis" could be reached between the conflicting tendencies of humanism and antihumanism (or, better said: the tendency that comes to terms with the nonhuman scale of the universe). Will to power needed to be replaced by will for solidarity, so much so that the rights of the individual and the rights of the people at large were equally respected. A social disaster, the historians warned, "will bring bourgeois conservatism down to the ground," involving in its ruin the entire European civilization together with its genuine treasures.

In their "unbiased" view, the authors of *The European Inheritance* had no doubts that only bourgeois conservatism could save the day. Sixty years later, a smug response to their conclusion would be no more than a cheap shot. Their diagnosis was accurate. If the remedy was insufficient, the reason was not only that it inclined toward bourgeois conservatism (which, as anyone could see, had been incapable of saving Europe from Fascism, Nazism, Francoism, and Stalinism) but also that the suggested medicine was the old concoction known as "synthesis." The real cultural "tragedy" of bourgeois conservatism was the inability to see that no harmonious polyphony was possible between humanism and antihumanism. On the contrary, precisely the strident, "atonal," yet inescapable coexistence of both paradigms was bound to be the cultural cornerstone of the new Europe.

The Gift of Nihil

Massimo Cacciari's entire "philosophy of Europe" aims to prove that the "synthesis" between such nonreconcilable forces is an ideological myth—exhausting at best, dangerous at worst. It also intended to prove that politics, if it aspires to be "grand politics" or at least effective politics, must situate itself in the gap that separates humanistic finitude from the vertigo of boundlessness, not necessarily deciding once and for all in favor of one or the other. This is the scope of his European trilogy: *Geo-filosofia dell'Europa* (1992), *L'arcipelago* (1997), and this volume, *Europe and Empire*, a collection of essays written between 1994 and 2012. The three works mark Cacciari's progression from political thought to geopolitical philosophy.[3]

Cacciari, whose life has always been divided between academic work, the activism of the public intellectual, and political engagement, was born and raised in Venice, of which he was three times the mayor. The history and location of the "city of islands" have given him the basis for the geopolitical model he has tried to apply toward an idea of Europe that harks back to the once powerful European "archipelagos" (the idea of Europe as made of islands, including continental Europe and not just the South, is also a theme in Braudel's *Mediterranean*).

Cacciari's geopolitics is also a Mediterranean response to the Nordic loss of the "law of the earth" mourned in Carl Schmitt's *The Nomos of the Earth* (1950). While the scholars engaged in the European Inheritance project were busy rebuilding the ruins of Europe with the magic wand of history, Schmitt had been outlining a fascinating yet rather fictitious morphology of the continent based on the juridical opposition between the *jus publicum europaeum*, which applied only on firm soil, and the sea, where piracy and absence of law were the norm from the onset of modernity through the eighteenth century. Here Venice comes into the picture. The city on water has been the geotheoretical tool that Cacciari needed to incorporate the most engaging traits of Schmitt's geopolitics while keeping at a safe distance from Schmitt's inclination to all-too-mythological reconstructions of the European political space.

The very presence of Venice, whose commercial and cultural power over the Mediterranean lasted longer than the Roman Empire, has always undermined the rigid distinctions between land and sea. Venice never fit into the category of *thalattocracy* or sea empire that Schmitt assigned to the maritime empires of the classical antiquity and the modern era. Venice has always been land *and* sea, a living contradiction in the heart of Europe, a simultaneous metaphor of localism and globalism. It was once what New York (another "city of islands") is now: a hybrid meeting place where friends and enemies were free to interact. Turkish merchants came to Venice to do business even when Venice was at war with the Ottoman Empire. Alexandria, Thessaloniki, Smyrna, Venice: they have all been the archipelago-city, hubs of tragic conflicts as well as economic and cultural innovations.

Each Venetian island has a "meaning"; each is singular yet connected to the system. Like a federalist state, the lagoon separates the islands while at the same time uniting and protecting them. In addition to being a living refutation of Schmitt's sharp separation of land and sea, Venice is also Cacciari's Southern answer to the rhizomatic utopia of the nomadic subject proposed by Deleuze and Guattari in *Mille Plateaux* (1980). A nomadic subject presupposes a desert more than it does an archipelago. Neither an "icy monster" (Nietzsche's definition of the state) nor a deflagration of uncontrollable subjectivities, the federation of islands abstains from the melting pot as much as it resists vagrant dissolutions of identity.

Venice escapes the North-South, East-West partitions. The Venetian perspective has allowed Cacciari to avoid being tangled up in the "defense" of Southern Europe against the Orientalist-Mediterraneist stereotypes about backwardness and the refusal of modernity that never cease to come from Northern Europe. (They also perpetuate themselves in the most complacent corners of Southern thought.) He does not ignore the issue. His criticism of what he calls the "Franco-Carolingian axis" (France and Germany deciding autonomously what is good for the rest of Europe, and too bad if the other countries do not keep up) is not, however, formulated in a rhetoric of wounded pride. His analysis remains political: an uncontested Franco-Carolingian hegemony will break Europe apart. Europe stretches from Dublin to Athens, from Moscow to Lisbon, from Stockholm to Sarajevo, and no Northern self-righteous authority lecturing the South will change that fact.[4]

Venice's archipelago is an ideal model, not the all-encompassing solution to the European crisis. Yet the issues of centralism versus federalism and globalization versus localism acquire a new perspective in the light of archipelago politics. Not only is no man an island, but also no island is just an island. Islands need to flourish as islands if they want to maintain their identity, yet they cannot isolate themselves; they must remain open to trade and the arrival of foreigners.

And what if the foreigners are enemies? Drawing from Santo Mazzarino's historical research on the ancient world, Cacciari digs into archaic Mediterranean geopolitics at the time when the geographical and cultural divisions between Europe and Asia were negligible. The Homeric sea knew only cities and harbors, passages from one island to another. There was neither peace nor harmony, but the political-ethnic distinction between East and West—between "them" and "us"—had yet to be born. Greeks and Trojans shared the same civilization and the same gods. They were enemies but not each other's "other." Only the Greek-Persian war forced the Greek archipelago to know the enemy, to *name* it, and to "know itself" in order to defend itself. The result of that epistemological change was the *polis*—which the East never knew—and the birth of politics. Greece is all about boundaries while Asia (from the Greek point of view) is chaotically boundless, and thus, given Asia, the Greeks could not ignore chaos. They needed the Dionysian, "Eastern" injection of chaos in order to define themselves as nonchaos.

Political tragedy and political philosophy were born from this necessity. In *The Persians*, Aeschylus captured perfectly this epochal moment in the history of the West. When the Persian queen Atossa dreams of Europe and Asia as two women who are divided, she is also aware that they are blood sisters—that their origin is one. Aeschylus even called the Greek-Persian war "*stasis*," using a term that has also been applied to civil war.

In opposition to Schmitt and claiming Aeschylus for his side, Cacciari points out that there is nothing primordial about the separation of friend and foe. Aeschylus recognized that friend and foe were united and remained united even when separated. For the same reason, we are "in friendship" with others not despite our differences but thanks to the elusive difference that stems from our unity. The Greek "form" (form of the state or logical form) is differential, defined by the exteriority of the formless. The wisdom of *logos* is the acknowledgment that unity is split into the infinite multiplication of differences. There is a common ground in war and war on common grounds, because what we have in common is solely the unending dissemination of our differences.

Geopolitics is older than Western philosophy. It originates from the traumatic discovery of the "other" and, as a consequence, of the "many." In its endless rethinking of the relationship between the One and the Many, Western philosophy quickly multiplied the differences among opposites. It did not take a long time. Parmenides does not contemplate the *polis* (his poem takes place in a divine-natural space). A few generations later, the *polis* is the very air Socrates and Plato breathe. The post-Parmenidean philosopher already thinks the One (the *polis*) in relationship with the Many (the multiplicity of subjects, plus the "other" subjects that can threaten the life of the *polis*), yet Plato, despite all his writings about *politeia*, does not provide a handbook of "political theory." His gaze is still sovereign, disenchanted, unpolitical (which in Cacciari's language does not mean a-political but *transcendentally* political, suprapolitical, overpolitical). It is only with Aristotle that politics becomes contract, negotiation, division of powers, a politics of "parts" and therefore of "parties." However, as Cacciari observes, the more Aristotle seems to believe that a good set of political instructions will in the end harmonize the city, the more Plato (together with Machiavelli and

Marx—and Spinoza could be added to the mix) looks more realistic to us on the account of his unpolitical side. It is a political or unpolitical paradox that in the long run extremism may turn out to be more realistic than the politics of the "right middle"—as long as it does not abandon Platonic pessimism, though, since even the most perfect *polis* is only a pale imitation of the Supreme Good.

The Greek *polis* was the coming of age of human unnaturalness. It was not supposed to wither and die like any other living creature; it could only *stay* in perpetual *stasis*, thrive, suffer, and affirm its power. In the name of the *polis*, every brutality was sanctioned, as long as it passed the scrutiny of "logic." For the *polis* has values, possesses *logos*, and can count metaphysics on its side. As we implicitly understand from Thucydides, it is in the name of *logos* that Athens destroys harmless Melos, not just because it can but also because it can call on *logos* to justify such a cruel and ultimately unnecessary display of force. Compared with the Athenians' blasphemous self-assurance, even Sparta's cold utilitarianism appears modest. Yet the archipelago sets limits to the amount of power that the *polis* (and *logos*) can amass. In the end, even Athens' hubris was short lived. So was Athens' democracy, soon replaced by Alexander's empire and the fragmentation thereafter. Yet in a civilization run by merchants and sailors no Eastern satrapy or absolute tyranny is likely to dominate forever. Thalattocracy and democracy are intimately connected. As Hegel said in his lessons on the philosophy of history, Asia largely ignored the sea, and as a result, it never knew democracy.

Hegel's statement is obviously debatable or at least needs to be supplemented by contemporary scholarship on the role of the sea in Asian empires, yet early capitalism is unthinkable without an economy based on the sailor's wits and the merchant's greed.[5] The fluidity of water parallels the fluidity of money, so much so that the Greek model will eventually find a new home in Northern Europe and the English maritime empire.

Asia never knew Roman law, either. Both Greek democracy and Roman law do have one thing in common, though. They do not form an organic community. Their political forms are in fact opposed to the notion of community, which on the contrary is the cornerstone of Judaism and Christianity. Yet for the Greeks the *nomos* is still divine. The law-abiding citizen is the god-fearing citizen, and a secularized *nomos* deprived of transcendence is a law without authority. The progressive separation of the *nomos* from its divine root is the story of Greece's decay. The Roman law is less divine (to Cicero, who outlines the legalistic foundation of the *civitas*, there is no citizen but the law-abiding citizen), yet it cannot be entirely separated from a religious component, albeit one limited to the worshiping of the family gods.

Long before Christianity became the official religion of the Roman Empire (a decision that in the end killed the very idea of empire), the Christians pledged allegiance to Rome "as if" Rome were enough to them, when of course it was not. If Rome's weak religious requirements had been sufficient, there would have been no need of transcendence and salvation—and no need for Augustine to write his *City of God*. The Christians were law-abiding citizens, but Christianity was antiterritorial and antiempire by definition. When it became the law of the land, it proceeded immediately to deterritorialize the empire. The Christians, who conceived of themselves as perpetual pilgrims, used the empire to spread the Word. They prayed for the emperor during persecutions because they recognized the imperial power as coming from God, not because they wanted the empire to last forever.

The Power That Holds Back

The only new political figure that early Christianity produced, aside from the role of the papacy, was the *katechon*, the mysterious "power that holds back" elliptically mentioned in St. Paul's 2 Thessalonians (2:3–12). Time is short, says Paul, but do not be impatient about the coming of Christ. First, the man of lawlessness (the Adversary) must be revealed. Only when the Adversary has established his power will the coming of Christ occur. But the lawlessness is held back by something (*to katechon, quid detinet*) or someone (*ho katechon, qui tenet*). When the power that holds back is removed, the final battle between the Son of Perdition and the Son of Salvation will take place, and the Son of Salvation will triumph.

The *katechon* is therefore the force that delays. It delays the rise of the Adversary, the second coming of Christ, and the Apocalypse. By delaying the sufferings that will accompany the end of times, the *katechon* is a power that wants to do good. But by getting in the way of the final judgment and salvation, it is not a good power at all. Eventually, the Christians will have to get rid of him (or it), but not before the lawlessness of the Antichrist (if the Adversary, the Son of Perdition, and the Antichrist are the same person) has taken over and the time is ripe. But exactly who or what is the *katechon*? According to the different interpretations that the Fathers of the Church, from Irenaeus to Augustine, have given of the convoluted Pauline passage (likely to be spurious but originating from his circle), the *katechon* may be a resisting force within the Christian community (those who claim to be Christians without acknowledging the divine, saving nature of Christ, and who are therefore anti-Christ, opposed to Christ); it may be the Roman Empire that "holds back" the evangelization of the world; it may be the church itself (although to say so brings one close to heresy), to the extent that the church has inherited the political authority of Rome and intends to delay the end of times until the Word of God has been announced in every corner of the world. Adversary, Antichrist, and *katechon* are sometimes distinguished, sometimes conflated.

Cacciari has given much thought to the *katechon*, which in fact has become quite an obsession in recent Continental political theory (Schmitt again is responsible for resurrecting the notion).[6] To a certain extent, it may look like a Catholic obsession, concerning primarily Southern Catholic Europe, without much currency in the Nordic, Protestant nations nor in Orthodox Eastern Europe, where the church never rose to autonomous political power. Yet even John Calvin discusses the *katechon*, identifying it first with the Roman Empire and then with the Antichrist. He also admits that the end-of-time lawlessness will not show its face before the Gospel reaches every corner of the Earth, implicitly assuming that the *katechon* will stay in place until that goal is reached.[7] And Cacciari's reading of the *katechon* (which spreads through *Dell'inizio*, *L'arcipelago*, *Il potere che frena*, and this volume) is not without relevance to the analysis of current political crises. Democracy too harbors a "power that holds back," preventing the *polis* from plunging into the lawlessness of destructive conflicts. With its constitutive indecision, democracy may be in fact the ultimate *katechon*, "holding back" the various forces (terrorism, religious fundamentalism, romantic revolutions, catastrophic capitalism) that despise the infuriating slow pace of democratic decisions and want free rein to hasten to the final showdown.

The three major monotheistic religions have neither the power nor the will to rebuild the spirit of the Greek *nomos*, a miraculous balance of human and divine law that appeared only once in the history of Europe. The church, the Word, and the imperative to convert the infidels have tipped the balance in favor of the divine. Democracy's *katechon* has the ungrateful task of keeping the divine at bay. Contempt for democracy, no matter from what section of the religious or political spectrum it is expressed, from the extreme left to the conservative right, harks back to the ancient hatred for the "katechontic" power of the Roman Empire, now transferred to the democratic institutions.

Once the Catholic-Protestant religious wars of the sixteenth and seventeenth centuries were over, the only political form that neutralized the antiterritoriality of Christianity was the modern state envisioned by Hobbes, where no theological guidance was allowed. The lack of transcendent values did not amount to the creation of a perfect machine-like state. Hobbes's state was paradoxically divine in its own right since it could operate only as a conventional god, as a soulless and faithless idol (an "icy monster" indeed). Yet the very lack of values on which the modern state was built was a value in itself (the value of being unaffected by values). The more it was groundless, the more "mystical" its force would appear.

After the crisis of Hobbesian absolute power, the "tyranny of values" (another Schmittian expression) moved on to political parties, in a true proliferation of icy little monsters. And now that the modern state is falling apart even more, its weakened power of holding back whatever needs to be held back is at risk of being nullified by the nihilism of globalization. The Cold War did not pit two visions of the world against each other; it pitted two techniques or technologies out to conquer the same world. Now that the utilitarian trend has won, we might say (as Cacciari observes dryly) that Europe truly wins only by losing, when its worst ideas triumph. Globalized nihilism ruled by the iron fist of "equivalent values" (everything must be equivalent except equivalence) still bears the European imprint. Nihilism, this most "unwelcome guest" (Nietzsche's words again), has been Europe's ambiguous gift to the world.

But where does it come from? From which Greek mountain, from which cave hidden in one of the thousand islands of the archipelago? Perhaps nihilism is just the obverse of the spirit of inquiry that has animated Europe from the onset of its civilization: never be content, always rationalize, always "make it new," always suspect, always destroy the values (the "illusions," as Leopardi would say) that the previous generations created, always be equally tempted by totalitarian order and social anarchy—but, most of all, always set out to sea to reach the next island, the faraway Strait of Gibraltar, the unpeopled world behind the sun (as Dante's Ulysses did), or a higher ground from where the future will appear in all its glory, only to be cast away as soon as it recedes into the past. In the words of the Italian philosopher Emanuele Severino (with whom Cacciari is in constant, implicit, "friendly disagreement"), European nihilism stems from the post-Parmenidean "folly" of positing absolute faith in Becoming at the expense of Being.[8] Drawing inspiration from Hannah Arendt, Cacciari also observes that the predicament of Western modernity may be indeed the ultimate revenge of the ancient European Gnosis, which now has touched on the whole world: namely, the assumption that the technoscientific project will finally "free" men and women from the boundaries of their worldly prison.

In the Homeric world, war is justified on mythical and heroic grounds. Beginning with Athens and its treatment of Melos, Europe has constantly tried to find a rational legitimization for the use of its power, not being content in justifying it with the mere desire to acquire new land or secure a new route of commerce. Obviously, this is not an excuse for the Crusades, Inquisition, the burning of witches, colonialism, or anti-Semitism. The point is that every power based on *logos* aspires to build the Harmonious City. Liberalism, the most recent harvest of this crop, wishes to achieve harmony through strict market rules and mild cultural tolerance. But tolerance is supposed to absorb all dissonances, even those that cannot be harmonically resolved. Besides, one can only "tolerate" what one does not take as true. Indifferent tolerance is ineffective at best and insulting at worst. To Cacciari, it is crucial that difference be taken at face value, as essential to the ontological connection among all the differences that resist harmonizing. The connecting factor among radically different entities is precisely their difference. Every difference affects someone else's difference. *My* difference affects *your* difference. Your difference may have a rippling effect on my difference and the difference of those connected to me by means of previous differences. Difference, not harmony, is what keeps us together, in peace as well as in war. But how to think the essential differences, differences supposed to remain different, without despairing about the actual possibility of living together with them?

Ramon Llull and Nicholas of Cusa may have been among the few Europeans who happened to "think the difference" in a way that did not minimize its otherness. While Llull was busy trying to convert the Saracens to the "logic" of Christianity and free Christianity from Jewish influence, he also wrote the *Book of the Gentile and the Three Wise Men* (1274–1276), the sweet parable of a non-nihilistic quest. A Christian, a Muslim, and a Jew explain their theologies to a doubtful pagan. When he announces to them that he has finally decided which religion to embrace, the three wise men do not want to hear his choice, fearing they would lose the pleasure of meeting again to resume their conversation. Similarly, Nicholas of Cusa in his *De pace fidei* (written in 1453, his response to the fall of Constantinople) tries to convince Jews and Muslims that Christian truth is theological, not mystical, and therefore more logical than their religions. The incarnation of Christ signals the epiphany of Truth, the necessity to live according to Truth (and not, we may say, according to indifferent harmony). Yet in the end, Nicholas admits that all the names and definitions of the deity are insufficient, the only true theology is negative theology, and all the conjectures about God can be true, for every conjecture is a sign of the ineffable truth.

This is the thought that Europe needs. It is within its grasp. It still could be its destiny, but only if Europe understands that such a destiny is shrouded in the evening light. The only course that Europe can adopt is to move consciously toward its sunset, which is not the same as twilight and certainly not the same as decadence. Europe's danger lies in its resistance to "setting," in its unwillingness to understand that sunset harbors more possibilities than any defense against it. Setting is Europe's destiny and Europe's only. It is not America's or China's or India's. It belongs to Europe alone.

It is destiny, but it must be chosen. Europe must decide for it (otherwise, others will decide). And setting is not an idle exercise; it is not weak ontology. It is a hard task. Europe must face the terrifying task of "letting go" of itself, opening up to the very possibility that immigration and a new, unpredictable multicultural landscape will change in few generations everything we know about the "European Inheritance," whatever it may be and whatever the present generation wants it to be. "For whoever wishes to save his life will lose it; but whoever loses his life will find it" (Mt. 16:25).

THE PLEASURES OF SELF-CASTRATION

Unfortunately, this is not what Europe is about today. In the eyes of the world, the European Union is still a UPO, an Unidentified Political Object. The historical agreement that led to its common currency has come with severe limitations on common politics, and the results of the monetary union have been so hampered by recession and crushing fiscal puritanism that the Europeans can hardly be asked to look serenely at the end of their day. The European Union, after all, was possible because after the catastrophe of World War II no state was strong enough to undermine it. Weakness has been Europe's best resource, but how long can one be strong by being weak? Before the market collapse of 2008, the undisputable principles of Europe were stability and irreversibility, as if no further political decisions were needed, only administrative ones. And the crisis has not changed significantly the frame of mind of the European bureaucrats. In a way, the model they were aspiring to reach was close to Francis Bacon's New Atlantis: a society of distant, benign technocrats and mild religious commitment fully healed from the constant pain of day-to-day politics.

Yet it is the European *homo democraticus* (Cacciari uses this term, whose history stretches from Tocqueville to Habermas, freely) who wants a strong economy and a weak politics. The European Union is not supposed to have a politics; it is supposed to protect the European citizens from it. Should this asymmetry be overcome? Or should we not, lest we stir demons better left sleeping? At any rate, the stability reached so far cannot be considered stable. In the end, political decisions are inevitable. But they cannot move toward a more powerful central government, which will lose political legitimacy in the individual countries. Cacciari has made the point innumerable times: nobody can unify Europe. After the fall of the Roman Empire, no one has succeeded. Not Charlemagne, not the Roman Church, not Napoleon. The only alternative is federalism, a Europe of cities and regions and not of national states. Europe's weakness can turn into strength if Europe can look at itself as an archipelago, a community of analogous, interconnected elements. To be sure, there is no real federalism without reversibility, without the chance to secede from the union. But who or what will secede, in a true federalist Europe? The real question is if politics beyond the national state is possible. Europe is still on the threshold that separates state and federation, unity of intent and multiplicity of subjects, politics and community; it is once again suspended, uncertain, Hamletic, *undecided*.

Being undecided is not necessarily the worst thing that can happen to Europe. Paraphrasing Carl Schmitt, Europe could learn a thing or two from the Catholic Church, which never really decided to be entirely in the world or out of the world. Nor has it decided whether human nature is saint, corrupted, or weak (Schmitt, *Roman Catholicism and Political Form*, 7–8).

Given the multiplicity of cultures that have shaped its history, Europe cannot decide to be *this* and not *that*. It is likely that even the common currency has been too much of a decision for Europe's inherent fragility. When Cacciari and Jacques Le Goff, in the interview in the final chapter of this volume, say, "we cannot only call ourselves Judeo-Christians," they mean that Europe must stay true to its original quest for the Unattainable, to its negative theology.

Thousands of years ago, Europe was the West the exiles from the East wanted to reach. Aeneas carried Troy with him when he reached the shores of Italy. In time immemorial, when Zeus tore Europa away from Asia and turned her into an exiled wanderer, a "sunset" (*arapu, erepu* in Acadian), whoever looked for her, like her brother Cadmus, became "European." *Everyone* can become a European, just like everyone, so we are told, can become an American. This was once the truth of Europe now put to the test every time a boat carrying immigrants or refugees sinks in the Mediterranean Sea.

Will Europe be strong enough to welcome the foreigners that will inhabit its sunset? Will the foreigners be strong enough to live in a land whose sun is setting and not rising? Contemporary European philosophy has repeatedly tried to make sense of Europe's suicidal tendencies (World War I and II) and then of the cowardice and impotence that followed, particularly striking during the Yugoslavian war of the 1990s. Spengler, Valéry, Husserl, Heidegger, Ortega y Gasset, Camus, Sartre, Weil, Arendt, Zambrano, Habermas, Derrida, Balibar, and Žižek (as well as Cacciari, Negri, Severino, Agamben, and many others) have repeatedly asked, "What is Europe?" (that is, "What has become of Europe?"), which also means "What is philosophy?" (that is, "What has become of philosophy?"). Under the scrutiny of their genealogical gaze, philosophy has been tortured to confess its secret. Which, in the wake of the Spanish philosopher María Zambrano (whom Cacciari often quotes), is philosophy itself, its will to power.

It is not a tautology. To conquer Europe, philosophy had to kill God and replace it with Spirit. Not the Holy Ghost but Hegel's *Geist*, a Ghost that has superseded the Father and the Son. The killing was so effective that the entire spectrum of European thought is now devoid of "presence" and universally "spiritualized" (Nietzsche, who foresaw pretty much everything, had already anticipated the outcome). The only true power, as Schmitt used to say, is the power to decide in a state of exception. Philosophy does not decide much (not anymore, at least), yet since Kant moved it away from ontology and toward criticism, philosophy too has lived in a constant state of exception. There is no philosophy but critical philosophy. Nietzsche's genealogical turn (the blueprint for all the turns that followed, with the possible exception of Husserlian phenomenology) has perfected criticism, making it the standard modus operandi of European thought.

In Zambrano's words, Europe is a *voz abismática*, a "voice from the abyss" that constantly asks the gods who and what they are. When the gods hear the question, they withdraw, leaving only their absence behind them. But philosophy wants to think presence, not absence. European philosophy has always tried to eradicate absence and substitute it with absolute presence. If God prefers to be absent, then philosophy kills the absent God out of philosophical love for the Spirit-God that can be made into an object of thought, an object opposite to the ineffable and unthinkable God exiled from the world. The love object of the mystic cannot be consumed, but philosophy is the opposite of mysticism: it is bent to devour the objects of its thought.

The god who was killed, we might say, was not the intellectual god of Descartes, Spinoza, and Leibniz. That god is alive and well, albeit turned into an object for theologians in the same way that science has its objects of research. To Zambrano, the god who was killed was the god in flesh and blood, the god who could walk on the face of the earth as a person and not as an abstraction. This is the god that Spirit has replaced. Ramon Llull and Nicholas of Cusa seriously wanted to convince Jews and Muslims that Christianity was logical. Thomas Aquinas was equally well intentioned when he tried to demonstrate that Aristotle and the Gospels were not incompatible. And he was right, but only to the extent that he succeeded (without Aquinas's legitimization of Aristotelian inquiry there would be no Western science). Yet Augustine had already stretched the looming formlessness of the Trinity into a Trinitarian logic. Augustine's gaze was still torn between pure transcendence, Neoplatonist intellectualism, and mystical proximity. Yet he too contributed to the philosophical disenchantment of Europe by making God understandable. Come modernity, and after philosophy killed every god that was left and turned it into "historical reason," the skilled murderer could only kill itself. Did it also kill Europe with it?

The Spirit is a mischievous God. Now it is the genius of the times; tomorrow it is a murderous ideology. It is a bad God. It claims to be thinkable, but it hides more than it reveals. It does not allow its truth to be stripped naked and show itself as the problem that it is. Philosophy has disenchanted the world. It was its mission, and it has been accomplished. The Europeans have become too sophisticated to believe in their beliefs. But all the postmodern attempts to scale down the problem of truth look like a desperate doctor who keeps saying that the patient is fine while it is the doctor himself who is sick.

The complete rationalization of Christianity, which was the task Hegel assigned himself (Trinitarian dialectics fully replacing Trinity), led to the possibility for the "last man," the *homo democraticus*, to kill God while hurrying up to his Sunday rite. This is what Nietzsche's *Gay Science* means when the fool tells the people in the market square that "God is dead" and "I am looking for God." Yet, as Friedrich Hölderlin problematically said (he was never sure about the matter), the absence of the gods, however despairing, protects men from an overwhelming presence. And, as René Char put it in clear terms, the gods wither when they linger too close to us. After more than two centuries of critical and genealogical thinking, Europe still does not know whether the spiritualization of God was a good "decision," a decision at all, or just the fulfillment of an ancient destiny.

Exasperated self-awareness stifles creation and the willingness to take a stand, and Europe's physiological indecision shows alarming signs of becoming pathological. Maybe the psychologists of the Second Foundation could give us an answer that lies beyond the historians and the philosophers' reach. Let us put it this way: after 1945, and having barely survived its second attempt at suicide, Europe decided to castrate itself. Noble renunciation of power was no longer sufficient. A more decisive, preventive measure had to be taken. The European Union and the common currency were the yataghans that accomplished the deed. The incestuous desire of the European man to violate its own origins (the mother of Minos, the first judge-king of Crete, was the nymph Europa) had to be curtailed. And Europe castrated itself. Not like Origen, who in the second century believed that the Second Coming was imminent and that bodies had to be pure to face the Final Judgment. Not to reach Paradise, and not even in submission to the powers who fought the Cold War over the skies of the European continent. It was not a symbolic castration, like the transfer of the image of power from the sovereign's body to his scepter. It was the real thing. Zeus's rape of Europa was finally vindicated. Europe castrated itself to enjoy the sublimated pleasures of impotence, the precious delights that in the courts of ancient empires were the precinct of the eunuchs.

The pleasures of self-castration belong to the *homo democraticus*, who cherish them dearly. He complains a lot, yet he has never been so pleasantly distracted from his sufferings. Or maybe he complains a lot precisely because the pleasures derived from castration (the sublimity of impotence, which Leopardi had foreseen) do not suppress desire. The democratic project needs a multiplication of individual appetites that only gadgets, the market, and popular culture (not politics or values) can satisfy. *Homo democraticus*, alternately a law-abiding citizen or the ravenous beast who cares about nothing but his private interests, is the result of the modern liberation of appetites. He is "logically," dogmatically certain of the goodness of his urges as much as Athens was certain of *logos*. The market economy supports his belief, and the separation of beauty from the good reaffirms his conviction. Yet he is not the master in his house; he is not an *Übermensch* who creates his own values and fights to defend them. He needs to be protected, and his relentless activism in defense of his next best deal pushes the society toward the same anarchy that he fears above everything else. His actions nullify the very principle of representation since he demands to be represented without political mediation, and immediate representation is a contradictory notion. His constant request for "freedom" from politics and the state coincides with an increased demand for protection and security. As Tocqueville, Canetti, and Bataille have repeatedly explained, the flip side of anarchic tendencies is a strong need for impersonal authority. The sovereign presides over anarchy, and anarchy feels safe under the hard heel of the sovereign.

The *homo democraticus* may very well be Nietzsche's "last man," one of the most puzzling characters in *Thus Spoke Zarathustra*. The last man can neither rule nor obey; he hates everybody but loves his hate. He is Dostoevsky's "man from the underground," always resentful, always complaining, a true icon of the "end of history" that has already occurred and therefore may go on forever. The opposite of the last man is Nietzsche's overman, but only to the extent that he or she (the *Übermensch* is not necessarily genderized) is understood as will to power that has reached the ultimate goal, the power to will or not to will.

In Cacciari's interpretation, the overman is essentially he or she who is dissimilar, neither a founder of cities nor the charismatic leader of communities.

In the wake of Derrida's *Politics of Friendship*, Cacciari understands the overman as the community of those who are without a community, those free to meet and leave any time they want: an "unpolitical" community not dictated by the constraints of biopolitics (which is the domain of the last man) and whose reciprocal gift is not nihilism but difference. The hint of an unpolitical community is also Cacciari's answer to Agamben's "coming community," which in its metaphysical élan may still owe a debt to Feuerbach's utopianism. In fact, building the unpolitical community would require an alternative genealogy of Europe, one hidden in the corners of European philosophy: Emil Lask's reflections on the nontheoretical dimension of life (irreducible to the logical form); Michel Henry's approach to life as affection and potentially free from the stranglehold of biopolitics; and María Zambrano's "blessed ones" (*bienaventurados*), who correspond to the voice from the abyss (correspond instead of obeying it) and act by necessity. They are not just individuals; they are singularities. Yet they can communicate, and the event of their communication creates a ground for a joy that Europe has long forgotten.[9]

The unpoliticals, the blessed ones, have only one duty: to be friends in their being strangers. It is the ultimate utopia after all other utopias have failed, but in fact it is deeply rooted in the heart of Europe, for the "stranger god" is none other than Christ: "I was a stranger and you welcomed me" (Mt. 25:35). If the last man is proof enough that resentful happiness is the surest recipe for depression, the unpoliticals are the ones who can "let go" of their pursuit of happiness. The two figures sum up our age. Unfortunately, while we are surrounded by the self-representations of last men, we have very few representations of the unpolitical community.

True, the gathering of the blessed ones has all the flavor of an aristocracy in exile (María Zambrano was for many years an exile from Franco's Spain, in Mexico and Cuba, Italy and Switzerland). Nor can one "decide" to leave the watchful eye of biopower, unless one is prepared to live in the woods or die in a gutter. The unpolitical community is hardly a revolutionary alternative to the current state of things. Yet Europe has always been the community of those who have their differences *in common*, united by centuries of war and peace, hatred and alliances: occasionally enemies, tangled in the same conflicting relationship, and therefore occasionally friends. What is true for the friend is also true for the other. Europe is now very good at thinking the other. It is not very good at welcoming it. Also, it is not very good at fighting it, not without the help of the United States. The connection is crucial, and one cannot be naïve about it: the power of welcoming the other cannot be separated from the power to fight it. If the other is really other, no one can predict whether the encounter will be between friends or foes, or sometime-friends and sometime-foes.

But, when it occurs, friendship is a miraculous moment, the calm in the middle of the storm, even if it collapses in the next instant when a decision must be made and the thrust of the sword will decide who will be the friend who cries over the tomb of the friend he has just killed.

THE SPIRIT AND THE CROSS

The Europeans have read Nietzsche for more than a century now, but they seem to have forgotten his most important lesson: that ultimately you have to *let go* of everything, including your master who told you to let go. Has the time come, perhaps, to put into question disenchantment itself? Is it now the right moment in history to exorcise the demonic obsession of European philosophy, the drive to "genealogize," in an eternal return of the more and more complex? And isn't it the ultimate metaphysical superstition to pretend that even the lack of logical foundation must have a genealogical foundation?

Cacciari's tormented, self-reflexive, spiral-like, multilingual style, whose full power, to some extent lost to the English reader, is unleashed only in its original, multilayered Italian-Latin-Greek-German-French-Spanish lexicon, is the perfect stylistic analogy of Europe's fetishistic compulsion to philosophize, especially because the author knows very well that philosophy always comes after the fact as the rationalization of an event that has already taken place, namely, the mystical apparition of power, the mysticism of politics in action *before* the intervention of political theory.

The political philosopher is fully aware that political theory *does not work*. If Plato ever thought otherwise, he was disenchanted enough after his trip to Syracuse. In fact, the assumption that theory should work, that it should be no different than action, is in itself the worst superstition, the end of political possibility and the beginning of totalitarianism. The absolute coincidence of theory and praxis, the presupposition that outside of what is practical there is no autonomy of thought, is pure nihilism. A political theory that does not ask what are *polis* and *politeia* is barely good for a think tank. Critical language cannot be turned immediately into a political project without leaving a remainder, a residue, a *difference*. The task of political philosophy is not to provide a blueprint to political action but to keep the difference open between theory and praxis, so that the unpolitical event (in the sense of Badiou's metapolitics) may happen. The unpolitical is the transcendental of politics, not its transcendence; it is not too pure for politics, and it is not the beyond of politics. It is the form, the notion of the political to the extent that politics will never coincide with its notion since its very existence depends on this noncoincidence.

Let us go back for a moment to the central issue of the death of God. This is where the noncoincidence of theory and praxis is caught in a tangle. Europe may very well be the land where God was killed, yet in "Europe or Christianity," the densest chapter in this volume, Cacciari points out that the impossibility of the Cross, the true scandal of Christ's *agape*, was not killed because it was impossible to kill it. The announcement "God is dead" is only a fake scandal because the entire history of Europe is the history of putting God to death. Among the "superior men" in the fourth part of *Thus Spoke Zarathustra*, the pope knows that God died by transforming itself, by becoming. (Incidentally, this is the reason why Severino in *Gli abitatori del tempo* has argued that Christianity partakes of nihilism by allowing God to become, have a history, and be other than itself.)

As we have seen, "God is dead" and "God is Spirit" mean the same thing. The immanentization of God was necessary to the extent that in Hegel history is the history of the relationship between master and slave and of how the slave must free himself, not be freed by an external savior (Benedetto Croce, a tangential Hegelian, got Hegel right when he said that there is no history but the history of liberty). The spiritualization of God implies that the slave refuses to be freed by God's sacrifice. There is no Kingdom of God if there is no freedom *from* God. Even the Son must be free from the Father.

In a supratemporal overview of Christian theology, Hegel could be considered a follower of Marcion, who in opposition to Paul insisted on the absolute difference between Judaism (the religion of the Father) and the new creed (the religion of the Son). On the other hand, it is the passion for logic inside Christian theology that provides Hegel with his best atheist ammunition. He just takes theology a step further and gets rid of God altogether, but not without implicitly putting the death of God on God himself. God wants us to be free in truth. He dies like the seed that gives birth to the sapling. The end of time happens *in* time. Yet the question of eschatology is not resolved. If the end remains anchored to the will of the Father, and if the Father dies or withdraws to reveal His will, then the Age of the Son (which is the Age of the Slave or, better, the history of the slave's liberation) will never be over. Atheism may be the fulfillment of Christianity, but if this fulfillment is a gift from God, then history is comedy, the slave will never be free, nor will the Son. Jesus, who is Lord of infinite power but also the one who has come to do the bidding of the Father, cannot escape the conundrum.

What does Jesus' Word reveal? That the Kingdom belongs to the poor, *now.* Not the world, which will never be theirs, but the Kingdom. The poor did not ask for it, but the gift of Kingdom (which is the gift of self-sacrifice) is perfect in itself. Only the poor can fulfill Jesus' commandments (only the poor have the time; the rich are too busy). Still, here is the issue: Jesus himself is the perfect poor, yet his actions show the impossibility of the fulfillment He promises. He is the Kingdom, and He prays that Kingdom will come. He is free and prays to be freed. The Cross, whose efficacy depends on Jesus' perfect desperation and the certainty that God has abandoned him, stands for the final contradiction. The paradox is not existentially "absurd." The standard to apply here is not humanistic. The desperation of the God-Christ on the Cross is *impossible* (it is real, that is, but without ever being a possibility). Here there is no allegory and no theo-logical solution. Compared to the impossibility of the Cross, Hegel's substitution of theology with dialectics shows that logic is not up to that specific task.

The political alliance between Christianity and the world stems from the necessity to live side by side with this "illogical" impossibility. The Kingdom is here, but "here" is also where we have history, institutions, and politics. "Here" is where the "folly" of the Cross becomes organized discourse and meets the *realpolitik* of the Empire. The church cannot eliminate the paradox (getting rid of the paradox is the heretics' obsession); it just wants to be its keeper. But the paradox is not "beyond"; it is not transcendent. It resides in this world, as the Unattainable of this world. If theology and theological philosophy ever believe that they can reach a reasonable deal with the paradox, they must also cease to listen to the True Word of the Perfect Poor. The two cities (the church and the City of Spirit, which stands for secularization) cannot be separated. But it takes a logic of analogy (*communitas analogiae*) to understand what they have in common. The church is both an eschatological force and a force that "holds back" the faithful from the *eschaton*. The City of Spirit, on its part, rejects the *eschaton* and wants to be immune from the *eschaton*'s otherness. No matter which city we want to belong to, the enemy is with us, the enemy is *us*. The paradox "contains" it.

Together, the Spirit and the Cross have shaped the history of medieval and modern Europe. The church has gradually become more and more spiritualized, which was the only way to keep up with the growing spiritualization of modernity. On the other hand, the spiritualization of modernity has taken a Gnostic turn and has increasingly embraced Gnostic liberation in various forms (liberalism, capitalism, communism); even the early cyberfreaks who dreamed to be liberated from the chains of physical reality were agents of the Spirit and so are the champions of various posthuman philosophies. Cacciari is not a believer, but there is a high degree of religious empathy in his final assessment of the paradox of the cross. The "end" of Christianity (not the *eschaton* but the end pure and simple) will come when men are convinced that everything is in their power and that they are wading into a river of infinite possibilities in which no impossible (no real Real) is allowed. But the Kingdom is revealed only in the moment of defeat, of abandonment and desperation, when the Real takes over. And what is true for theology is also true for politics. There are no Pauline reversals in Cacciari. No exclamations such as "Where, O Death, is your victory?" (1 Cor. 15:55). Cacciari's political theology is remarkably free of the passion for the Second Coming that can be found in post-Marxist or born-again Marxist thinkers from Negri to Badiou (the first time did not go very well, but just wait and see when He returns!). If the enemy will not prevail, it is only because he too is contained in the impossibility of *agape*.

Europe or Empire

Every decision Europe makes about a common constitution, federalism or centralization, monetary union or fiscal policy, immigration reform or tightening of the borders, carries the guilt of not having made the opposite decision. Europe is in "agony" because it has an "agonic" essence (it is always in *agon*, in a conflict). As a consequence, Europe can carry out its program only by emptying its program of values. To the extent that the European apparatus aims to be all encompassing, it must come to terms with its constitutive impotence. Indecision brings the pleasures of passive freedom

(Europe does not have to colonize the world, not anymore, nor "bring democracy to the Middle East" or obey other God-given mandates), but if this freedom does not make many enemies, it does not make many friends either. The European dance on the edge of indecision is infuriating to the same Europeans who enjoy the benefits associated with it. And it is small consolation to know that Europe is still the best *katechon* available against the consolidation of a transnational, ultraliberalistic empire.

Cacciari's treatment of Empire is often in disagreement with Negri and Hardt's. In their bestselling book *Empire* (2000), both adopt the term in a nonterritorial, decentralized fashion (which is also Cacciari's approach) but also in a decidedly nongenealogical way, to the point that Empire becomes almost synonymous with the flow of globalization. The major difference between Negri and Cacciari, stemming from their common apprenticeship in 1960s Italian neo-Marxism and *operaismo* (worker-based Marxism), has always been in the unequal emphasis they put on the autonomous power of the various players in the social and economic arena. In Negri, labor acts (not only blue-collar workers but all labor forces, including the intellectuals), and capitalism reacts. The Empire is capitalism's answer to the reality of labor internationalism. Cacciari, on the contrary, has often stressed the capability of capitalism to navigate creatively its own crises.

Negri and Hardt see in the Empire the possibility for the multitudes to produce new political subjectivities and refine their capacity for testing new forms of social antagonism. In a way, they could claim to represent the multitudes that, as the British authors of *The European Inheritance* feared, intend to crush the sane forces of bourgeois conservatism.

On his part, Cacciari regards Empire as *the event that is not happening.* Whatever happens in the world today takes place in the absence of Empire and unfolds its possibilities largely thanks to the Empire's absence. National states are heading toward a long sunset, but it is not necessarily time for Empire to rise. There are transversal empires, from finance to crime, but no actual Empire. In fact, the growth of globalization generates an increasing desire to be sheltered from globalization, and local demands—no matter how pointless they may be—ask for more powerful and protective local institutions. The Cold War ended with one clear winner, which felt endowed with a mission to an empire with no end. But the American empire, as Negri himself admits, is not territorially imperialistic, and Cacciari points out that it is a maritime empire like Carthage and Venice (its power over the sky is an extension of maritime power), whose armies are employed primarily to "tame the proud" (*Aeneid* 6.853).

Empire is not a destiny. The current stage of depoliticization amounts to wild interventionism and catastrophic capitalism, not Empire. *Imperium* is the Latin translation of the Greek word "hegemony." Today, hegemony has absorbed the *imperator*, who is not a person but a collective Prince, without the exceptionality that the Romans associated with the term. (Here, however, we may add that whenever American exceptionalism creeps in, as for instance after the events of 9/11, it creates readymade imperial presidents who see themselves as constituent powers and establish new rules of peace and war. The ensuing depoliticization of presidential decisions, based on an assumption of moral superiority, is fully imperial in its own way, yet it faces the impossibility of moving beyond the "taming-the-proud" stage, since nation building in the Middle East has proven impossible to achieve.)

The Greek *polis* was based on the myth of autochthony. Rome was the opposite. It was a city of refugees, a revolutionary political experiment sustained by the idea of obedience to the boundaries. The Greek *polis* intended to stay; the Roman *civitas* intended to grow outside the city's limits. In two chapters of this book, Cacciari deals extensively with the concepts of "growing city" (*civitas augescens*) and *translatio imperii*, namely, the "transfer" of Rome's political model outside the empire itself. It happened when Byzantium (the "second Rome") and then Moscow (the "third Rome") claimed to be the inheritors of the Roman Empire. The *translatio imperii* was feasible because Rome was not a community but a pact. The Romans even worshipped the gods of the vanquished peoples, welcoming them in Rome (more gods, more power). The Jewish God and the Christian God were exceptions, since they refused to take place among other gods. But where is a similar pact today?

Globalization has not produced that form of empire. Where is the hospitality offered to foreign gods? The United States is better prepared than anyone else to be the "fourth Rome," but is it moving in that direction? There are many centripetal forces, too much "American religion" at play, still a great amount of disdain for foreign gods (to the conservative forces in America, Islam is approximately what Judaism was to the Roman Empire).

Things have changed since Cacciari wrote the pages that we have introduced here, and things are still changing while we write. Yet the consequences of 9/11 have demonstrated that no state today can exercise actual world empire and that the very idea of victory is quick to slip out of the hands of the victors. The future is not Empire but a global supersociety without true political authority and immersed in a multitude of local conflicts. The only alternative could be a universal and global federalism. Which of course is likely to be the ultimate utopia.

In the meantime, the state, confronted with the deterritorialization of politics and the crisis of territorial sovereignty, has fully entered the *katechon* mode, embodying the force of resistance, the force of the past, the "curbing" force. Even the confinement of the European Union to administrative functions has been a form of resistance, a way of joining your enemy (depoliticization) if you cannot beat him. The contradiction dwells deep inside the system, not between globalization-Empire and the occasional anti-globalization resistance (the no-global movements can thrive only in a reverse Empire). Cacciari includes in his discussion the political prophecies of an unpolitical thinker (Ernst Jünger) and a superpolitical one (Alexandre Kojève) to make clear that the state is not becoming unreal (as Kojève would have it) and that beyond the state there is no World State (Jünger) waiting for us. Like Europe, the state is approaching its sunset, but it will not go away. The gap between the state and world order will not be bridged anytime soon. If Empire will come into existence, it will be a "great space" (a Schmittian expression), but it will not be universal. It will be a political form among other political forms.

We might also add that depoliticization is still a political form, pursuing political decisions based on a state of exception or on a "general will" supposedly embodied by public opinion and the media. If Empire manages to dissolve politics into society, the outcome will not be Roman splendor but Roman submission. Or, as Tocqueville put it: "The Roman law carried civil society to perfection, but it invariably degraded political society, because it was the work of a highly civilized and thoroughly enslaved people" (*The Old Régime*, 223).

The absence of state religion and citizenship offered to the vanquished (a double-edged generosity, to be sure, yet unthinkable today) were the most palatable traits of Roman history; slavery and the brutality against the "proud" who would not submit were the other side. In the end, Rome failed (the unthinkable—Christianity—happened), yet the question has never ceased to haunt the European soul: is Rome still a guiding light? Cacciari does not seem to share Simone Weil's distaste for Roman cruelty, but he is attentive to frame the issue in a nonreactionary fashion. As of today, the truly Roman question is: who is ready to turn the defeated into citizens? One would like to ask the United States that question, if it were not that the United States is always careful not to defeat their enemies *too* much, lest the issues of permanent occupation and citizenship arise. The election of Barack Obama to the presidency has marked the end of the unsustainable faith in the "infinite just war" (the end of the faith, not necessarily the end of wars), the expansion of civil rights, and, possibly, a more relaxed immigration policy. Other than these results, which are not insignificant, the state of exception in which the world has lived since the first Iraq War is not over, and universal citizenship is nowhere in sight.

But why should change start with the United States? Why not Europe? Why not India or China? An international law exclusively based on universal (Western) human rights is not feasible. A Latin empire is impossible, no matter how much Kojève would have liked it; a Nordic empire that looks at the Mediterranean as if it were just its messy backyard is equally impracticable. A polycentric globalization is necessary. Europe could still provide the blueprint, but who are the constituent subjects who want Europe to pursue that goal? Negri would say that the intellectual workers of the European states (who are now the new proletariat, or *cognitariat*) are the first in line. Less optimistically, Cacciari points out that until there is real European citizenship the European subject will be missing. Europeans may freely cross borders without changing currencies, but they do not take part in common decisions and do not form a common society. They live in the ambiguous promise of a society that is appealing to the peoples that are not part of it, especially in Central Europe, but disappointing to those who are in it.

On a more theoretical but also operative level, the most urgent need is to rethink who is the stranger and who is the guest. Once they were both *hospes* (guest, host, stranger). Stranger and guest cannot be separated, and not much grammatical distance separates guest (*hospes*) from enemy (*hostis*), either. Most of all, we need to recognize the stranger in ourselves. If we believe that our identity knows no internal difference, then we cannot but turn the guest into an enemy, and no welcoming of the other will be possible. Only women and men who feel in themselves the strife of different forces can be *hospites* (hosts) to *hospites* (strangers, guests) and even *hospites* to *hostes* (enemies). If this is a political project, it is so to the extent that it is profoundly unpolitical and therefore open to a politics that transcends the straightjackets of identity politics.

THE DREAM OF TIMARCHUS

In *De genio Socratis*, included in his *Moralia*, Plutarch has Simmias telling the strange story of Timarchus of Chaeroneia. Timarchus was a friend of one of Socrates' sons, Lamprocles, and a young initiate to Socrates' philosophy, or so Plutarch wants us to believe. To acquire a better understanding of Socrates' daemon, Timarchus underwent a shamanic ritual of death and rebirth: he descended into the cave of Labadeia in Boeotia, where, according to Pausanias (*Description of Greece* 9.39.5–14), the oracle of Trophonius, son of Apollo and founder of the temple in Delphi, would reveal divine messages in a dream. Timarchus remained in the crypt two nights and a day. His family was already lamenting him as dead when he came out of the cave "with a radiant countenance." As he told afterward, in the darkness of the cave he felt that his head had been struck and his soul released. Lifted up into pure and translucent air, he caught the whir of a pleasant sound overhead:

> Looking up he saw no earth, but certain islands shining with a gentle fire, which interchanged colors according to the different variation of the light, innumerable and very large, unequal, but all round. These whirling, it is likely, agitated the ether, and made that sound; for the ravishing softness of it was very agreeable to their even motions. Between these islands there was a large sea or lake which shone very gloriously, being adorned with a gay variety of colors mixed with blue; some few of the islands swam in this sea, and were carried to the other side of the current; others, and those the most, were carried up and down, tossed, whirled, and almost overwhelmed.
>
> (*Plutarch, Discourse Concerning Socrates's Daemon*, 2:407–408)

Timarchus's vision is a hologram of the sky. The sea is the celestial sphere in its apparent diurnal motion or perhaps the Milky Way in its nocturnal movement. The circling islands are planet and stars, and the smooth sound they make is the music of the spheres. The planets do not complete a perfect circle. They rather describe a spiral that corresponds to their motion combined with the motion of the celestial sphere. The swimming islands are constellations, and the current is the celestial equator. As the vision goes on, the sea containing the islands is inclined, like the zodiac. From two openings (the intersections of the zodiac and the galactic circle), the sea receives two rivers of fire (of light) that turn its blue color into white. What Timarchus sees, however, is far from entirely beatific. As soon as he looks down, the scene changes dramatically:

> But when he looked downward, there appeared a vast chasm, round, as if he had looked into a divided sphere, very deep and frightful, full of thick darkness, which was every now and then troubled and disturbed. Thence a thousand howlings and bellowings of beasts, cries of children, groans of men and women, and all sorts of terrible noises reached his ears; but faintly, as being far off and rising through the vast hollow; and this terrified him exceedingly.
>
> (2:408)

Then Timarchus hears the voice of someone who remains nameless. The higher regions belong to the gods, the voice says, but the lower side is the portion of Proserpina or Persephone, "which is one of the four that we govern." It is marked off by the course of Styx, the river that circles Hades. Styx extends upward and even touches the world of light, but its path drives downward. Timarchus holds to the beauty of his vision: "I see nothing but stars leaping about the hollow," says he, "some carried into it, and some darting out of it again." Then you have seen the daemons themselves, says the nameless voice. The stars that are apparently extinguished are the souls that have sunken entirely into their bodies and are therefore distracted by passions. The stars that are lighted again are the souls that float back from the body after death. The stars on high are the souls of men who possess understanding.

Then the voice fell silent. Timarchus turned his head to see who the speaker was, but he felt a sharp pain in his head, fainted, and when he recovered, he found himself lying on the floor of Trophonius's crypt. The vision of Timarchus encompassed Heaven and Hell, the higher regions of the blessed ones and the pit of those who cannot free themselves from the chains of the material world. But what if the islands he saw, in a meta-allegorical interpretation of his allegorical dream, were a poetic transfiguration of the islands of the Greek archipelago, the harmony of land and sea shining over the marvelous surface of the Mediterranean, and the reality of pain and suffering down below, the grating sound of discord that no superior *concordia* can silence? The preachers of harmony dream of the upper portion alone, as they should, but it is the inferior region—not just Hades but the entire lower hemisphere of the universe—"that we govern." The nameless voice likely belonged to a daemon. But the daemons speak with the voice that is in us, and, as they did to Socrates, they tell us who we are.[10]

December 2014

PART I

Thinking Europe

1

THINKING EUROPE

Any idea of Europe and its future has to come to terms, first of all, with what Europe *is*. After the tragedies in Eastern Europe during the 1990s, one is understandably tempted to end the discussion by simply stating that, politically, there is no Europe.[1] However, to do so would only be a sign of romantic impatience, of "political romanticism." Truth be told, I believe that the clearest demonstrations of Europe's most recent political impotence will be found in the origins of its current politics. The extreme difficulty facing Europe, or even its powerlessness in taking the lead when past solutions no longer work, and where conflicts can no longer be kept in check, has to be explained by drawing on the leading ideas of European politics. In short, if Europe seems today to be an unidentified political object, could we interpret that as an expression of its *political* essence?

For, in reality, the second half of the twentieth century ends with an absolutely extraordinary fact whose political and symbolic importance is undeniable. The creation of the single currency brings to an end a process of economic and commercial integration that took place precisely because it was rigorously conceived within strict limits.[2] Namely, a political vision, the limits of which many knew, was able to pursue greater integration over the last fifty years even though constrained economically and financially. The lack of identification that constitutes Europe's present vision of politics is the product of a political strategy. To assert, as many do, that the question of European political form really exists now for the first time only is, once again, political romanticism. The remarkable success of economic and financial integration is owed to the political weakness of the powers par excellence of modern history: national European states. If we forget this, we cannot understand anything about current events and Europe's "future present." If it were only a question of the power of the European states, we would certainly have had only the never-ending European "civil war," since the victory of one of these states was and is inconceivable. This is the tragic lesson of the "long century" that runs from 1848 to the end of World War II.

Because of the extraordinary weakness of the European states by the end of their century-old civil war (and not in spite of it), the conditions for integration were created. Utilizing this weakness, or, should I say, exploiting the epochal crisis of the national European state driven by globalization (economy, finance, technology, culture), an exceptional political result was obtained, namely, the single currency, that is, the creation of a unique space of monetary politics across all of Europe.

How can we think Europe now? What are the ideas that give shape to how it is actually configured? Europe's origins deeply underpin its current state and its future transformations. Can an organism, which has made of its own weakness the fundamental weapon of its affirmation, move beyond the present? Is immobility even an option? In its current state, can we recognize the seeds that can give rise to positive change? Or are such changes conceivable only through catastrophe?

We can only begin from ideas that are dominant in the European political arena today. There is truly a Maastricht philosophy, which is not too difficult to define, one that is entirely determined by the history that precedes integration.[3] Its fundamental principle, *fundamentum inconcussum* (although, and especially as foundation, it remains indemonstrable), is called stability. All the traumas and all the anxieties surrounding the great European civil war have demanded stability. The value of stability extends far beyond mere criteria of the financial sort. Even here, it is a question of political decision: it is imperative to prevent those political decisions able to interrupt the network of reciprocal interests and economic advantages that have underpinned European integration.

But that isn't enough. A corollary of the stability principle is its irreversibility. Integration cannot stop since to do so would jeopardize stability. In order not to endanger its foundation, such a development must appear irreversible. That is, the ensuing stages must appear predictable during the current phase of integration; they must appear essentially inherent to it. Not decisions or arbitrary choices but evolution, "natural" growth of the stability that has already been achieved.[4]

To look more closely, at stake here is the entire "philosophy of time," that is, the entire significance of the modern "project." Time is conceived as a linear function of the equilibrium between the elements of the present state, and its contents can be extrapolated from the analysis of this equilibrium. The best approach would consist, therefore, in working out the optimal growth of the given elements and then taking into account the relation of stability to their equilibrium. It would be too easy to criticize the old-fashioned epistemological rigor of such a model for seeming to reflect a naïve vision of history and progress. Actually, presuming an indeterminate and probabilistic point of view would put into question the entire body of the principles that maintain, today, European integration. No matter what we assume about the "possibilities" that cannot be reduced to the primacy of the "act," the model would entail that the next phases of integration do not simply evolve out of the present state and so cannot guarantee equilibrium. In short, these possibilities are conceivable only as political decisions, which is precisely what the "fundamental principle" of stability was to avoid. It is absolutely essential that the decisions are depoliticized and that they are transformed into administrative calculation. The depoliticization of the process of integration, once again, is the essential political weapon to guarantee the very integration's development and success.

Can such a strategy work? It can, but only on one condition, one that always is part of any progressive and liberal philosophy of history, namely, that the stability as well as the irreversibility of the system be immanently guaranteed with respect to the laws of the market and free exchange.

The idea of stable progress or progressive stability obtained through mechanisms that are presumed to be self-functioning or, in any case, "anonymous," which is to say removed from causality and arbitrariness, is, of course, an old utopia. Furthermore, it is the quintessence of the utopian form. What does utopia stand for if not a condition of development of knowledge, technologies, and well-being in the absence of conflict and political decisions? But in the case of European integration, utopia has been introduced with renewed vigor and with a different sense of what is real and what is not. Renaissance utopia rose at the dawn of the European states' will to power; the "irreversible stability" of Maastricht atones for its part for the irreversible decline of such a will to power. The effectiveness of administrative automatism is different now: no state today would think of redesigning Europe according to its own sense of its national power. On the contrary, the principles of integration themselves redesign the power of the European states. And their power is that of the rules of competition and of the market.

Yet a more fundamental reason can be found, an anthropological one I would call it, that today renders "realistic" the utopia characterized by an irreversible depoliticization of Europe. Europeans today understand Europe as a space of safety and protection, that is, a "protected place," as well as the guarantee of an ever more effective defense of their own economic interests. They understand the process of integration as the definitive waning of the need to turn to political decisions in the proper sense. It is by relying on this deep-rooted need that national states in Europe have been able to overcome ideological and cultural oppositions in order to be a part of the communitarian structure. This fundamental trait of the European situation constantly goes missing whenever one laments the political absence of Europe in situations of crisis. The governments of the European Union could never persuade their own citizens to adopt a policy of active intervention, with all the resulting military risks and economic costs. In fact, they would run the risk (if such intervention were to become a meme of European politics) of provoking strong reactions in their own countries against integration. The European *homo democraticus*, the rightful heir to the one described by Tocqueville and Nietzsche, requires an economically strong and politically weak Europe.

Can such a hybrid stand up? Will the situation continue, or will it quickly fall apart? It seems clear today that the principal idea underpinning the construction of the European Union (that is, a stability that can be obtained only through the homologation of the European space to the mechanisms of competition and the market) corresponds deeply to the idea of politics that the Europeans have developed after the tragic experiences of the twentieth century, that is, of politics as basically the cause of crisis and conflict. Perhaps we might venture a comparison: Europeans are prepared today to recognize themselves in the European Union against political conflict, just as they recognized themselves in the modern state, the "artificial god" (*deus artificialis*), against the religious wars.

On the other hand, the entire construction of the European Union (consciously or not, it matters little) implicitly creates mistrust in the capacity of politics to offer stability (hopefully, stability in the form that is irreversible). This is made clear from those organisms whose structure depends on an obvious asymmetry. The new supranational bodies are the economic and financial ones. The source that legitimizes their power is absolutely metapolitical. As guardians of the "fundamental principle," they receive legitimacy in the exercise of their functions from their very obligation to provide stability. On the contrary, the "old" bodies that have to look after the real political functions of the union are able to operate only on the basis of intergovernmental agreement; therefore, they continue to draw their own legitimacy essentially from the sovereignty of the different states.

The real question is not if it is possible to overcome the asymmetry, which appears to be what preoccupies so many today. The real question is whether we actually ought to wish for the end of such an asymmetry. From what direction could such a change come? On one hand, it certainly will not be in reactionary terms, that is, by trying to swim against the current of integration and globalization and thereby reconsolidating old powers. On the other hand, attempts aiming to confer democratic legitimacy on new powers would dramatically expose them to a greater number of changing demands from the people, which is the main feature of the current "society of entitlements." It is essential for European unity—it is at the foundation of the very idea of unity—that the powers responsible for the essential functions of stability draw, so to speak, their own legitimacy from "above." European equilibrium is, by its very nature, deeply asymmetric.

Is such an equilibrium stable? How to face it administratively through what has been called the "incompatible quartet" that rules the union's agenda? It is in fact a question of harmonizing monetary policy (which is the exclusive competence of the European Bank), budgetary policy (destined to have radical repercussions for the fiscal policies of the member states), social and labor policies, and, finally, regional policy. The "four" constitute, looking at all evidence, a unique system, while the areas of competence remain deeply differentiated, when not competitive. Because of such a fundamental asymmetry, to which we referred earlier, it is clear that the new economic and financial powers work within extremely restricted national budgets, with weak social and labor policies and with limited distributive powers. Vice versa, it is inevitable (and the tendency will grow proportionally to the strengthening of the Central Bank) that the political powers, appealing more and more to their democratic legitimacy, will try to enjoy increasingly greater margins of freedom when applying the fundamental principles of stability and irreversibility. Moreover, the crisis is likely to explode at any moment as a result of a further worsening of labor problems and imbalances among regions. The crisis is not inescapable, but it is inevitable that in order to deal with the above-mentioned "incompatible quartet," issues of an essentially political order, of political decisions, may take on new importance in the European Union.

New powers cannot be left to their own devices since to do so will put into question the whole asymmetric equilibrium that currently exists. Is the European Parliament up to the task? This will only happen if the European Parliament "binds" itself to the decisions of the new supranational entities and metapolitical organs. Such a move will not violate, in principle, the postulate of stability, but only on the understanding that the European Parliament is ultimately European in nature and is able to resist at a minimum the expectations and issues emanating from the national states. Not an impossible prospect, perhaps it's again inevitable, though certainly it isn't doable immediately. The reason can easily be understood. On one hand, Parliament will be called on to become a European system, that is, a political guarantor of the irreversibility of integration, by removing itself as the safeguard of individual states. On the other hand, Parliament will have to make itself increasingly the bearer of the need for recognizing the particular regional and urban realities that make up the European political space.

The epochal move to the decline of the great construction of the modern European spirit, that is the national state, is in fact dominated by two forces that are not necessarily destined to come together: technoeconomical globalization and the network of autonomies and intermediary bodies that the national states have throughout the course of their history always tried to absorb. In European jargon, there are at play here both the meaning and the limits of what it means to be subsidiary (*sussidiarietà*).

We know how this principle derives from the need to counterbalance the dreadful homogenizing forces at work in integration. It is not only a question of achieving the objectives of competence and economy. To avoid a useless call for greater levels of government involvement entails, precisely, acknowledging the need for autonomy coming from the European regional-urban network. But no one has been able to establish where such a principle ends. The quality of being subsidiary can point to a synergy, in a federalist structure, between the different jurisdictions and the different institutional levels.[5] Or, on the contrary, it can signify that when the essential factors of stability are not at play, other public or private subjects can take on ancillary knowhow, that is, complementary with respect to those of the central administrations. It seems to me that the principle of being subsidiary is essentially being interpreted today in the latter sense, that is, as a weak antidote to the standardizing mechanisms and the strong metapolitical powers of the European Union. The European Parliament, however, will not be able to hold such a view, unless it wants to appear as the parliament of a new macrostate. It is also true that by ratifying the resolutely bureaucratic and centralist perspective of the new institutions, the European Parliament would lose the democratic legitimacy that is crucial to it if it is to compete with these institutions.

Even here the decision, ultimately, will be political; it will only be the product of a political contest and conflict. The two great trends in competition will be the strong centralistic one (founded on a weak conception of what is subsidiary and the absolute sovereignty of the "fundamental principle" of stability) and the federalist one, which is based on the synergy among not necessarily weak sovereignties (all conceived as original and not as byproducts of others), though still responsible and competent across well-defined fields of interest and expertise. Still, one should be careful in choosing too quickly which may appear to be the obvious choice. If we adopt the federalist perspective, that is irreversible stability, such a perspective could in no way be guaranteed. Integration, in federalist terms, is only conceivable in terms of negotiation-agreement, in terms of the possibility of reversal, according to patterns that remain highly variable and open to risk.

What kind of federalism are we talking about? If we understand Europe as a confederation of sovereign states, undoubtedly one ought to recognize that they have the right to secede from the union. If we understand federalism, instead, as an authentic one, then defining the federations' sovereign institutions that are valid for all the member states and to which all European citizens are directly subject, without mediation, is needed. Only then will Europe be reconfigured as a Europe of cities and regions according to parameters free from territorial boundaries and from the territorially determined sovereignty of the old states. Is such an alternative feasible, and if so, how, with the new powers I spoke of earlier, and with internal peace, which the old states alone seem able to guarantee?

Deciding to move toward a technological government of the union, a government that would regulate the monetary-commercial relations, where all the other competences would be ancillary—can that be seriously renegotiated today? It is one thing to determine, as we have tried to do, those issues that seem beyond the intervention of a technological government and those that can be faced with other means. When we speak of technological government, we do not mean to use the expression reductively. "Technological government" means government of technology (*tecnica*) as the all-embracing dimension of European life, that is, as a form of government that derives its own legitimacy from a sense of our present lifeworld (*Lebenswelt*) and not from "archaic" democratic procedures. A form of government that makes sure to support and promote not the interests of this or that group but the fundamental impulse of today—namely, the progressive and irreversible supremacy of technology, the definitive metamorphosis of technology from involving a collection of instruments to what we consider our own habitat.

An extraordinary revolution that disrupts the traditional relations between economy and politics, means and end; a revolution that brings us back to the waning of politics as perhaps the great political event of this second half of the century. (And I ask myself: was this second half of the twentieth century not in fact the beginning of the third millennium?)

To conclude, what we can imagine for the future is this: if the principle of "sound becoming on the solid sod of the earth" (Hegel)—that is, if the principle of stability and ratification were to prevail—Europe would no longer be Europe.[6] If European space were to be transformed in mere "solid sod" devoid of fluidity, an inhospitable space of protection and safeguard, afraid only of danger and its own failure (how can the West avoid having to deal intimately with its own decline?), it will not be Europe but Europe's oblivion.

Without a doubt, European law (*nomos*) is being written today according to principles that bind it to a hierarchical order and to fixed parameters. But the same uncertainties, contradictions, and doubts that its structure exhibits and that we have tried to point out, far from being wounds to be healed as soon as possible, constitute, in my view, openings for new possibilities. Through them could pass the federalist idea that "re-collects" in the most pregnant sense of the term—that is, which brings back to the heart of the idea of Europe its being an archipelago: a network of distinct individualities, united precisely by what appears to distinguish them the most, given to dialogue and to listening, unable to know themselves without reflecting on what is other from them. What the medieval doctors would have called a *communitas analogiae* (a community where no element can be stated univocally, yet not condemned to an indifferent ambiguity, to relativistic dogmatism) requires political communication. Its language cannot be the same as technological information. Can Europeans reinvent new forms of communication beyond the form of the state? Can there be politics beyond the state?[7] This is the great challenge that awaits the European people today.

2

EUROPEANISM

Europe and philosophy share the same "restless heart."[1] Since Europe is a problem—even the origins of its name, its etymology, its *etymon* remain an enigma. No generalization is able to encompass the "terrifying" freedom of responses, forms, and languages, the uncertainty of relations between parts and the whole, between states and nations, which characterize European history. Europe has never defined its borders to the outside because inside its figure is a perennial metamorphosis that does not tolerate a stable determination (*determinazione*). It is irreversible rootednessless. It is *experimentum*: process, way (*via*), danger. It only possesses itself as a destination to reach something that is absent in the present. Pure "already" and "not yet" (*iam et nondum*). Europe is not. It will be.

This is how Europe endlessly represents itself, even in this era, as is said, full of secularization and utter nihilism. This is also what Europe's representatives repeat: Europe will be "truly" such when the Atlantic and the Urals meet . . . when it "truly" comprehends in itself the entire Mediterranean space (when "our sea," the *mare nostrum* will become once again a sea among its lands) . . . when it becomes able to give itself a "real" foreign policy and common defense, when . . . . The European demon declares all its times in the future, and the future is always the overcoming/coming true of the present. This explains why European space is a variable geometry: not a universe but a multiverse.[2] All its frontiers exist so as to be crossed. They exist only in that variable distance, impossible to capture, which separates and unites those who dialogue and those who fight. Europe's parts have always been within a "network"; they have always looked at themselves in the light of conflict-harmony (*polemos-harmonia*). Each part lives because it absorbs energy from the others and transforms it. And no empire has ever succeeded in besting this archipelago.

Europe, therefore, designates neither a physical-geographical reality nor a politico-cultural state. Europe is *logos* in the etymological sense of the word: an idea that gathers in itself different languages and different questions and then tries to express them. The *logos* that is Europe gathers and expresses the different ways through which it has attempted to respond to the enigma "know thyself." That Europe has always looked for an identity, for "one" identity, can only be put into doubt by the "nationalist nonsense" that has separated the peoples (and it was Nietzsche who said it!).[3] But an identity, "one" identity? In what sense? It is only a question of the One that lives in relation to the Many. Once again, philosophy. "One," which is reason, but also history, theory, which is praxis. Universalist as well as pluralistic philosophies without *logos* both betray the sense of the European search for identity. Caring for difference entails the desire (*eros*) for the principle that gathers them all together. And the principle is alive because it gives itself to itself in the manifestation of the differences.

"Europeanism" can mean two things: to designate what Europe appears in its essence or to assert a kind of supremacy. We have already spoken of the first. The figure of Europe emerges from the defining, axial age—from the great tempest that cuts it away (de-cides) from Asia. It is a "scission" (de-cision) that Alexander's utopia cannot heal and that is renewed and fulfilled in the battle of Actium.[4] To be sure, neither the myth of Troy nor the history of Salamis and Marathon are absolute separations. With a powerful image, Aeschylus in *The Persians* represents Europe and Asia as beautiful and divine women, "blood sisters of the same lineage." In the *Gorgias*, Plato entrusts to the judges from Asia and Europe the fate of the souls of the dead. Rhadamanthus will weigh those who come from Asia, Eachus those who come from Europe, but the supreme appeal lies in the hands of the Asian Rhadamanthus! Aristotle too in the *Politics* is very careful not to break the harmony between opposites, Europe and Asia, and entrusts precisely to the Greeks the arduous task of mediation (*metaxy*). The Greeks occupy the central position, and not only geographically: they too partake of both sides. They represent the courage and the strength of Europeans and the intelligence and ability in the arts typical of Asians. Greece is the outpost of Europe; therefore, it could only imagine itself as confining (*con-finis*), close to, contiguous, near Asia. Yet it is a question of harmony among true opposites, as deep as it is difficult, since it is always on the verge of breaking.

One recurring theme, one *topos*, dominates the history of ideas of Europe from its origins to today: Europe represents indomitable freedom, "true speech" (*parrhesia*), the discourse that seeks and questions everything. Asia is seen as tame obedience. A servile nature supposedly characterizes Asians and barbarians. They tend to indifferent unity, to the indistinct, and to the absence of definitive form. Their beauty is grandiose but immeasurable. On the contrary, the beauty of the Greek is perfectly visible and in a comprehensible form that proceeds enclosed in the rhythm (in the *number*) of the figure. The Asian One devours in itself the many; the Greek One communicates itself. It is self-diffusive (*effusivum sui*).[5] Its unity is generating. It is *physis*. It is birth. And its science-philosophy (*episteme*) is called on precisely to understand in the light of the origin the multiplicity of beings, to intuit everyone's essence (*ousia*), what its being truly is. Similarly, the "city of Europe" cannot be imagined as simply, abstractly "one." Its very root points to the plurality and also, as Vico claimed, to the conflict (*polis-polemos*) that inhabits it. Cities (*poleis*) are dialogue, contrast, exchange, conflict. And this is the energy (as Machiavelli teaches us) that makes them strong and makes them grow.

Does the sum of these factors produce Europeanism as a value capable of expressing "rightly" its superiority or "ordained" dominance over other cultures and civilizations? There is no doubt that Europeanism was lived within such a perspective. Even the values of tolerance that stemmed from it wound up reestablishing and relegitimizing just these sorts of claims. The ideas of perpetual peace and universal republic are the great stratagems of the European spirit, products of its history and of its law. They are not universally "human." Can we rethink them in such a way that they don't simply reaffirm the spiritual-political power of Europe? Can we, by working precisely on that paradox of which I have spoken, make Europeanism a way for recognition and for welcoming beyond the rigid logic of exchange and friendship among nonequals? The path opens to an ethical and political search that we cannot follow here. Once again, Europe's search for itself coincides with its philosophy.

Today's political and practical Europeanism—if we really want to be realistic about its chances—still remains entirely deaf and blind to these questions. How can we think Europe now? And where does the current situation point? To what possible changes? After World War II, the founding figures of European unity thought of Europe essentially as a commercial, economic, and financial community on the basis of the two pillars mentioned above: the stability and the irreversibility of the process of integration. The underlining assumption was that community itself could be attained through self-functioning mechanisms dictated, precisely, by the economic-administrative rationality now removed from the more or less arbitrary "occasionalism" (*occasionalismo*) of the political. Having just emerged out of the twentieth-century civil war as a suicide, it was decisive that European politics set out on European integration almost for the purpose of disappearing within it.

However, the hybrid nature of a Europe in constant economic progress yet permanently weak as a political power today displays all of its innate fragility.[6] Europeanism reached its critical moment when the single currency was instituted: either it moves on from here to political success, or political decline will surely follow. The asymmetry between economic progress and political weakness was able to withstand the Cold War between the two titans victorious in 1945. It is, however, no longer sustainable. The first challenge is to put to the test the "incompatible quartet" that rules the agenda of the European Community now that the entrance of the new members has made it even harder to manage: the monetary policy, the budget policy, the social and labor policy, and, finally, the regional policies (that is, the state of being subsidiary [*sussidiarietà*]). As I noted earlier, the four constitute a unique system, and good government compels them to move together. In reality, nothing of the sort is happening. On one hand, the new economic and financial powers, which now believe in their own full autonomy, will work to restrict national budgets, make social and labor policies extremely weak (as evidence, consider the so-called Constitution, where the themes of welfare are dealt with according to a classically liberal style of free trade), and produce a complementary and residual state of being subsidiary. On the other hand, the old political states, appealing to their own democratic legitimacy, will always open increasingly dangerous gaps in the application of the fundamental principle of stability.

Beyond this, there are geopolitical decisions that Europe will have to make. Europe's vision of the future international order, after the definitive end of the twentieth century (1989), will also influence its choices in matters of expansion, common defense, and presence in the United Nations and the other extranational organizations. In the past, it was easy to disguise economic and financial problems as technical issues, but today no longer. These, instead, are essentially and exclusively of a political and cultural nature. Will Europe take on a role and a commitment to effect international stability marked by a multipolar conception of the world? Or, simply, for a multilateral one? The former presupposes the definition of "large spaces" (Schmitt) that are culturally and historically homogeneous, that is multinational, and in some ways "imperial," capable, precisely, of constituting actual polarities. The latter is simply based on the consistency of a network of agreements, deals, and compromises among the nations at issue. Both visions, however, contradict the unilateral hegemony asserted in that "other" Atlantic Europe, which actually has, as its indisputable foundation, the strength of a full, total victory over its ancient enemy. If Europe were to choose to represent only the interests of the other bank of the great American island, Europeanism would then be synonymous with Atlanticism, that is, mere acceptance of America's supremacy. Could we still speak of Europe in this case? Certainly not as archipelago, as harmony and composition of distinct entities; certainly not in the sense in which we spoke earlier.[7]

Plato tells us how Athens, before confronting the challenge that threatened to engulf it in Asia, had to answer the will to power of Atlantis. The land in between, Hellas-Europe, can be a bridge that unites, a harmonic middle, to the extent that it remains conscious of the risk of being swallowed by the East or the West. Europe is not only the West. Its heroes go to the West, but always looking behind them to where the sun rises. Aeneas does not abandon Troy. Columbus himself goes to the West because he misses the East. If Europe is able to "resist" in this duplicity, it will have to remain itself, that is, in search for itself. The day Europe believes that it has been "healed," that it has reached a single stable and well-founded identity, it will at that point not only be at the end of its true power but at the fading of the very idea of Europe forever.

3

TWO GERMAN SPEECHES

THE "SECOND THOUGHT"

If I may be allowed, I would like to share first of all the honor that I was given with friends and colleagues in Italy who for so many years have been studying and publishing the thought of Hannah Arendt through conferences, translations, and essays.[1] In fact, it may not be an exaggeration to say that the attention given to Arendt in Italy really has no match in other countries. Beginning in the 1980s, an entire generation of philosophers and political thinkers came to terms with her work with exceptional commitment—a commitment that was not only historical and philological but above all theoretical. If I may, I would like to remember, beside works of a general nature such as that of Simona Forti (*Vita della mente e tempo della polis*), at a minimum the discussions included in the very important volume edited by Roberto Esposito, *La pluralità irrappresentabile*, with essays by Franco Volpi, Remo Bodei, Pier Paolo Portinaro, and many others. I would also like to recall the special number of *aut-aut* (one of the leading philosophical journals in Italy), edited by Alessandro Dal Lago, who has been a tireless translator and student of our philosopher.[2] All the most important Italian political philosophers of the last twenty years have measured themselves on Arendt's work, from Roberto Esposito—who has also written a study on the relationship between Arendt and Simone Weil—to Carlo Galli, from Bruno Accarino to Augusto Illuminati, from Paolo Flores d'Arcais to young scholars like Luca Savarino, who recently published a very good essay on the relation between philosophy and aesthetics in Arendt. This is a body of work that certainly does great honor to our universities and to Italian philosophy, which should receive credit, more than my own work, for the attention that you are giving me today and for which I am truly thankful.

I do not wish to provide you, nor could I, with a new interpretation of the thought of Hannah Arendt or demonstrate its relevance. There are so many specialists present here who can do this better than I can. I would just like to point out, very generally, some problematic aspects of my research that have arisen during my dialogue with this great thinker whom we celebrate today.

It is often repeated, sometimes on the basis of a misreading of Carl Schmitt, that the techno-economic-financial globalization, the assertion of goal-oriented capitalist rationality upon the entire planet, could well put an end to that "great construction of the European spirit" that is the state. To be sure, contemporary space can no longer be represented and governed from the perspective of a state that is territorially determined, of its sovereignty rooted in territorial identity. Certainly, we are faced today with a "spatial crisis" of the Leviathan. But does this crisis contradict in catastrophic fashion its underlying logic, or does it represent, instead, a logical development of the same logic? Seen from the point of view of Arendt's critique of modernity, the universal "general mobilization" of today continues that systematic *Aufhebung* (namely, the overcoming of differences of location and "now" in the a priori forms of space and time) that is the transcendental condition of the sovereignty of the Leviathan. Globalization presupposes the systematic reduction of the person to an individual, "naturally" nonpolitical (that is, the utter abandonment of the classical perspective of the *zoon politikon*, of the animal that as such is political relation), and the reduction of politics to artifice. Moreover, it radicalizes the consequences of such a reduction by putting into crisis the form of the state and by uprooting the individual from it. The pure artifice of economy takes on the highest practical and symbolical power (*summa potestas*). Increasingly intolerant of the ancient "artificial gods," of their national character and their boundaries, economy now demands that politics "serve" it as its minister, in the etymological sense of the word (minister and *minestra* [soup] are in Italian the same word!).

Hannah Arendt's thought is a school of resistance, but, above all, her thought is a school of resistance to the philosophical premises of modernity. *Gnosis* defines its essence—yet a gnosis deeply connected to Europe's philosophical tradition.

The engine of universal homologation (as well as the primary cause of the irrepressible feeling of envy and uncertainty that the individual has) can be found in the removal of spatial-temporal distance (and, therefore, of any proximity, since distance and proximity are the two dimensions of any possible dialogue). It will be found as well as in the "passion for equality" (falsely linked to the idea of liberty featured in democratic ideology, and in this sense Hannah Arendt is a good reader of Tocqueville).[3] Both engines mirror the most tenacious dream of our reason, that is, to reduce every difference to the articulation of the One; to contemplate in the One every distinction; to deduct from the One, "purely" intuited, the Many. Hannah Arendt did not want to call herself a philosopher since philosophy is intrinsically metaphysical, and in the metaphysical tradition she discerned the same gnosis that at the beginning of *The Human Condition* she pointed to as the foundation of the modern technoscientific project: "to free" men from their worldly prison, that is, to break the tie between men and the earth, to render life artificial as the inescapable conclusion of the artificial reconstruction of the political. Isn't this the same project that ends Hegel's *Phenomenology*? Finally reconciled, man appears as the *Künstler*, the perfect artist, independent from any natural premise, capable of creating by himself the ground for his own works, that is, capable of producing an authentic new nature (and it is on this basis that Hegel's most original twentieth-century interpreter, Alexandre Kojève, speaks of the "end of history").

To be sure, history will end if production no longer reveals the agent, that is, if the technopoietic dimension of production absorbs that of action (*agere, prattein, dran*)—namely, the risk of the action that "de-cides" (in the etymological sense of "cutting itself away from") the automatic, impersonal course of daily life. To be sure, history will end if the individual can indeed be "resolved" in a modality of production that is so much more effective the more it radically excludes any risk of being shared. But is such an end thinkable? Can the thought of such an end be formulated? Will its compelling violence ever really "convince" (in the etymological sense of "winning together") those who do not want to be "won over"? By insisting on this question, Arendt's thought becomes an active, positive resistance.

As soon as thought exits from the illusory world of the purely thinkable—as soon as thought truly questions itself—then it is plain that every thought and all knowledge are inseparable from the life of language. There is no thinking (*cogitare*) that is not speaking (*loqui*). I speak because language exists. My speaking-thinking presupposes the language that others speak with me. I think, therefore we speak, and we are being spoken (*cogito ergo loquimur et locuti sumus*). I think, therefore we are (*cogito ergo sumus*). Plurality is the fundamental condition of discourse and of every action. If I think, then I belong to a community of speakers, and as a matter of course I speak to them and with them. To understand is to misunderstand each other in every sense and peril of the term. Even if no logical calculation were to allow me to assert that I and others have a world in common, I would still be forced to admit that language is our common horizon, which is continuously transformed and which nonetheless contains my every action.

In this deconstruction of modern metaphysics (a deconstruction that proceeds from within) lies the foundation of the "second" character that thought always takes on for Arendt. Not only thought requires "a thing thought through" (*un pensato*), and in this sense it is always afterthought (*nach-denken*), that is, always a meditation around problems, a concrete reality that challenges us and strikes us. It isn't only thinking that is undistinguishable from the *pathos* from which it originates, but the first problem that thought must "think through" is also that of the language in which it dwells. And here is where we discover the irreducible *plurality*, which is what Hannah Arendt calls the "Law of the Earth"![4]

Every language is a network of relations, a plurality of languages. A language cannot be defined by itself just as the individual in his solitary existence cannot be defined when that individual speaks and therefore thinks. Every language reflects and expresses the fact that not Man but men and women dwell on the earth. In meditating on language, we see how every identity not only exists in relation to what is other from itself but is in itself relation—how it not only presupposes a plurality but is plurality itself. No identity is immune from the "com" of *communitas*—only the unaware, immature identity fears it and will try to find shelter under the shadow of totalitarian ideologies.[5]

But if thought is always "second," an after-thought, *nach-denken*, then, for Arendt, the need for distance is also coessential. If thought is the *logos* of plurality (that is, the ability to connect and link the manifold, not to deny it or overcome it), then thought will never be able to resolve in itself what it has "thought through." It will never to be able to erase the distance between itself and what is thought. Action is what preserves the distance among acting subjects, among the different practices. To the distance conceived as space that guarantees an exclusive identity (an identity that sees in the other the enemy or the threat, having completely forgotten the original affinity between guest [*hospes*] and enemy [*hostis*]), Hannah Arendt pits an idea of distance that allows a correct vision as the precondition of making-seen and making-known (but also to listen and to *cor*-respond).[6] Distance allows action to reach an effective acknowledgment of the other and impartiality in judging him or her. Distance is, on condition of the correctness of action (or maybe even of a new sense of justice), not the applying to everyone of an equal right but acknowledging the right of everyone—somehow, justice as "love for the stranger" (*philoxenia*). And if city (*civitas*) means city that grows (*civitas augescens*), if authority and power (*auctoritas et potestas*) are not synonymous but dimensions in perennial conflict—then the justice of the city that grows, the justice that is the author of the city, can only be *philoxenia*: power to welcome and to give.

The Latin *hospes* is the most appropriate translation of *xenos*. The other, the stranger, is the guest, the friend. The Russian *drugoj* is the other and *drug* the friend. Let us listen to language. It invites us to remember that to us, inhabitants of Europe, nuptial bed of Hades, is given (and continues to be given) the chance to consider our city as community and pact, (*communitas, foedus*), federation among guests and friendship among strangers. Outside this horizon, there is no "politics beyond the state" but the end of politics—or politics reduced to the impersonal and inauthentic "they" (*man*), or to the merely economic and administrative. Is that our destiny? Hoping against hope that a counterblow may take place? I believe that Hannah Arendt would say that only by following this line of thought can we find a sign of freedom. I prefer liberty with danger to peace with slavery (*malo periculosam libertatem quam quietum servitium*).[7] I prefer to think against any hope, on the basis of the most desperate realism, than to give up thinking and so conform to the fact by declaring it true. Not even a god will save us if we abdicate before the idol of total immanence, if we banish risk from our actions and the wonder from our gaze.

THE LANGUAGE OF EUROPE

Europe as *problem*. Europe as something intrinsically worth questioning: such an approach is by now what historians, sociologists, political analysts, and geographers have been tasked with. The exchange economy unifies everything, but it does so only by making prominent places and universalizing individualities. The scene is a network of relations. European unity will never be the mere result of calculation and purposeful rationality. It can only be defined historically: one European duality of reason and history. But here lies the problem. Europe is inquiry (*interrogazione*), but the status of the inquiry is paradoxical. It tends primarily to void any tradition, to doubt any transmitted value. On one hand, when inquiring, truth is always the product of a search but never the premise, and it therefore is the product of the very same doubt that accompanies any search. On the other hand, no inquiry can begin if something did not set it in motion, if some "voice from the abyss" (as María Zambrano calls it) did not demand it.[8] We always question what it is that searches for us. The language of inquiry is based on the Augustinian paradox: never assume, yet one must assume the existence of what we are searching for. It is as if through inquiry that we remember a lost intimacy with what we still ignore: the past future.

The emergence of the problem of the language of Europe leads to the decision. We can preserve that loss, that absence; that is, we can make of our language the sign of such absence, or we can see it as a totalizing discourse, as the full presence of Babel. European language can decide to absorb the absence in itself, to free itself from that premise that the "voice from the abyss" calls us to inquire, or it can conceive all its own signs (because "we are signs . . .")[9] as ad-verbs, *ad-verba*: not *verba* already settled in perfect adherence to the designated object but indexes or images of the "coming one," the *adveniens* that is not—images of its absence, of its present silence. In Heideggerian fashion, either European language does not care at all for no-thing (*ni-ente*) and dissolves in the actuality of practical-instrumental knowledge (the *Machenschaft*, which is the essence of nihilism), or it opens itself to the listening of "what" speaks in the form of silence, that is, by not presupposing the no-thing (*ni-ente*) as nothingness (*nulla*).

I believe that around this problem the turning point for Europe has occurred or will occur—and therefore the turning point of the entire world because today's globalization means Westernization. Language, our languages, are they just conventions, instruments to be arranged as decoration? Tools at the service of the technological domination of the world? All reducible to a system of signs that can be manipulated technically at the service of pure information? Or, rather, will Europe, or will Europeans, remain loyal to a transcendental vision of language as condition of the possibility of intuiting, seeing, and building objects? It is a question of choosing practically and politically in the most meaningful sense of the word. If we subscribe to the first way of "dwelling" in language, then the meaning of words will coincide with their use: they will designate only facts and will not set in motion new modes or communicate new perspectives. They will not be "open," and they will inform without communicating. The term "poietics" (*poietica*), the word that is work (*poiesis*, *opus*), will be valued only as ornament.

Has Europe already made its decision? Many things might lead us to think so, yet . . . Are you familiar with *The Book of the Gentile and Three Wise Men* by Ramon Llull, *doctor illuminatus*, the first European to write philosophy in his vulgar tongue? (Dante is the second!) Llull imagines that at the end of a hard-fought discussion on what is true law, neither the wise Jew, nor the Moslem, nor does the Christian wish to declare a winner. On second thought, they want to remain "in common," precisely, to keep in common their research. They depart asking forgiveness for any involuntary offense, and they "decide" nothing else except to continue their conversation until they reach the Unreachable end.

Can we still imagine Europe as the paradoxical space of such an openness? Or has Europe already decided that the Unreachable is actually nothing (*nulla*) and that what counts is only the easily computable space of practical-economic action? But do we "do nothing" when we follow Llull's wise men on their way to the Unreachable? To do so would undoubtedly be the verdict of every instrumental-pragmatic conception of language (and of every theological and philosophical dogmatism). Is it rather the case that by accompanying the three sages can we recognize language as the place where we conduct our research? If we didn't move toward the absence of the end, we could renounce all the places where we hesitate, where we reflect, and where we practice wonder. Were it not to experience this pathos—a nostalgia for the no-thing (*ni-ente*) of the end—our logos would discover nothing (*nulla*). Language that is not driven by the question around that "what," which no representation exhausts, becomes a dead language. Neither Plato's Greek nor Lucretius's Latin are dead languages. Instead, those who forget the question about what remains unsayable to them speak in dead languages.

And so, once again, is our language dead? It would seem so. It would appear that Europe desires indeed to become a stable state, to become a law of the soil, forgetful even of its Mediterranean roots. The very contradictions and difficulties of Europe's construction, of its union, however, demonstrate that Europe still believes that a counterblow against indifferent homologation, or inhospitable self-sufficiency, is possible.

Europa, a tragic name. She lived in Asian Europe, daughter of Agenor and Telephassa. Agenor had come from Egypt to Canaan, the same way taken by Moses! Here Zeus kidnapped her under the guise of a bull, a disguise very dear to the father of the gods (the same god who in the Mesopotamian civilizations and the Semitic-Anatolian areas has always been the image of the rumble of the thunder that threatens the coming storm and the imminent disappearance of light). Only then, when torn from Asia (whose root is perhaps *Eos*, *Aurora*, from the Acadian *asu*, meaning "to rise"), the young woman becomes Europe, exiled, foreign, a "sunset" (*arapu*, *erepu* in Acadian, means sunset; in the Greek *erebos*, darkness, we find perhaps the same root). Tragic destiny: from dawn to sunset, but comprising the same metaphor! Asia is in Europe and Europe in Asia. Cadmus goes in search of the sister who has disappeared, and his name is certainly Semitic (*quadmu*, meaning the first, the most ancient, the guide). But even he, in tracing the steps of his kidnapped sister "to the West," becomes an integral part of Europe: the founder of Thebes and the bridegroom of Harmony, of she who does not erase but creates contrasts, daughter of Ares and Aphrodite, and the goddess of Heraclitus.

What boundaries can we possibly impose on these genealogies? What rigid terms could these myths of our history tolerate? It is hard to bear the contrasts, just as it is difficult to maintain the contradictions. Yet it is impossible to forget them without forgetting Europe. As Nietzsche says, Europe is sick, that much is clear, but it is a patient we would most certainly kill if we thought we knew how to cure it.

4

EUROPE OR PHILOSOPHY

INFINITE SEARCH

Hamlet is certainly one of Europe's most revealing masks or personae. Like Hamlet, Europe remains undecided about its own roots. The father appears firm and "certain," but the mother? Is the father alluding, perhaps, to a crime she has committed, to some betrayal? To the son it is forbidden to act as another Orestes, yet how can he detach himself from that womb?[1] Metaphor aside, how can Europe choose only one of the spiritual currents that flow into its origins without betraying the others? How can it define itself on one of its possibilities without being considered guilty with respect to all the others? Europe is the Undecided that is always called on to decide. Like Hamlet, Europe cannot escape the destiny that forces it to take action—that forces it into the drama of action that "cuts away" (de-cides). Yet no decision will eliminate its deep *insecuritas*; there has never been a *secure* decision.

Europe is suspended in its geographic configuration. It is a place that from one era to the next appears constantly to require redefinition. This feature can be heard earlier in the Greek term *topos*, or place. In fact, *topos* does not mean a container in which different elements, however distinct, are collected but rather the extreme limit, the *eschaton*, where these same elements "end up."[2] Therefore, one recognizes the place only when the threshold, the limit, is reached, that is, there where place turns into its own border (*cum-finis*), near, close, contiguous to the other from itself—where it reveals something "in common" (*cum-munus*) with the other. Europe is there where it "touches" the extraneous, the stranger. Europe does "know itself" only there where it encounters, in every sense, the wonderful and frightening face of the stranger. Its idea of place, we could say, is centrifugal. Until it reaches its "extreme" (*stremo*), which can change over time, Europe is not (Dante calls Byzantium the *stremo* of Europe).[3]

Therefore, can we say that Europe is the place in which history is invented, that is, where historical becoming becomes the essential trait of being, and this because Europe occupies the same "place" of becoming?[4] Yet Europe's name doesn't measure up because it cannot be reduced to a state of being, and in so doing it escapes univocal denotation. Europe is always a name, which is a sign for what Europe will be, wants to be, or must be. Since its origin cannot be determined, its figure is presented historically as a task, an imperative that is undefinable, which does not mean by any means without end (*sine fine*)!

In order to understand Europe we need first of all to pinpoint its direction. What direction does it look in? Where does it mean to arrive? It's opposite to the direction that the Phoenician Europa traveled, abducted by Zeus. It is to the East that Europe has always aimed, either to differentiate itself from the East, or with nostalgia, or with a spirit of conquest. The Mediterranean was supposed to be the sea among its lands. It is the same direction where the empire was transferred (*translatio imperii*) from the first Rome to the second Rome (Byzantium), and to the third Rome (Moscow). The relation of conflict with the immense land of Asia was at the center of European identity. Then the age of discovery—the age in which the *logic* of discovery is established—changes Europe's direction and with it the sense of Europe.[5] Europeans move toward the West, transgressing "the narrows / where Hercules set up boundary stones,"[6] always to reach the East. But the East is reached by erasing that earthly dimension that had belonged to it and that had both dismayed and seemed insurmountable to the early Europeans. The European had been reaching the East by sea, on that "house" which is the ship, from the time of the ephemeral Athenian empire. He discovers the East through a mode of transport that in his opinion is foreign to the essence of Asia, and precisely for this reason he believes that he can make Asia his own. The immense expanse of the sea is felt to be rich with promises. Only the rule of the sea guarantees the conquest. To rule only over lands means to be prisoners of the sea. The last and decisive *translatio imperii* is from the Mediterranean (already "in crisis," no longer "ours," *nos-*

trum) to the great island in the Atlantic, lady of two oceans and bridge between them.

Only to the extent that this *translatio* works out from its center can Europe fully become the future city (*civitas futura*), a traveling community (*in itinere*) in which the true solution to the problems and contradictions is expected to come in the future.[7] Even the ancient *eros* of philosophy and science had always been "homeless" (*a-oikos*), extraneous to any fixed dwelling, a son of that poverty that always compels it to search, a son of those "ways" as well, of those "means" that make it possible to reach the goal. Rome too, even though always maintaining its roots in the city, the *urbs*, displayed its own essence as *mobilis*. The Roman *civitas* exists only as always growing and enlarging (*augescens*). Yet only at this crucial point (under the powerful sign of the Augustinian theology of history) does Europe show itself as noncontainable spirit, as a will to power that cannot be established territorially, as project of a will to planetary conquest whereby, paraphrasing Hegel's *Logic*, every determination is removed and overcome at the very moment it is posited.

Can there be gods where there are no borders? Ernst Jünger asked himself this question. Can the sacred be there where the very idea of border (Hegel again) is only a moment soon overcome in the very act of thinking it? Europe's secular status, the European political, must also be considered in this perspective. The boundaries between sacred and profane are shaken at their foundations. The Christian religion could appear to romanticism as well as to idealism, in all their variations, as the ultimate or absolute religion precisely because it was after all a nonreligion. It was liberation of the abstract separateness between the secular and the religious, between faith and reason (*fides et ratio*), between progress of the earthly (as well as the marine!) *civitas* and the Dantean "outlasting" (*infuturarsi*) of the Pauline celestial city (*politeuma en ouranois*).[8] Even in Erasmus of Rotterdam, the nostalgia for the ancient God Terminus, god of boundaries, resounds. The herm (*erma*), however, is a two-faced Janus that unites the opposites, peace and war, rather than differentiating between them. In the fifteenth century, Europe had become almost synonymous with an irenic hope of reconciliation whose purpose was to counterattack the rampant Ottoman offensives. But at the heart of this hope even more lethal contradictions were being born, ones that Machiavelli mercilessly laid bare (and it is under the sign of the tragic that Italian humanism should be read). European identity was and is an identity in conflict. Europe's agony (of which María Zambrano has eloquently spoken) signifies the being agonic of Europe.

How could anyone "leave in peace" who finds no peace within himself? The pacifist appeals to peace (as if to make peace meant, precisely, "to leave alone") ignore the essence of European identity: an outward (*ek-static*) existence in every sense, whose aim is to communicate, open up, and convince in the sense of "winning together," convincing the enemy of the winner's cause.

To want European identity to be expressed in different forms means inventing the impossible. The difficulty consists in making peace with Europe's agonic essence and in discovering a sense of peace that is not antonymic to the will to communicate and convince. This is also and necessarily a will to wound and be wounded.

Power is knowledge (to have the "idea" of everything is to occupy a place from which one can gather a panoptic view), and knowledge is power. Far beyond any spiritual connotation, to care for the soul means, first of all, to care for that which makes possible seeing and anticipating, planning and discovering. It is the discovery as well as the ability to discover that in the end gives "legitimacy" to conquest.[9] Nevertheless, I don't know myself when I sharpen my gaze. I know myself only through the eye of the other, when I see myself *recognized* by the other. Knowledge is power but in the sense of reciprocal acknowledgment. I attain my identity only when the other freely acknowledges my worth. If it were not done freely, the acknowledgment would not mean anything. Deep in its soul and in the intentionality expressed there, Europe does not only want knowledge-power or power over those who are forced to acknowledge its power. Europe passionately desires that it be the value of the other's freedom to testify to its own value. Is this impossible? How can this burning desire not end up by being carried out as "liberation," that is, as eradication of the other from every place as well as imposition of "our" idea of freedom and "our" form of rationality and knowledge, a liberating intolerance, on them?

Let's leave open for the moment this question and ask instead: does this powerful bond between knowledge and power (*Kennen-Können*) lie on the shoulders of the "heroic idealism" (Zambrano again) of the European philosophical tradition, of its claim to attain unassailable truths? Still, European philosophy (which is without doubt "the original phenomenon of Europe," as Husserl remarked), even if based on unquestionable principles (insofar as they are believed to be self-evident), elaborates, interprets, and lives science essentially as an endless search.[10] If the truth of principles is unconditioned, science develops and is conceived of as an infinite horizon of tasks. Moreover, science attributes the character of mere approximation to any "factual" truth each time it touches it. The vocation (*Beruf*) of European science is to stop an impenetrable border from being imposed. What changes in the course of science's affirmation as the paradigm of rationality is not by any means the open and experimental character but the pure epistemic claim (from Plato to Husserl) that a radical difference exists between the theoretical approach (the love for research in which is realized the love for knowledge, *sophia*) and the techno-practical dimension. For Kant, technology is still conceived as mere application of the laws established by the science of nature, a science driven exclusively by the pure having-to-know and having-to-discover. But the "desecration" (whether it is devaluation, *Entwertung*, or disenchantment, *Entzauberung*) of this purported purity does not take place only through the line that runs from Nietzsche to Heidegger but also and perhaps especially through Giovanni Gentile's reading of idealism. More so, indeed, than in Marx, for whom the idea of the superiority of praxis dominates, and, in particular, that praxis which has leisure, *scholé*, as its final aim. The faith in technology is so little in contradiction with "heroic idealism" that it ends up actually fulfilling it. The idea of science as research and task guides the "always beyond" of the technological enterprise. The vehemence with which technology desires the permanent transformation of the world is already entirely immanent in the praxis of philosophy and not in the abstractly contemplative.[11]

Nos interrogantes—we who ask questions. Europe: a plurality of subjects who conduct research. Absolutely different styles of research, yet, even at unbelievable distances, the questioners wind up recognizing themselves. Hegel sees Anselm, he of the *quiddam maius* ("something greater than what can be thought"), as the greatest of medieval thinkers.[12] Nietzsche's overman recalls in his infinitely similar traits Eckhart's "noble man"; Gentile recalls Nicholas of Cusa's "learned ignorance" when he explains the "not yet" (*nondum*) that casts doubts on every scientific discovery but from the inside. None can tolerate a boundary: not the mystics who raise themselves to what no thought can attain nor the idealists whose Ego is not so much the point at the center of a circle with infinite radius but rather the very radiating to infinity of the power of thought, a thought that takes place in every moment. Faith is the gift that supports the mystic in ecstasy, a state of no limits, not even that of the Supreme one. At the same time, the questioning of the philosopher advances the claim of not depending on presuppositions. Yet both present themselves in the form of a never-ending search. This is a search for what is lacking, in the sign of absence (*apousia*) rather than in that of presence (*parousia*), in the sign of the "always coming" (*semper adveniens*) rather than in that of the event already been, of the "it is finished" (*consummatum est*).

THE ABYSS OF THE COMMON

Has the European spirit been dethroned? Is this just another chapter in the list of "long bestsellers" on Europe's loss of its position (*Entkrönung Europas*)? I don't believe so.[13] The twentieth-century political suicide of Europe was the product of the will to hegemonic power of territorially determined and "bounded" states. To be sure, they wanted to extend imperialistically their borders with force, but only so as to assert their own closed identity. Imperialism is the projection of traditional state sovereignties, not their overcoming. States aim at the subjugation of other states, not at the acknowledgment of anyone's freedom. The project of domination was called on to put an end to searching (understood as subjugating discovery), not so as to reinforce it. The most important cause of why twentieth-century philosophers could so radically err about totalitarianism is that they saw in it precisely the "liberation" of mankind from the limited horizons of liberal individualism, which relegated individuals to the isolated voice of their responsibility. They imagined the relation between man and the totalitarian state as founded on the positive freedom of man that is "for itself" to the extent that he is "for another" (*ad alium*). They imagined the relation between state and people to be based on the dialectic of recognition, and they looked for the moment when the truth of their own philosophy would occur. They kept on searching for an essence that had to be synthesis, that is the supreme reconciliation of theory and praxis—but they sought it in a politics that represented its reversed image: the conclusion of infinite search (*skepsis*), an act that became a revolutionary regime, a universalism proclaimed by nationalisms, and lastly an acknowledgment of responsibility that ended up in surrendering to "presupposed" powers.

Can we really say that with Europe's fall a corresponding fall has taken place with regard to its philosophy? Or, rather, can such a demise after Europe's civil war of the last century help us understand Europe anew? Can Europe's decline as political power, in the former sense of the term, represent the beginning of a new and different direction? Hegel used to say that ripeness is achieved concurrently with the beginning of decline. The same understanding of decline returns in Nietzsche. Philosophy has accompanied Europe throughout all of its history. Can philosophy strike a counterblow today?

Any perspective on such a philosophical undertaking has to be realistic. Isn't a united Europe perhaps "necessary" today to the extent that the collapse of its states, big and small, with all their imperialistic ambitions, seems to fulfill, even too well, Nietzsche's prophecy? In 1885 Nietzsche had this to say: "The small States of Europe—I refer to all our present kingdoms and 'empires'—will in a short time become economically untenable, owing to the mad, uncontrolled struggle for the possession of local and international trade. Money is even now compelling European nations to amalgamate into one Power." And he added: "For the tasks of the next century, the methods of popular representation and parliaments are the most inappropriate imaginable."[14]

If we judge the efforts of the European Union today to forge a constitution, can we say that Nietzsche was wrong? Do we truly believe that Europe is uniting because of anything other than world trade and commerce and that money is not the main reason? That the form of its government is democratic and parliamentary in the sense we know of from the history of Europe's national states? All answers we might give today are more or less apologetic or filled with disappointment. They are also ideological in both cases; we deal either with feeble realism or with the melancholy of a "beautiful soul." Truth be told, the work for a European Constitution and the events that will follow constitute a formidable benchmark for a "search for Europe." They have made the case, once again, about an *undecided* Europe that has to decide, and they have clearly emphasized the terms of the decision. Europe began the process of integration by appealing to its own political weakness. On geopolitical questions, it could not have a voice, and its founding fathers ingeniously exploited just this state of inferiority.

Removing the issue of an identity around a political culture, or explaining it in meaningless traditional terms, anaesthetized and rhetorical, has been a key factor in the speed with which economic-commercial integration has ushered in a monetary-financial one. All of us know that the integration continues. Its logic, however, is blindingly clear, and it is the logic whereby the economic and social structure, which now rules the entire planet, redefines radically, more than erasing it, any sovereignty, which is reduced to a checkpoint or transmission belt of the logic's own empire.

There can be no doubt: the basic principle that informs the so-called European Constitution perfectly adheres to the meaning of this empire. The constitution declares only one end to be non-negotiable, beyond those principles that constitute its preamble and rhetoric (I use the term not in a derogatory way): free competition and "freeing" the economic-social space from any protectionist barrier. Obviously, even this is to be pursued gradually since harsh resistance may be encountered. Yet it constitutes the undeniable pillar, the fundamental principle (*fundamentum inconcussum*) of the European Community's construction. The old political subjects—states—may be able to exercise a right of containment with respect to it—that is, they may slow it down or soften it—but the line is drawn, and the entire building will collapse if antiprotectionism were put into question. This fundamental principle affirms that the idea of liberty and the source of any of its concrete expressions is the freedom of the market. Political freedom, citizens' rights, etc., are thought to be generated from it, and without it we cannot even conceive of them.

Thus, Europe can carry out its own "program,"[15] which can be extrapolated from its history, one that is indeed founded on acknowledging in disenchanted fashion its insurmountable political misery as well as the premise of the irreversible neutralization of any autonomous political action. This does not mean that the program can be easily carried out and not even that the result is guaranteed. It only means that it is based on secure data and on an absolutely realistic calculation. The logic of the program excludes taking into account factors that by their very nature are not reducible (to quote Leibniz) to the phrase "let us calculate!" ("*calculemus!*"). In other words, Europe is utterly incapable of taking into account any actions beyond that freedom of which we have spoken. The program functions to the extent to which it is devoid of values (*wertfrei*).

It is not important to criticize the value-free character of the program. It is important to pose the question whether Europe can be held *responsible*. Being responsible entails the ability to respond. One truly responds only to a task that cannot be simply deduced from the present state of affairs. Responsibility for a task cannot be extrapolated from the calculation of factors given and from predicting the outcome of their dynamics. Responsibility means having a listening capability and then "obedience" with respect to a task that transcends or that is subsequent with respect to the immanence of the system. Can Europe undertake such a project? A task that lands a real counterblow and not one that is an abstract, unrealistic, and fanciful negation of its program?

The European task was always conceived philosophically, within the framework of questioning and seeking. Yet it was also moved by an unshakeable will to comprehend the totality of beings—by a compulsion to order. Understood this way, a task for Europe cannot be separated from a program for Europe. The imperative we know so well to cancel all distance; to reduce differences to the operative, functional compartments of the overall system; of assimilating freedom to a formal legal equality before the immanent laws of the latter—all these features are naturally stressed again. Seen from this point of view, the European program embodies perfectly the mission that philosophy seemed to have entrusted to Europe. Fulfillment of philosophy, then, or its survival as pure hermeneutics, as the comprehension and interpretation of facts?

In philosophy, however, there is no interpretation without critique, and critique is applied first of all to that "world picture" that claims to turn itself into a system. Such an image is incomparably antinomic. A system of everything is not feasible, just as it is impossible to formulate *the* law of nature. A system is effective (and the laws that are formulated in it will have predictive value) only if it is self-limiting, that is, protected from external noise. A disturbing noise in one system is the language of another, however. The logic of the system, correctly understood, presupposes the existence of insurmountable differences. It does not homologize and equalize but distinguishes and analyzes. Insofar as philosophy is a critical exercise against any collapse of the limits of intellect and its language, its dominant project today could be to entrust to Europe the task of dismantling the dominant *idola* (whether idolized or apocalyptically repelled), all of which are included in the apparently unavoidable affirmation of those economic, social, and cultural relations that can downsize the world to a mere system.[16]

However, no task (*compito*) and no responsibility can be found in the pure exercise of criticism. When we understand that the world-system contradicts the final cause (the "main cause" for Thomas Aquinas!) of that *agon*, of the pairs conflict-dialogue and relation-conflict, which constitute the essence of European history, only then can we gain a glimpse of what is really entailed. Europe's "final cause" is to acknowledge that the free person searches for and receives from another subject, that one recognizes another's value, and that freedom is not at all negotiable. There is no satisfaction except in this: to recognize my being-free through and in the freedom of the other. If I believe I am the maker of the other person's freedom, his or her freedom depends on me and ceases to be freedom as such.[17] And my satisfaction is also not as great since to be recognized by someone who depends on me will never attest to my worth. I cannot be certain of myself if I am not certain of the value of the other, nor of my freedom if his recognition is due to me. Satisfaction is possible only if the other stands before me in all his or her value and, therefore, if no easy "equality" brings our conflict (*polemos*) to an end. Equally unconceivable is the "final cause" for each of my actions (and that form of acting which is thinking itself) if an abstract separateness breaks the relation or if the relation is established by norms, procedures, and authorities transcending the subjectivities at play.

Relating is an act of bringing-closer (*avvicinanza*) that is never concluded, a being-together in the distance—but in a distance acted upon, crossed through, suffered, and never simply measured or contemplated. The more the identity of the other appears to me well defined and insurmountable in its value, the more the relation is satisfying, since it is on the part of such an identity that I pursued the recognition in the first place. In fact, the relation with the other satisfies me more deeply where the "inequality" with him or her appears the greatest. The relation brings closer an understanding of distance, which is not mute separateness but rather the rhythm of the relation. Only a thinking so organized, one that is metaphorical and analogic, will be able to salvage that idea of satisfaction/joy (*Befriedigung*) which is the "final cause" of *pathos* and *logos*: the idea that we know ourselves in the value of our being-free through the recognition that an "equal" person donates to us—equal to us in his or her own being-free. Such thinking will declare suffering intolerable not out of the goodness of my heart but because it would make my joy impossible: the look of who suffers, of who is forced into a position of dependence, will never be that free gaze in which I can find my worth. To paraphrase Adorno, not even the most trivial state of well-being could stand on the existence of the damned.

This idea supports a research and a questioning, but not the one that we find in the mere logic of *discovery*. Always research: a coming-closer, precisely, which is expressed by conjecture, by metaphor, by analogy—but which will never reveal the essence, the goal, the *eschaton* of the other, or of the other that I am to myself. It will have to be a research that demonstrates realistically the division that does not come together in any "deep peace" or *pax profunda*[18] but that sees in the distance the compatibility (*com-pathos*) and in the *logos* of the distance sees what gathers and binds distinct beings together.

Can Europe remember this thought? Only through the critique of the idea of liberty that has underpinned each European discovery and will to power: liberty, that is, as "that which" Europeans possess and that measures what they possess, liberty as "that which" Europeans are called on to impose and with which they want to "baptize" the world. On the contrary, in the play of nearness with distance, which is what makes bringing-closer possible, freedom is, instead, "what" nobody possesses: "what" makes possible that open space where the relation happens and expresses itself. "What" exists in the relation without ever being able to be exhausted by it.

Irony, the most European of commodities, as Walter Benjamin called it, is to be employed ruthlessly against the idol of liberty as the jealous possession of the single, the property of the individual—a possession he or she claims to be able to demonstrate and to prove. Freedom is revealed in the "twilight" of any claim to possess it, a claim that is the foundation of every *philopsychia*, or "love of life" gone awry.[19] Freedom is expressed in the search for the common (*xynon, communis*), which, because it is such, belongs to none. One cannot reduce this good to mathematics and calculation. It is not *mathema* that can be communicated as is, yet it is the premise of any communication. In fact, communication itself leans over the abyss of the common, which, as such, is not "sayable." The common only shows itself, we might say, as the possibility of the event of communication. This is the freedom to which we correspond and that we express in being responsible, that is, in aligning ourselves with the radical question of the other's recognition and to the irrepressible necessity to bring satisfaction and joy (*Befriedigung*) closer.

Europe can decide that it ought to be represented within the program of techno-economic "enframing" (Heidegger's *Gestell*), or within the notion of a pact (*foedus*) among those who "save" their freedom in the recognition that comes to them from the freedom of the other and, therefore, among those who ironize on the claim of possessing freedom for themselves—among those, again, who conceive freedom, analogically, as the impossible Good. Europe is called on to decide between "ruthless, intolerant monism" (as Isaiah Berlin would say) and the love for the impossible that guards the distance in the most insurmountable relation (the one, precisely, that connects the absolutely distinct).[20] The wish to construct the unity of the world-system on the premise of the absolute truth of one's own "identity" seems today, instead, to be the best way of finishing any possible future "bringing-closer." To quote Berlin once again, if we cannot tolerate—but in the sense of *tollere*, to elevate, to show in their stature—values in conflict, if we accept the dogma that they must be reduced to One and that the world has a great Design and it is a question of putting together the pieces, each in its proper place—if we do that, we will eliminate any expression of freedom.[21] We shall reduce it to the extent of our own power. And then, certainly, Europe will have at that point forever decided, for it will have decided to make itself disappear once and for all.

5

EUROPE OR CHRISTIANITY

We have seen extraordinary things today.

—LUKE 5:26

THE TWO KINGDOMS

The history of Christianity or Europe is as agonistic as the faith that founds it.[1] It is impossible to think Christendom apart from the contradictions that mark its living relation to the Christian religion (*traditio christiana*). Revelation is a given, but one always need to inquire into it (*veritas indaganda*), in the sense that it implies, namely immanently, the "exacting" interrogation of itself. Revelation excludes, and this is true from when it was first posited, any merely apologetic attitude.[2] Christianity is embodied in the history of answers that dare to challenge Jesus' question: "Who do you say I am?" (Matthew 16:15). This is the challenge that the Christian religion carries within itself, and Christianity is only the history of the renewal or reforming of the challenge. Christianity is called on at every turn, that is, always to return to that question, to check its "bottomless" quality and to attempt to answer to it. That is why the tone of conversion (*conversio*) is so radically distant from that of change of heart (*metanoia*).[3] The mind in the latter is able to arrive at the contemplation of the Unconditioned and can dwell there in peace. Christian conversion, instead, seems to be authentic only because of its perpetual renewal in time. It is as if conversion does not erase doubt but, on the contrary, appears to be fed by doubt. In short, the premise of our argument is that to think Christianity entails understanding the sense of its endlessly being questioned, which means, first, to address those questions—raised by its own history—that claim to constitute both the judgment and fulfillment of Christianity. Only with respect to the challenge these questions represent can we ask whether the reconversion of Christianity to a Christian religion is still possible today.

Where should we begin, if not from the sentence "God is dead"? In the marketplace, no one ignores that it happened, but only the madman goes around crying, "I am looking for God! I am looking for God!"[4] And his search does not provoke any scandal, any serious atheist argument, but instead just boisterous laughter. What can such amusing indifference produce? How can one explain that in the marketplace the tragic character of that sentence seems so outdated, the mourning for that death so perfectly "consumed"? The reason is that the entire history of Christianity or Europe is the history of putting God to death. We have killed Him, and to search for God can only mean now to understand the will of His murderers as well as to establish a Kingdom of the Earth where God is only the formula of "every slander against the 'here and now.'"[5]

But among Superior Men, men perfectly "desperate," prophets of the necessity of nihilism, only one, the old Pope, possesses the true science of God (*scientia Dei*). He also knows how God died.[6] God died by transforming Himself, by becoming other-than-Himself in the process of His metamorphoses. If His death were a mere having-been, He would still transcend the act of thought that establishes the kingdom of the earth. The sentence "God is dead" does not express the establishment of a fact but the actuality of a thought that presumes God's transformability. Nor does the sentence point to an absolute against which man is unable to manage anything new, but on the contrary it points to the complete availability (*disponibilità*) for man, that is, of the totality of beings. "God is dead" means God has become Spirit (*Geist*), the law (or principle) of the contradiction that vanquishes over any abstract identity, while affirming itself in the process as the truth of differences. Here we find the great leap toward unbelief. Having become Spirit, God is known. In the argument that posits substance as process and in the identity of concept and time, faith expressly fulfills its potentiality: more than simply theology, philosophy becomes theosophy. In the case of theology, always present is the painful awareness of the insurmountable difference between the theological *logos* and the *logos* to which theology testifies. For Nietzsche, the decisive leap in unbelief, therefore, is not the result of those who "don't think." It is not the outcome of the fool, the *stultus* who negates the existence of God, but of those who think of Him, radically, as Spirit, as an immanent logic of the Being of which we speak, since Spirit is itself *logos*, speech, becoming. In a word, Nietzsche is referring directly and forcefully to Hegel. Taken literally, "God is dead" might be just one of the arguments of the fool, but as the great theosophical formula "God is Spirit" shines behind the mask, the "scandal" that ensues is absolutely momentous for Christianity.

Christianity hangs on the translations that it is able to provide of the following: "The coming of the kingdom of God is not something that can be observed, nor will people say, 'Here it is,' or 'There it is,' because the kingdom of God is in your midst" (Luke 17:20–21); "The kingdom of God has come upon you" (Matt. 12:28); "The Secret of the Kingdom of God has been given to you" (Mark 4:11). The last hour, the supreme *eschaton*, the revelation of the spirit of man to himself as Kingdom of God (the identity of Kingdom of God and Kingdom of the Spirit, *Gottesreich* and *Geistesreich*), is already here.[7] The absoluteness of Christianity for Hegel is real and is based precisely on the Word. And, to the extent that every externality or transcendence sinks so deeply in the inwardness of the Spirit, it's impossible to imagine a further sublation of such a move downward. What can be done is only the work of "thinking the foundation" of the kingdom of God so announced and of a radical critique of any misrepresentation.[8]

In particular, on one hand we need to keep in mind that evangelical expressions asserting a separation between Kingdom and World only have a propaedeutic polemical function and are proper to a church not yet firmly established in its theological self-consciousness. On the other hand, doesn't the parable of the wheat and the mustard seed tell us clearly how the process whereby the Kingdom is claimed for us is already contained in its beginning? Whether one sleeps or is awake, the earth gives us the stem, the sheath, and, finally, the grain. The seed came, and the wheat was sowed. The Kingdom was placed within us. But in order to be truly ours, we have to learn how to recognize it—we must truly know it. The necessary process consists of nothing else but this, namely the discourse on God, at the end of which any belief can be vanquished and any division between faith and reason finally reconciled, in a philosophy that for its part will be Absolute Knowledge.[9]

The weight of the decision brought on by affirming the Kingdom is self-evident and cannot be softened. No compromise is available between the unveiling of God as Spirit and the compassionate care of the millenarian-eschatological traditions in which the Kingdom appears in the figure of the unforeseeable and ungraspable *adveniens*. Obviously, at stake is much more than Hegel's critique of contemporary conceptions of faith as matters of feeling or simple aspirations of the heart, that is, as only a vague and vain nostalgia. If God is Spirit, we no longer need parables. No longer is there any mystery. Philosophy is now fully reconciled with religion (with that religion which we find profoundly in the history of religious representations), and Athens, ultimately, can understand Jerusalem and save it. The rigorously atheist consequences of this discourse (which is a borderline example of atheism in Christianity) are even more radical than those pointed out by Nietzsche and before him Kierkegaard.[10] (Both Nietzsche and Kierkegaard were led astray in their criticism, as was Marx, by the theological form of Hegel's idealism—an absolutely necessary form, given that only in the language of idealism, by living it and transforming it, could philosophy be manifested as the fulfillment of the history of Europe or Christianity.)

It is not enough to know that the Kingdom is in us, that it grows in us, and that it is embodied in the contradictions of our history, even after we save them from mere chance and an understanding merely intellectual and abstract. No external appearance is done away with, nor any mastery of the hereafter. Only by implicitly leaping into unbelief does Hegel actually begin! Certainly, the dogma of incarnation, that is the Christian *logos*, vanquishes the figure of the Master by seeing it as an incomprehensible imposition with respect to the power of our spirit, thereby transforming it in the Father who sympathizes and allows us be His perfect heirs. But never, according to the basic logic of Hegel's argument, is it possible to overcome fully the figure of the slave.

The slave remains as such even if pitied and freed. The slave is confirmed in his position at the moment when he is made heir. The slave must remain a slave until he frees himself. Therefore, he is obliged to refuse the gift of the divine self-emptying (*kenosis*). The translation of the Kingdom of God (*Gottesreich*) in Kingdom of the Spirit (*Geistesreich*) clearly implies this refusal. To manifest the Kingdom in himself, man will have to make that gift to himself, negating it as such and reintroducing it as of his own making. As long as man depends on the gift of the Father, as long as man's foundation for freedom continues to be that inheritance, man cannot claim to be free, and, therefore, the Kingdom is not in him and for him.

The radical sense of modern-contemporary atheism, that is, as an understanding of the destiny of Christian religion via an interpretation of the history of Christianity, appears only in Hegel, which in the end renders worthless all those readings of Hegel offered in the key of a too-easy compromise with a properly theological dimension. The "kingdom in us" requires that the gift of divine *kenosis* be only a moment, a passage; that the growth of the Son's self-awareness contradict the Father—the Son who is called on to free himself from any externality and any conditioning; that Father and Son, in analogy with the Master and Slave, overcome the distinction of their own *figurae* and so recognize the fundamental unity of the *personae*. Thus they put an end to any mastery, except the mastery of the Spirit over the totality of beings. In short, the position of the Father is still an immediate relation to be overcome but not to be subverted in the equally immediate affirmation of an Age of the Son. The reason is because the Son, to the extent to which he is heir, the "prodigal son," and the receiver of the Father's gift, remains dependent: no longer slave but still not free. He cannot limit himself to welcoming the gift and giving thanks. He must embrace it to seize and take on its power, accept it and negate it at the same time. He cannot limit himself to witnessing the drama of the divine *kenosis*. He will instead have to act on it. He will have to transform it through his work. He will have to reintroduce that divine voiding as the result of his work, of his art. Only then will his desire be satisfied: no longer fathers and sons, no longer slaves and masters, but only Kingdom of the Spirit, that is the *Geistesreich*: a Kingdom that will not tolerate inequality, dissension, wounds; a Kingdom in which man finally will be rid of all the abstract, critical conditions that have disfigured his face over the course of time.

This is a project, we repeat, that is a great deal more radical than the establishment of an Age of the Son that, however, is premised in the complete overcoming of the Mastery of the Father. But herein lies the catch: on one hand, the Father of the New Testament is fully enclosed in the progressive unfolding of the *logos*; on the other hand, He must be radically differentiated from the Father of the Old Testament. The absoluteness of the Christian religion implies above all removing the Father from that relation and its Judaic roots, which the church, from its origins on, and often desperately and contradictorily, has always held and defended as necessary.[11]

The freedom of the Kingdom of the Spirit understands those relations of dependence-obedience as mere "history," that is, those that characterize the chosen one with respect to God. The chosen one, in fact, has to transgress the commandment in order to show himself, first, worthy of inheriting the Kingdom and, then, capable of reproducing it by himself. The dialectic of sin is essential if the process is to become alive in order to eliminate in the Father any trace of mastery and dominion. Yet the fulfillment of this process remains unthinkable within the sphere of Judaism, but it constitutes, for a theosophy of Hegelian cast, the quintessence of the Announcement.

We are witness here to the powerful return of Marcion's Paul, a Marcion purified of any Gnostic trait, who is focused on the concept of the absoluteness of Christian religion (absoluteness that would not be possible if Christian religion were Gnosis).[12] The transgression of the Law, as the founding act of the victory over servitude and, therefore, of the establishment of the autonomy of the *Geistesreich* (an essential element of the Marcionite spirit) helps us understand the Hegelian edifice (and the entire world that it reveals) even more than the Pelagian trust in the cooperating effectiveness of good works.[13] No good work has any value if it does not manifest itself as the abolition of servitude and therefore of the Master who has imposed it. No good work liberates if its time and forms are dictated to us. If work is called on to respect conditions and limitations that do not derive from its own will, from its immanent reason, it will move away from us, and the Kingdom will not be realized.

THE SALT OF THE EARTH

Still, as we have already seen, if the Kingdom is now the *eschaton*, or if its closeness to us must be understood as the presence of the ripened fruit in the seed, it will be even clearer how necessary it is to maneuver the sword firmly between the Old and New Testaments. There is no room for compromise with eschatology or with messianic promises. The contemporary Kingdom of the Spirit distinguishes itself from any Joachimism not only because the latter is always conceived in the form of the "not yet" but even more so because the apocalypse of the Spirit is present as grace and gift. It couldn't be otherwise. Contemporary eschatology, by which I mean those visions of the world that treat history according to an end (*secundum finem*), still conceiving this end simply as potential and also believing in a man to come who will plant the seed, cannot be assimilated conceptually with Hegel's discourse (even though it can imitate the dialectical system). From the latter's point of view, contemporary eschatology is an absurd contamination between the evangelical "Kingdom in us" and Jewish messianism.

If, indeed, we grasp the logical foundation of Christian faith (and therefore we overcome it as belief), if we understand that final settling of the eternal in time, which implies the incarnation of the *logos*, then not even the "hereafter" (represented by the "not yet") can be defended. The servile *Dasein* is not only dependent on the past of the Master; it is also dependent on the future that conceals the servant's freedom. The *eschaton* is now; any expression concerning its proximity has to be radically demythologized and purified of any messianic expectation. The fullness of the ages is reached, and the future is likewise without the mystery of God insofar as God is Spirit. The *eschaton* is near (*prossimo*) just as the neighbor (*prossimo*) we are asked to love. Millennialism and messianism reduce what is already an object of science to an object of hope. Both can be the expression of the effort of the Son to overcome the Mastery of the Father, but they cannot be the expression of the Son's highest understanding, namely, that his negation of the Father is at the same time the negation of his own immediate figure. Yet because any contemporary representation of both Father and Son must take into account Hegel, today's millennialism and messianism cannot in any way accept the idea (essential to ancient messianism and Joaquim de Fiore himself) of salvation coming *from* God. Therefore, millennialism and messianic tendencies find themselves compelled, on one hand, to lean on the most "sectarian" atheist secularization of Judaic eschatology while, on the other, on not being able to escape from the latter. Far removed from their origin, both tendencies are even more remote from the revolutionary consequences that Hegelian science develops of the actuality of the Kingdom.

We reflect our world in the mirror of this knowledge-science, where even the laughter that accompanies the madman in his search for God is the result of a *scientia Dei*. The madman does not know that his search is over and that man is no longer in the condition of need (and therefore of faith), that the negativity of his labor has succeeded in dooming any externality, and that the future is only the unfolding of his freedom fulfilled. The man who searches for God outside of himself is dead, and the death of this man is the secret of the "death of God." God dies like the seed, so that man can be—the man beyond the man of poverty and need, belief, and longing, and beyond the feeling of being severed from knowledge. Such a man-beyond-man is the Kingdom. With him history ends but not time, or, at least, what comes to an end is history in its dimension of unpredictability, ruled by the struggle for recognition, by the unfulfilled need for freedom. The time begins of man who can freely create, who is freed as well from being God's heir. This is a man who is infinite in productivity, in his power over beings. He is unconditioned, just as unconditioned as his freedom to philosophize had been declared in the past.

What can withstand, if something ought to be withstood, the fulfillment of Hegel's idea of *veritas*? Such a truth inquiries after itself and is self-made. It also has in itself the necessity of the inquiry and the self-making. A truth that is its own becoming-idea, as I have tried to show, is absolutely inconceivable when not located in Europe or involving Christianity. Is it because Hegel's *veritas* claims to draw to its logic the unavoidable consequences associated with the evangelical "Kingdom that is in us"? This idea (around which the entire modernity revolves) is at one and the same time an interpretation of Christianity and, if you like, Christian heresy. How can we offer resistance if indeed we ought to resist? Not just theology but Christianity as a whole has tried to come to terms with this question. Our answer will not come, as was often the case in the past, carelessly, by extrapolating some fragments from Hegel and them employing them to counter the whole system.

So, if eschatological persistence is not reduced to infinite struggle (*Streben*), to an image of "bad infinity," to delusion and impatience (in short, as a psychological-sociological issue), then it ought to be posed, both theologically and philosophically, as the problem of the eschatological character of the *Now*. "Now" refers to the end of time in time, to the relation between process and fulfillment, which is Hegel's problem. It is a losing proposition to reassert the "eschatological reservation" in the context of every stage of becoming as if it were a mere moment, as if it were nothing but a step toward a goal naïvely conceived of at the (chronological) end of time. In the light of Knowledge, such a process is integral to the idea of the outcome. Essential is the *appearing* in the difference of its moments. Yet if we understand the radical, heretical character of the way in which Hegel posits the relation between Christian religion and Judaism, we will not be able to fight it simply with the "reasons of the heart." Judaism is root and memory even in Hegel. The question is rather another. The fully formed grain—will it be Christianity and Judaism? Or is the root "overcome" in the sense Hegel intended? Lastly, how are we to understand being "heir"? Can we discover the necessity of obedience (of not only listening, the listening *logos*, the silence in the word, but also of dependency, conditioning) in the form of perfect autonomy, that is, of complete freedom? Or is Hegel right to the degree that insofar as the heir receives his legacy and is "busy" with it, he still serves? The freed slave is still subject to the agent who has freed him. But how is it possible for a Christian not to be liberated? How can a Christian not *pray* for liberation? How are we to understand, then, the dynamic of the prayer in order to counter the logic of the demand for recognition and satisfaction?

Let your Kingdom come. Nevertheless, give us *today* our bread, and give it to us in such a way as to free us precisely through your gift. Your Kingdom is closer to us than even the closest relation we have to ourselves, yet it is always to come. It is always beyond. Such a contradiction does not wait to be resolved. This contradiction is in itself redeemed, as it knows how to move in response to the demand of the ending (*compimento*). It knows the ending in terms that show the comprehension and the overcoming of its Hegelian form. In short, is a tragic form of an ending imaginable? Any other question is distant from Hegel's answer, which begins with the one formulated around the already-and-not-yet. Does it imply the same process indicated in the parable of the seed? Is this process truly necessary? And if it is, we really ought to know how it ends. This is Hegel's position. Or is the ending solely believed? If that is the case, then why ought we to believe it if *now* it is said that the Kingdom is in us? And then: how can believing manifest itself as believing the Truth, when it admits of not knowing it?

The Truth, if Truth, persuades completely. Or is that End, which is to say the appearing of the Truth without enigma, simply the Future? If so, it will have to be understood as the future in the radical sense, that is as what is absolutely unforeseeable. Therefore, our faith and our hope can also deceive us. And to what does the ending remain "hanging"? Is it to the will of the Father? If so, then the era of the Son continues to be (as implicitly held by Hegel) a moment of the Master-Slave dialectic. Or will it remain dependent on faith, that is to the heir's hope and faith (even if the heir is still child, *nepios*, incapable of authentic *logos*, still unable to speak, *infans*)? Isn't such a moment the clear representation of the Son's Promethean effort to free himself from his being-Son in order to reproduce through his own power his own perfectly liberated world? Is there a compromise between the two paths able to open up the door to all sorts of anthropomorphisms and seductive rhetoric, halfway between the "suffering God" (*Deus patibilis*) and all-too-human finitude? If we declare that the ending depends essentially on the inquiring and the making of man and that Truth consists in the power of his mind and of his labor, that this is the will of God and that God "withdraws" precisely in order to express and reveal this will of His—well, then, this is actually how Hegel explains the modern. Atheism is the fulfillment of Christianity. If we rather affirm that such a fulfillment is steadfastly promised by God, guaranteed by His Word, and that our age is the ripening of the fruit from the seed, then history is comedy, the slave will never be able to free himself, even if he lives eternally in the happiest of the heavenly Jerusalems.

There doesn't appear to be another way to think of fulfillment, that is, of the Kingdom in us, in all the fullness of its meaning. It doesn't seem possible to find, precisely in the fulfillment, the necessity of the relation with the Other beyond any conciliatory dialectic, which is to say to find the tragic form not as a moment-movement of the interrogation and the search for Knowledge but as division in and fulfillment of itself as it is perfectly aware of itself. Therefore, the Now *is*, and this is the real scandal: He, the Son, forgives our sins. He gives us life. He is the Lord of the Sabbath (that is, the Lord of infinite power). His very presence manifests Truth. The meaning of the fulfillment gathers in his discourse and in his being the *logos*. But He also declares that He was sent to do the will of the Other and that obedience is essential to his Mastery. Is this just an absurd contradiction, or is it instead a necessary consequence after having posited the being-free in genuine continuity with the eschatological nature of this Now? Is it a residue of religiosity, or is this the most radical demonstration of the irreligious character of the Christian Message?

What does the *logos* reveal? It reveals that the Kingdom belongs to the poor, that those thirsty for justice, the compassionate, the pure of heart, and those persecuted in his name possess a great treasure and therefore ought to be glad and rejoice. *Today* for them is a time of joy even as they are being persecuted, because they are the salt of the earth. They are the "taste" of the world, and what gives taste to the world the world rejects. The poor reveal the sense of the world, but the world is unable to acknowledge it. The King-

dom belongs to their figure, and therefore fulfillment is in the form of extreme misery. This explains why the world does not recognize it, as the world
cannot fathom how the *eschaton* can be revealed in the greatest poverty of
the here and now. No knowledge, no *sophia*, can grasp it, not even Hegel's
science. Why then do we refer to it as fulfillment (*compimento*)? On the
strength of what *logos* can we indicate this situation as End?

The poor, the truly naked one, expresses the perfect abandonment and
suffers it all in himself (if he didn't suffer it, he would contemplate, remain
extraneous to the world, and therefore no longer be the salt of the earth).
Yet he asks for nothing, expects nothing, and does not depend on any
alms. The poor do not fight for recognition; they do not try to impose their
will, nor do they accept any gift other than the gift of being able to give. But
the gift is perfect. It is a perfect end in itself, when it is turned to the Absent,
that is, to the invisible one, to the one who has abandoned us or who is incapable of recognizing us. The satisfaction, which presupposes the necessity
of asserting one's own will, extinguishes, instead, either in the legal form of
the contract-compromise or in equality with the other. In the former case,
the satisfaction is unable to represent fulfillment, that is, real peace. In the
latter, it depends on the overcoming of difference, on one will imposing
itself over another in the struggle. But the poor who gives freely to the Absent does not depend on the overcoming of the absence. He does, in fact,
save this distance. Only when we have a relation among what is "absolutely
distinct" is the relation truly necessary for the poor and not at all causal.
When the "com-" of commonality can be affirmed among the never united,
it will always have value and never be lessened into mere equality or identity. The relation is eschatologically thought through when it is thought as
insurmountable, when it is never to be transformed into an abstract separateness or an actual unity. Such appears to be the relation of the poor with
the Absent. The latter is the one who has abandoned the poor and who, in
his abandonment, is precisely with the poor and forms with them the Kingdom. The poor assert themselves and exist completely at the height of this
"tearing apart" (*lacerazione*). The poor establish the *communitas* as communion with the Other, and the gift that they make of themselves is the
nourishment of the communion.

The poor man is *eschaton* because he captures the relation in its most
tragic and overwhelming form. And on this foundation he recites his "commandments" (which appear as the fulfillment of the Law, just as his figure

is the realization of the Kingdom): never become angry, pay your debts, avoid any occasion for scandal, never swear because one's word must be the Word, turn the other cheek to those who hurt you, love your enemies and pray for your persecutors, just as it rains over the just and the unjust. The sense of the fulfillment, however, is perhaps best encapsulated in these two: do not covet, and do not judge. Coveting and judging, in fact, are the weapons of the dialectic of satisfaction. Here we can station the "either-or" (*aut-aut*). On one hand, without desire for recognition and without expressing the will to power over another's will, the manifestation of the Spirit is inconceivable. This desire, in order to manifest its power, is expressed as judgment, *Urtheil*. It divides and opposes one to another (*Ur-theil*); it is fever of the negative, labor, in every sense of the term. Here, though, is the counter-melody: you have heard that one must judge (the sinner, the adulteress) and that it is necessary to separate the chosen from the gentile, the friend from the enemy. Such a chain cannot be broken, as only the ancient Law promises that. On its bases satisfaction always "will be," since the Law is nourished by the negative, and even when becoming has consumed it, the end of the Law, nevertheless, will be grounded in the force of its past. And its memory will haunt us.

Only self-sacrifice, the emptying of any misplaced attachment (*philopsichia*), the metamorphosis of one's *logos* in welcoming listening, can make man "an end" (*teleios*), that is, can represent the eschatological figure that is man. Perfect as the Father: only so is the Kingdom in us conceivable. Only in this form does the Kingdom of Heaven cease to appear as unreal hereafter. The need to think the relevance of the Kingdom remains. No longer, however, does it do so through the dialectic of recognition of wills, which is the great hypothesis of the modern generally. Only a *logos* that maintains the distance between the word and listening, listening and silence, word and judgment, only a *logos* that is the "salvation" of all the contra-dictions without pretending to name them and judge them, only such a *logos* can be the sign of the Kingdom's event.

THE THEOLOGY OF PARADOX

Yet the Prayer is addressed to the Father who is in Heaven and asks Him to free us from evil. It is the Prayer that the *teleios* dares to say because it resounds in every sense at the end of the divine sermon on the fulfillment of the Law, that is, at the crowning of man's liberation from desire and judgment. Why, then, does the *teleios*, perfect as the Father, keep this "religious" tie with the Father? Isn't there here a contradiction that makes reopening that process whose conclusion is the "death of God" inevitable? No contradiction exists, however, if we can imagine fulfillment as in itself tragic. The Word was pronounced and has become flesh in the figure of a truly naked man, a perfectly poor man. Time, therefore, is complete. And at the same time the impossibility of fulfillment is shown. Mind, not the "not yet" but its *radical impossibility*, is shown. The fulfillment is very real (it is this Word, this figure, in flesh and blood that discloses it) and at the same time it is *im-possible*. In the fulfillment emerges an infinite distance between the event of the Word that reveals it and any measure of human possibility. Yet the impossible we speak of is not in abstraction the negation of the possibility but rather is its end, its *eschaton*.

At the ultimate height of his possibilities, man can be that figure who pronounces that Word. For all that, this height is man's impossibility. There is no dialectic, no describable method that can lead us to it. The Event is, walks, eats, speaks before us; it is, therefore, the possible and at the same time the impossible of all our possibilities. The fulfillment is this paradox, and since it appears in this form, here is the sense of the Prayer: the End that appeared as man (*teleios*) is, simultaneously, here and now, beyond man. Man in his figure appears at the same time both himself and beyond himself. He is the Kingdom, and he prays that the Kingdom may come. He is free and prays to be freed. If the fulfillment could be conceived as complete realization of the impossible, this would signify the man's full divinization, the metamorphosis of man in divine com-possibility (*com-possibilità*), which is to say, the negation of man and God. The Prayer points out, instead, that the impossible is such because impossible and that the *logos*, which manifests, welcomes, and obeys the impossible, is the Kingdom, in which we are glad and rejoice.

A discourse that shows the coming of the Kingdom in the necessary unfolding of all its moments (as the expression of all the possibilities of man until the manifestation of the fulfilled freedom of his power) would cause no scandal at all. Instead, such a *logos* scandalizes (Matt. 15:12) that gathers in itself both the possible and impossible. In so doing, it shows the *eschaton* of the possibilities of man as an impossibility. It also states, at the same time, that this is the last Hour. This is the *logos* of the Cross (1 Cor. 1:18), that is, of the Cross as last contradiction. The reason is because if it were only a passage, that is, if its "folly" were only a moment, then the fulfillment could only reoccur in the form of the "not yet," and the "not yet" could only appear as certain hope of perfect reconciliation. If hope is certain, however, it must also be known, and the Hour of reconciliation is precisely what the Spirit knows. Each theology so designed ends up being reintegrated in Hegel's system. Equally, we cannot oppose to it the simple display of the folly of the Cross, for this folly knows that depending on the desire of recognition will not produce the Kingdom but instead will negate it. The folly knows that the necessity of the relation is conceivable only in the form of perfect abandonment. It knows that perfect love can only exist in the form of a free gift, though it also knows that this fulfillment is the impossible, which is revealed, made flesh, heard—but, precisely, as impossible. God can do the impossible, which is to say, the *logos* of the Cross is the impossible, and this event "appropriates" us. It is our *eschaton*.

In this sense Kierkegaard's paradox cannot be confused with the "I believe because it is absurd" (*credo quia absurdum*).[14] The paradox states that everything is possible for God and therefore that God can also perform that possible which is the impossible. It is conceivable that man can raise his potential to the height of perfection (*perficere*), but man cannot render possible the impossible. Man does not possess in himself the measure of the perfect com-possibility. The fulfillment and the Now are thought of in Hegel's system as the perfection of the possibilities of Man, that is, as the end of man's history. In spite of that, and precisely on the basis of that paradoxical idea of the *eschaton* that leaps in front of us in the Christian Event, we know that the thought of the fulfillment, which results from the struggle among wills for their own recognition, leads to impossible aporias. Satisfaction only lies in giving oneself now to that impossible that nevertheless is in the Word and in the "acting" of the Word (*en ergoi*). Man is *teleios* in the distance between its possibilities and this impossible tragically fulfilled in it. The absurd would consist in believing that man can be saved by having him coincide with that com-possibility which necessarily contains in himself the impossible. Or better, that this End (*telos*) is able to be the salvation and not the negation of man. There is, however, nothing absurd in being reflected in the mirror of the impossible that exists here in the Word. The Christian religion calls man to judge himself, freely, by himself, using the yardstick of just such an impossible.

Undoubtedly, man judges himself according to a nonhumanistic standard and is fulfilled according to a measure that transcends his possibilities. All the same, this transcendence is positively the character of his fulfillment, the sign of the Kingdom.

To provide reasons for this paradox by distinguishing it radically from the absurd is perhaps the task, today, of a conscientious theology. The paradox does not consist in the intersection of finite and infinite on the cross (which remains the rose of knowledge, blossoming on the cross) but in thinking the Hour (*Ora*) as indeed the last and, indeed, as impossible, as the presence of the impossible. The paradox, as its name indicates (*paradoxon*, "beyond belief"), maintains a fundamental relation with thought. If thought were to move beyond common belief (*doxa*) into the abstract, it would lose its meaning. It would only point, once again, to possible futures not known. It would reassert that separation between faith and reason that makes contradictory any claim to Truth.[15] Paradox, instead, reflects the Event, interprets it, and reworks it. The paradox states that the infinite measure of the sacrifice-gift is for us the impossible, and that only in relation to its infinite distance, with its absence from the realm of what is possible, are we at the End, and that this End is now, since we have already completely measured this distance and since the *logos* of the impossible has become flesh to the fullest: it reveals the whole measure of the distance to us. If the paradox cannot be neutralized in the absurd, nor can it be reduced to a metaphorical-allegorical game awaiting its theological or philosophical explanation.

Now, the "illustration" of the Christian paradox is, quintessentially, the program of the Hegelian dialectic. In fact, we might even say that the contemporary dictum, "we cannot but call ourselves Christians" is based on just such an "illustration."[16] Yet the paradox of which we spoke earlier either is explained in itself, or it is not. Indeed, it is not by translating and thereby alienating it in another language that we can understand it. The paradox cannot be explained thus; it can only be revealed. It lives on in its own dimension, next to its reflection and foreign to it, just as Abraham is a temporary dweller (*paroikos*) in the land that both gives him hospitality and is also his. In the Gospel, the paradox is boldly expressed in the form of the parable, an open form insofar as it remains untranslatable and is not a metaphor.[17] A radically analogical theology could indeed remain faithful to the parable's spirit, as it is capable of revealing the infinite distance in the nearest proximity, able to uncover increasingly greater differences while at the same time probing deeper and deeper into the parable's unity. Such is a true theology of the cross (*theologia crucis*), not the simple and immediate affirmation of the abyss between finite and infinite, which has nothing paradoxical about it, or their intersecting and dialectical lines, but as the revelation of the "com-," which is to say the commonality at the height of the "tearing apart."

Such a theology is based on the sequence of scandal, followed by parable, followed by analogy, and it is understood as the narration and construction of analogies. It is in tension with any Marcionite separation between the biblical God and the New Testament God. While a theology based on the premise "God is Spirit" understands the biblical story as essentially absurd and "transforms" it in metaphors of truth that can be understood philosophically, or in "preparation" for the Trinitarian God (*Deus-Trinitas*), a theology of the paradox in the sense above will find in the paradox itself the drama of the most exacting, suffocating, and obsessive proximity, of the most extreme distance, of concealment, and of absence as the unbreakable manifestation of commonality. The theology of paradox will also make us aware that in corresponding with such a form of the relation (the only one unable to be "to come," that is, *adventitia*) lies the impossible for man and that man must betray it or attempt to escape it. Jesus fulfils the Law precisely in the sense of showing in the figures of the greatest tension and extreme abandonment (in the most "servile" figures) the sign of the Kingdom. And seen from this point of view, his messianism could not but appear as absurd according to the rabbinic tradition. Just as there is a deep interweaving between the rabbinic parable and the Gospel's parables, so too the paradox of the Son that love flagellates, persecuted by love, makes *inseparable* the never-to-be-united religions of Israel and Christ. The religions form the flesh, the blood, and the history of the analogy.

If the madness of the *logos* of the cross (that is, do I need to repeat it, the madness of a discourse that lies "beside" other forms of discourse, that has in itself the element of reflection) can only be grasped again as a theology of the Spirit (that is, as a moment, however essential, of the always-assured unveiling of the whole), it also seems that not even the fundamentally mystic tradition of Christianity can answer to it because mysticism is inspired by the Platonic and Neoplatonist traditions, which prevent, despite appearances, the development of a logic of the analogy. A method that is noetically founded, or one that is ultimately rational, leads the mystic to abandon the consideration of the multiple in favor of the speculation around the supraessential One. The various stages are all clearly definable, and even if they are reflected differently therein, their co-presence is still representable. The mystic language is essentially, "heroically" speculative and is aimed entirely at overcoming that essential contradictory nature of paradox and analogy. That, or it is transformed through a dramatic play of similes and metaphors in the attempt to express the "missing word," that is, the "great inadequacy" (*inopia magna*) of our discourse. Even Nietzsche saw that classical idealism enjoyed a deep affinity with the great tradition of Christian speculative mysticism, which confirms, in a more problematic and disturbing form, what we have already seen. The "death of God" distinguishes the history of Christianity and constitutes its mystery, which is beyond any esoteric meaning of the term. Indeed, such a death is greatly in evidence today as the *scientia* of the contemporary market, inasmuch as this history is interpreted and is claimed as the mere affirmation of the Kingdom of Spirit.

For all that, could the preaching of the Announcement, the testimony of the Event, remain silent at the scandal announced in the parable and described in the analogy, Christologically founded? No external factors are at play here. In truth, the history of Christianity is to be read according to its own principles and not as a series of compromises that had to be made. Or, better, precisely the compromise between Christianity and the world has to be reflected in the paradoxical character of the Christian religion. It is then that we shall see how Christianity's distance from the *logos*, which is expressed in the forms of an impossible mandate (*mandatum*) for man, is in fact imminent to *logos* itself. When the *logos* knows how far its own *eschaton* is beyond man, the *logos* is "perfectly man," incarnate in the history of mankind, again both foreigner and resident, alien god (*theos xenos*) and the singular evidence of the mystery itself. The preaching of the *verbum* will have to be analogically faithful to the paradox of its own structure and, therefore, will have to distance itself from its own conspicuously eschatological features. The more such preaching attempts to bring these features to memory (and the more it becomes aware that it can no longer tolerate them and thus tries consciously to weaken them), the more difficult will it be to counteract. The analogy works via the law of unintended consequences, and it is in such a light that the history of Christianity ought to be understood theologically.

Therefore, such a history can by no means be a history of ideas, beliefs, and visions of the world. The *eschaton is*, that is, the being-here is to be understood eschatologically, but the being-here is also culture, politics, and institutions. A theology oriented toward such a paradox will be a political theology not in the banal sense of that which reflects the social relevance of the evangelical message or, polemically, with respect to any "civil religion" (*religio civilis*) but because the *logos* is "true speech" (*parrhesia*). It requires public questioning; it challenges the play of interpretations. For them it is a scandal that never ends, and for this very reason it lives on in the difference between the perfect laconism of poverty and nakedness in opposition to the discourse of history. The *logos* demands madness in the world. As St. Francis of Assisi says, "and God told me He wanted me to be a new fool in the world" (*et dixit Dominus mihi quod volebat quod ego essem novellus pazzus in mundo*). Madness and the world will meet and will be forever divided. The analogy doesn't produce reconciliations, but it does explain the dynamic, that is, the energy whereby madness and the world echo the other and cross each other like the arms of the cross. Madness preaches a mankind beyond man, but this same folly must be organized; it must be embodied in a discourse, which is to say in a "politic" that contradicts madness in the name of its own rationale. In fact, if madness were to pretend to have been converted back to the reasons of the world, it would cease to be such. It would be manifested according to a logic that the world would find persuasive—in short, madness would convert to the world. The conversion of the *logos* of the cross to a rational system, to a logic of history, is precisely the grandiose project of theology and of the philosophy of Spirit.

Heresy—indeed any form of heresy—represents the attempt to overcome the contradiction by making paradox absurd. Heresy takes on a clear feature of the antagonism that characterizes the analogical form, and, on that, it builds its own system. Although they may appear different, the methods of every heresy are essentially similar: either they "free" the *logos* from the cross (that is, they de-cide: they cut the *logos* from the cross), or they absolutize the cross as a madness without *logos*. In both cases, they negate the paradoxical character of the antagonism. Either we have a sectarian (heretical) affirmation of the divinity of the *logos* or a profound forgetting of the problem of the Kingdom in the here and now, to which the *logos* of the cross testifies. In actuality, both the heresy that tends to the perfect spiritualization of the *logos* and the one, seemingly the opposite, that tends to abandonment abstractly understood, of absence and silence, have the same outcome: they rationalize the paradox, eliminate its scandal, and explain the meaning of the parable, thus destroying the freedom and openness of the parable. The same occurs in all heresies of the millenarian type, where what is broken is the eschatological simultaneity of the different dimensions of time (past immemorial, here and now—*nunc instantis*, always to come— *adveniens semper*). Given the impossibility of seeing the Kingdom here and now, we will need to "outlast one's life" (*infuturarsi*) in order to reach it. Or, since the Kingdom is only announced, we must will its realization. In both cases there is no *para-doxon* but only pure *doxa*, chatter, which no rhetoric on the "principle of hope" (or on the "principle of despair," which is simply its negative) can conceal.[18]

THE ENEMY WITHIN

The Roman Church has always fought against heresies using different means, but it has always done so with a firm conscience. Indeed, we might also say that its tradition is based on its safekeeping of the Christian paradox. But heresy itself is constitutive of that paradox and therefore cannot be eradicated. More profoundly still, it explains why the church will never gain the upper hand against the motivations underlying these heresies. Heresy states, in fact, the fulfillment (present or future doesn't matter) of the possibilities of the *mind* of man, which cannot be put aside. In fact, such possibilities are preserved in the notion of the impossible, which is decisive for Christianity, since the impossible is the *eschaton* of the possible. It is simply naïve to see either-or as the form of an abstract decision. The separateness of the two dimensions is not tragic. What is tragic is that the either-or constitutes a necessary whole. The church guards the paradox and (trying at the same time to transform it historically once again to the realm of what is possible) represents it as a knot destined to be disentangled; as a contradiction that will eventually give way. The church fights heresy by accepting its quintessential premise, namely that the historical process "fulfills" the Truth and that if not the Truth itself at least the Truth in us is "daughter of time" (*filia temporis*). And what would the Truth be if it were not also manifestation, that is, if it were not a phenomenon? Still, this is no betrayal of the paradox, if not in the sense that the paradox contains its own betrayal (just as the Truth must contain in itself its own negation). The impossibility of the

Announcement can only be manifested near the possibility that declares the former absurd and contradictory. The impossible is not the *eschaton* that the possibilities follow, is not their "project," and is not the final objective of this world. It is of this world as what cannot be attained. In actuality, it is important to repeat that what cannot be attained in the great mystic speculation is perfectly attainable by the mind alone (*sola mente*). That is, we know perfectly well that there are things that cannot be comprehended. Much as Paul Natorp explained it years ago once and for all, the "beyond" of Platonic Being does not lead at all "beyond" Being and thought.[19] There is no way to guard the impossible except by "reflecting" it in the history that transforms it into a possible (or into an incomprehensible). This is the only way that the absolute distinction—the absolute distance between impossible and possible (the distance that only analogy is able to express)—can always be affirmed.

Only in the light of the paradox, which is the basis of the Christian religion and therefore of the church as well, does the history of Christianity become meaningful. The compromises between the church and the world cease appearing as objects of a simple political, sociological, and moral consideration in order to become symbols of the Christian paradox. It is not a matter of explaining the compromise between the absoluteness of Christian religion and the wisdom (*sophia*) of this world. One has to understand that absoluteness (in the sense that we explained) is based on the analogy between the impossible and possible. If the analogy is broken—and the analogy can always be broken—we will have, on one hand, the immediacy of what cannot be attained upon us, while on the other, we will have world's *sophia*, which will rightly claim its own fulfillment. The drama of Christianity ceaselessly unfolds between the Kingdom as absolute contradiction (analogically speaking) and the Kingdom of the Spirit, which is conceivable and realizable only within the "pure mind" (*sola mente*).

Have these two polarities ever appeared as "pure"? History would seem to be the phenomenology of their reconciliation, yet a clear dissymmetry emerges. Since comprehending God as the Highest Being can only take place as a culmination in the mind (*apex mentis*), and affirming the Kingdom can take place in the concept, and, since comprehension itself can only be fulfilled by interpreting the Highest Being as the totality of the process as it is ultimately finally known—then this is the outcome: while the paradox must necessarily be seen and must, therefore, maintain distance from the *doxa* (and the *logos* of the cross must also be "the" *logos* to appear in its own paradoxical nature), the onto-theological discourse (which ends necessarily by leaping into the statement "God is Spirit") will have to count as the perfect overcoming of any paradox, any analogical demand, which is to say, any "folly." The impossible "receives" the possible; the dialectic of the possible must instead posit the same *eschaton* as nothing but a possible. The univocal discourse of the world's wisdom requires the tearing apart of the paradox, and the paradox must also guard in itself the discourse that wants to negate it. The paradox can only be maintained as incarnate in the world, but the discourse of the world cannot recognize it. The paradox attains its fullest measure by addressing those who will not listen, namely, the wisdom of the world, whose power depends precisely on its ability not to listen to the impossible. Would the power of the Spirit be displayed if the Spirit had actually listened to the *logos* of the perfectly Poor?

This is no question of banal compromise. The Roman Church must embrace within itself what by necessity will undermine its foundations. The nature of the church as great political form consists in this. Any other explanation of the formula captures only the external aspects of the symbol under discussion. The church cannot simply condemn what negates it; the church must love its enemy. Note that the church has to declare it an enemy and at the same time must love the enemy. Therefore, and on the basis of its original paradox, the church cannot do without the enemy in order to manifest the fullness of its mandate. The enemy, however, cannot but wish for the church's dissolution because its principle demands the realization of the Kingdom, now only in us, but also "outside" of us, by means of our Spirit. Herein lies the power differential, which is the energy of Christianity or Europe.

To say that the church, as what foreshadows the City of God (*civitas Dei*), preaches its truth to the City of Man (*civitas hominis*) from the outside is an absolutely vulgar way of understanding Augustine. The two cities are never separate. The church can be understood as *communitas* only if it is entirely not immune from the principle that radically negates it. This is why the church is "on a journey" (*in itinere*) and therefore does not "happen" to sin (as a recent trend would have us believe). Rather the church *is* a sinner. Even for the church the *eschaton* is the actuality of the impossible. In fact, the church must be the keeper of the *eschaton*'s ultimate knowledge; it must announce that the Kingdom is in us, but—insofar as it is recognition of the impossible—as that which belongs essentially to us; it is our "proper." The church must announce it to the "other" that it has in itself and with which it forms a *communitas*—the other that will not "obey." Will the church be able to resist this force that "does not listen," or must it give in?

In fact, the paradox can be forgotten, but it cannot abolish the "opinion," that is, the *doxa* that speaks in it. The *doxa* expresses itself univocally; this is its will. On the contrary, the paradox is necessarily an analogical community (*communitas analogiae*). The church seems barely able to withhold, to contain, the City of Man from becoming once and for all the face of the City of the Devil (*civitas diaboli*), literally the city that breaks, divides the symbol, cuts the analogy into pieces (de-cides) and forgets or rationalizes the paradox. Yet the church manages to contain the paradox within itself by taking on necessarily the character of what it contains.[20] Every onto-theology, just as every purely speculative mysticism, every "outlasting" eschatology that ignores the "Kingdom in us," every Kingdom of God, translated into Kingdom of the Spirit, exhibits the will to power of the city that claims to be perfectly free from any impossible and that wants to incorporate what is impossible within its reach. Every city wants to be the autonomous realization of the Kingdom, immune from any difference and distinction, from any otherness and distance. This is the enemy that inhabits the dimension of the journey (*in itinere*) of the church. In such a journey, which is the church, the enemy grows more powerful. The paradox must contain the enemy within it, and the church will remain the paradox until it succeeds in containing it. But for how long?

The answer cannot be found historically—and even less by invoking the spirit of prophecy—but rather only by investigating the sense of what we mean by paradox. When the powers of the Spirit are manifested according to their ultimate "capacity," only then does the absolute distinction between them and the impossible appear. The office of the church ought to be then to "sacrifice itself" to the powers of the Spirit so that the paradox that justifies the church's existence may come to light. The church, however, cannot do it. It can be perpetually tempted to do so (hence the never-ending sequels of compromise), but it will never succeed once and for all because its own reason for existence consists in "withholding" (*trattenere*) the passage of the *civitas hominis* to *civitas diaboli*. The church can be won but not convinced (*vinta, non con-vinta*). How so? Is not the same Kingdom that the church proclaims announced while the flags of defeat and abandonment are flying? Can the church bear witness to it other than in its defeat, or can the church triumph differently that in its decline?

Here is where the measure of the possible culminates. The Spirit of apostasy rises high above everything we call divine and sits in the temple of God, as God. And this Spirit is already at work (*energeitai*); it is neither an object of hope nor of fear. The Spirit dwells with the *logos* of the cross, and it exhibits its highest power (*en pasei dynamei*). The mystery lies here: this power, sent by God, is not in any way apart from its Kingdom; in fact, it is both foreigner and resident. *Evidence* of the mystery: the Kingdom preserves in itself the possible and the impossible in their infinite distance. One does not listen to the latter unless one captures the former in its finality, that is, in its *eschaton*. One captures the relation only at the height of abandonment. The church withholds this Spirit, indeed, it cannot avoid contradicting it given that the tradition the church embodies remains that of the *logos* of the cross. Thus, the church knows the "amount" of eschatological reserve of the impossible and can compare it to every amount of will and power. Yet this "withholding" doesn't permit the perfect unfolding of the apostasy (literally, the "diabolic" refusal of the paradox), which alone makes appear and then understandable the sense of the Kingdom. The apocalyptic symbol asserts (and asserts it here and now; history has no say in judging whether what it says is true or not) that only in the moment of the advent (*parousia*) of "he who opposes and exalts himself" ("*o antikeimenos kai uperairomenos*," 2 Thess. 2:4), only in the moment of the perfect contradiction against the *logos* of the cross, can the latter triumph. This outcome, however, is contradicted precisely by those who wish to bear testimony to the *logos* since they cannot stop themselves from fighting against the establishment of the apostasy.

This conflict, this *polemos*, is also a relation, and a knotty one at that, not only because fundamentally the church has to recognize the enemy (sent by God!) as part of the paradoxical nature of the Kingdom (which is why the church must love it!). In addition, it must do so because the enemy is an enemy insofar as it is capable of drawing the church away (*sedurre*) from that journey which dives deeper into the very depths of the scandal out of which the church itself originates. The church fights within itself against the idea of the adversary, the *antikeimenos* ("God is Spirit"), and it does so not because the adversary introduces himself as such but rather the contrary. Here lies the cunning of the adversary's reason. He pretends to be the exact opposite of the Spirit, so as to bring over to himself the testimony of the *logos*. The church only contradicts the adversary as mask, though in reality the church "imitates" it.

The truth of the *antikeimenos* is expressed in the spiritualization of every relation, that is, in the "liberation" of man from any spatial-temporal "prison," from any earthly tie, in the declaration that it is in man's power to posit any nature, that his mind is the center of a circle of infinite radius. Such a Spirit does not tolerate a plurality of moments and places but instead demands that the world be organized in a space. It also demands that at every point in such a space the mind that produced it can appear. The Spirit demands simultaneity and ubiquity. But in order to keep all the energies for itself, including those of the church, the adversary shows himself with the face of the opposite. "He advances masked" (*larvatus prodit*): as vulgar materialism, proprietary individualism, and eudemonism. But the *antikeimenos* is rationalization and spiritualization. It is eradication, general equivalence, the freedom of mind from any condition and from any presupposition. It is the reduction of language to the lone powerful and imposing form of "information." All other forms, and all ideologies and visions of the world that appear to define it, must end or will have already ended. Only this element remains: information as a strong and seductive power for the very power (namely, the church) that is called on to restrain and contain it.

Christianity preserves these antinomies: it is heresy and spiritualizing gnosis. It is omnipotence of the mind and *logos* of the cross. At the same time, the apocalyptic symbol (what Christianity reveals of itself) also says that Christianity is for its own ending. Christianity contains in itself an (anti-Christian) energy destined to eliminate the scandal and overcome the paradox. That energy will be withheld until nearly complete, that is, until all obey the idea that there is only the possible and that the possible is possible because we are able to realize it ourselves. Christianity contains and has kept in check thus far the fulfillment of the Kingdom of the Spirit, but it also says that such a fulfillment is inevitable.

The only loyalty to the paradox consists in demonstrating that the "Kingdom in us" is in truth defeat and triumph. The end of Christianity and the victory of the *antikeimenos* are, in fact, revelations of the last of the possibilities and, therefore, of the infinite distance that separates man from what is impossible for him. The Event has said this: the *verbum* "rises" at the moment of absolute abandonment. Here the Kingdom is revealed: no beyond and no hereafter. The *logos* of the cross has within itself the discourse that "carries" and "betrays" (that surrenders, in fact, to the cross).[21] The *logos*, however, knows also that the fulfillment of the "betrayal" will coincide with the triumph of the *logos*, that is, with the evidence of the scandal, which is to say of the paradoxical nature of logos. It is a true apocalyptic sign that the *antikeimenos* has put an end today to all the masks with which it had concealed the reasons for its "no" with regard to the scandal. Yet not even Christianity can deceive itself any longer concerning the nature of the enemy and the outcome of their conflict. Yet Christianity can preach this *verbum*: in the end, in the Hour, the enemy will not prevail. It can preach that yes, that enemy as any enemy, as any power of the Spirit, is "contained" in the im-possible of the *agape*.

PART II

The Idea of Empire

6

WHAT IS EMPIRE?

The political form of empire wants to answer a situation of nonhomogeneity and fragmentation of the sociopolitical body, a situation perceived as intolerable and threatening to bring about the end of all "legitimate violence." Yet if the idea of empire is to become viable, it is necessary that from within crisis a clear hegemonic power can emerge, which brings about new values and is capable of being legitimized as universal. A will to imperial power must be produced from the very heart of the crisis. Not every crisis, however, is able to do so. There may only be weak energies, or it may be that only reforming tendencies will prevail, or simply forces that aim to reach a deal, an accord, or just an armistice between two opponents. For an empire to become reality, the crisis must emerge in such a way so as to require an epochal change, to make the beginning not only of a new politico-institutional phase inevitable but, indeed, of a new state of Being (*epoché*).[1] It is also required that the subjects fighting for affirmation live fully aware of such a perspective. War par excellence, that is, civil war (*bellum civile*), which exhibits in its purest form the relation friend-enemy, is the moment-and-movement that brings with it empire. Every genuine will to empire must be tempered in the cauldron of civil war. The political form that is supposed to provide the most stable representation of itself is produced, therefore, by the most violent contradictions. The memory of this guilt is constitutive of empire. Its ideology is represented essentially as a metabolization of that original sin. Virgil's *Aeneid* remains the best example.

Given this background, empire is able to take on different forms. The centralizing tendency can prevail. The political, cultural, and ethnic differences that constitute the imperial structure are considered, then, essentially, as the legacy of the past that needs to be eradicated. The agreements (*foedera*) that link the parts together are entirely fictitious. They are simple masks. It is the capital and the culture of the capital that dominate and repress all autonomy. The imperial form of the Soviet Union was of this type. The Roman form, for its part, was entirely different: it always respected the political realities of the conquered "nations and peoples" (*nationes et gentes*). Rome is certainly at the center of the system, and all roads, indeed, do lead to it. However, the novelty (*novitas*) that is Rome must not weaken the memory of the Hellenic cities (*poleis*), the value of their traditions, and, also, the value of the different people that Rome subjugated (on the Roman condition that they recognize the destiny of Rome's rule).

A different form of empire is the one that we could call symbolic not in the sense that it lacks substance but in its proper sense (implied in the use of the term "symbol") of holding together the different realities that form a common idea thanks to the legitimacy that derives from religious and cultural forms deeply felt as shared origin. This is a traditional form of empire that is essentially different from the Roman one. Rome guaranteed harmony by the power of its laws and its military force. The Christian faith (*fides Christiana*), instead, is the condition of the medieval *Sacrum imperium*, which is always bound to respect the compromise that binds it to the authority that certifies such *fides*, namely, the politico-spiritual authority of the church.[2] This form of empire, therefore, is subject structurally to centrifugal pressures. They become decisive there where the ultimate forms of the legitimacy of the empire do not reside in the same political authority that wields them. In other words, to the "full" idea of empire is connected some form of "civil religion" (*religio civilis*) in which the spiritual dimension cannot be entirely distinguished from the exercise of power (*potestas*). The imperial *auctoritas* stands as symbol of sovereignty and ministry. A symbol, to be sure, is always questionable and always has to be revived. But when a secure foundation goes missing, for extraordinary philosophical and theological reasons, the imperial form comes to an end. This exemplifies the empire's constitutive fragility within the Christian Republic, but most of all, it explains the immanent crisis that the spreading of Christianity generated within the body of the Roman Empire. All of a sudden, the empire's *auctoritas* cannot be reduced to its root (*augere*, "to grow," "to expand"), that is, to its function of making the state expand until it acquires a universal value (from city to world, *urbs* to *orbis*). The new *auctoritas* entails the establishment of a new order (*novus ordo*), a new era of Being that is all-embracing. And an empire that has all the spiritual keys of its era outside itself is an empire halved, whose authority staggers from the start (*ab origine*).

From the political point of view, empire (*imperium*) certainly means the capability to rule during a state of emergency, that is, beyond the given laws. *Imperium* "must not be called into action there where it is possible to make use of the existing laws" ("*nec utendum imperio ubi legibus agi posit*," Tacitus, *Annales* 3.69). Still, the legitimacy of this extraordinary action cannot be based solely on politics and calculation. One is permitted to rule (*imperare*, and also *imperare arma*, to prepare weapons for the conflict, for the *bellum* called on to decide) only if one embodies a metapolitical vocation of a spiritual-religious order. The empire aspires to reach the highest heights (*ad summam rerum*): the role of generals (*legati*) is to heed the *praescriptum*, that is, the command they have received (to be "tied"—that's the meaning of *legati*—to the given law). The role of the emperor-Caesar is to be free (*libere*), beyond the law, to establish a new universal order. If this feature of the empire is contested, the integrity of the form is put into question. From the previous considerations one can now see how mistaken it is to attribute the hegemonic imperialist will typical of modern states to the idea of empire. Imperialism develops from the territorially determined sovereignty of the state, of which it is a typical expression, and from the nationalist ideology that permeates the territorial state. Imperialism is essentially the manifestation of the state form, that is, the product of the victorious criticism launched by the modern state against the universal idea of empire. The fundamental contradiction of imperialism consists in the will to assert universally what by its own nature, by its origin, can only be partial. It is therefore unavoidable that, on one hand, every state, having reached a certain level of power, develops imperial tendencies. On the other hand, all such states flounder eventually in their ephemeral imperialisms.

Does the decline of the state form and of international law, as the expression of the totality of agreements freely stipulated on the part of these sovereign subjects, make possible once again the formation of an imperial *auctoritas*? We use the term "empire" today to mean different and often confusing things. We speak, for example, of an "empire of crime," but no empire is conceivably founded on its operating effectiveness alone. We speak of the empire of the great economic-financial capital, but the term doesn't really apply. No form of legitimate rule can be based exclusively on market law (*lex mercatoria*), notwithstanding universal recognition. In this respect, we can perhaps only speak of "transversal empires." Still we cannot rule out that an imperial order can be confused with these. In reality, an imperial order appears possible today only for the following reasons: (a) a great crisis, a titanic *bellum civile*, has finally come to an end (articulated in two moments: World War II and the Cold War), and a single power has emerged, undeniably the winner (as Rome won unquestionably over Carthage); (b) this power interprets its own role as a mission: to establish on the planet a lasting peace under its own sign (*in hoc signo*); it believes its own imperium to be truly without end (*sine fine*) by representing it as a politico-spiritual *auctoritas*; (c) this imperial vocation is not expressed imperialistically: it does not exhibit a will of territorial annexation and is animated by a nationalistic spirit solely because it interprets its own nationalism as an authentic universalism. In this sense, the post–Cold War empire accentuates the federalist character that was essential to the Roman Empire. Its military power is essentially functional to prevent any secession from the alliance (*foedus*) and to "tame the proud" that rebel against its laws.[3] Military power, far from being the foundation of the empire, is its instrument. The empire has a capital and has its own roots in it (just as the Roman world, *orbis*, was born from the very origin of the city, *urbs*), but its spirit can be transplanted (*Roma mobilis!*) anywhere autonomous governments recognize its superior value. Militarily, this form of empire qualifies as a "maritime empire," one capable of preventing, controlling, and repressing disturbances through the intervention of its legions, which are located everywhere (*ubique*). But its legitimacy is cultural and spiritual. It is deterritorialized and truly synergetic to the present form of globalization.

This form of empire, which combines creatively many of empire's traditional characteristics, is for the moment only hypothetical. But its possibility is real. What we can argue now, in a historical and philosophical context, is that empire must try to prevent the formation of competing powers and that competing powers will nonetheless inevitably spring up. The doors of the temple of Janus always remain open when the empire is committed to the realization of its universal peace. Yet where is Christianity able today of renewing Augustine's and Orosius's accusations with regard to the history of Rome? Or is it rather Eusebius who triumphs?[4]

7

THE MYTH OF THE GROWING CITY

The *mythos*—together with the rituals and the cults that accompany it—brings to presence that origin which is the foundation of the present state: it makes origin present and reveals at the same time that the present time is still contained in its origin. The myth is therefore always the result of a "work," a narration that discerns, interprets, and imagines. There is no myth that is not mythology, and there is no mythology that by means of intervening on its own material does not become an act of mythmaking (*mythopoiesis*).[1] More generally, no memory exists that is not imagination and the perpetual re-creation of the past.

Mythology, this work of interpretation-transformation-metamorphosis, establishes any associated order, any pact (*foedus*) endowed with real virtue. A political order that ignores its own origin appears to be without a foundation. At best, only a simple, contingent cohabitation (*synoikia*) can stand without a proper *mythos*, but this is not true of a political reality, nor a *polis*, and certainly not a *civitas*. Could or can the modern national state exist without its own myth? Can that paradoxical rootless community that we are today still narrate its own origin? Can it reimagine its own *mythos*? Of our states only history remains, but the writing of history (*historein*) will never be able to represent that character that is not ephemeral and not transitory and that supports and shapes (*in-forms*) the becoming of the city. In fact, *historein* ultimately aims to destroy precisely the validity of that foundation that the mythos "imagined." History, by its nature, demythologizes.

Neither *polis* nor *civitas* can be imagined in their substance, disembodied of their founding *mythos*. This, in fact, is what the *mythos* says: who founds the city? Which demon or character guarantees its power? In other words, only the origin (*arché*) is myth's true champion. Still, how are we to understand the *arché*? How can it be portrayed? The well-known passage from Book 5 of Aristotle's *Metaphysics* speaks of the different ways of predicating the *arché*. It is the beginning but also the first and immanent cause, and it is also the most essential and original part of a being. Furthermore, it is also what guides and rules a process, and it is the principle of a knowledge as well as the premise of the demonstration of that knowledge. It certainly isn't easy in reconciling these definitions. To be sure, *arché* appears as what explains a process (and therefore what remains stable as the foundation of the history of a city). Nonetheless, this potentiality in no way coincides, necessarily, with the origin of the same process. What guides and rules, what holds supreme command is not as a matter of course manifested as the first in chronological order. Therefore, the tenet (*principium*) that must be recognized as the most important part (*potissima pars*) of everything does not necessarily sum up in itself the character of the first (*primum*) and highest (*summum*).[2]

What power or force, then, guarantees the life of the city? The things that come first (*prima*) or the highest ones (*summa*)? And what dialectic exists between the two? Mythical thought is called on to grapple and "work out" these problems.

Dumézil cites Augustine's quote from Varro with regard to the relation between Janus and Jupiter at the beginning of the most interesting chapter, for us, of his work on archaic Roman religion. To Janus belong the first things (*prima*), but to Jupiter belong the highest ones (*summa*), and the *summa* prevails over the *prima* (for this reason they have the *arché*).[3] The power of the beginnings (*potestas primordiorum*) has less *dignitas* than that of the Capitoline god whose presence safeguarded Rome. Janus comes first chronologically; his "value" (*timé*) is established on exordia, on births (and in this he pairs with Juno), as well as on transitions and passages from one state to another. Janus is the first of his kind (*primigenius*) but absolutely not *maximus*. This is how we can say that Janus is principium but absolutely not *potissima pars*, not the most important part.

His figure appears to be primordial even with respect to Saturn, whereas Janus and Saturn form a unique structure clearly subject, in the end, to Iupiter Optimus Maximus. The historiographic compilation *Origo Gentis*

Romanae (*The Origin of the Roman People*) narrates how Janus had taught the barbaric natives rituals and ceremonies. Yet this is not enough to found a city. Only Saturn, by teaching the shared use (*communis utilitas*) of the art of cultivating the land (*disciplina colendi ruris*), brings men to order their life together (*ad compositam vitam*). A significant mythos is the rite of the "cultivation" of the gods (*ritus colendorum deorum*), that is, of giving the gods their due. Religion does not free men from their primitive state; they continue to live by hunting and pillaging and remain "people uneducated and scattered among the high mountains" ("*genus indocile ac dispersum montibus altis,*" *Aeneid* 8.321). Religion does not build a real community. For a community to appear, Janus's first things (*prima*) must join up with Saturn's first things: the cultivation of the gods with that of the land. The cultivation of the gods must reside on cultivated land, for only then do we have the conditions for a *civitas*. This is a particularly Roman trait: for a multitude to give way to a genuine people (*populus*), religion must be embodied in the laws, that is, in the system of laws: "it must be converted in the law, as faith in an order of absolute value."[4]

Accordingly, Janus and Saturn come first (*prima*). The principium, insofar as "only" *primum*, is divided in religion and law, which means that it falls to religion to overcome itself in law in the sense of the Hegelian *aufheben*, resituating itself in a superior order at a higher level. Two clearly distinct dimensions must be reassembled in the superior unity of the *prima*. Moreover, their exchange is made even more obvious by the fact that while Janus (the religious principle, at a more proper mythological level) precedes Saturn (the political principle), at the level of the history of the city it is Romulus, the political agent (*auctor*) par excellence who appears as the first (*primigenius*) with respect to Numa, the religious king (*rex religiosus*).[5]

Nevertheless, the *prima* do not belong only to Janus and Saturn. Roman mythology also includes another figure, one who is not as easily "workable," a figure much harder to bring round to the *potestas* of Jupiter, and that is Fortune. As fertile (*fertilis, ferax, bona dea*), Fortune certainly does not contradict the structure Janus-Saturn/Romulus-Numa. Yet insofar as Fortune is also linked to *fors-sors* as the expression of the unforeseeable and the ungraspable "accidental" (*fortuitum*), it seems to point to a primordial (*primigenia*) dimension with respect both to the religious and the political. In Praeneste, the most important place of its cult where the oracle is the essential element, divination "is based exclusively on chance." From a sarcophagus, a boy (*puer*) draws "the asked-for response, after having mixed the *sortes*—inscribed pieces of oak which, according to the myth, were found inside a rock." The cult of Fortune exists in Rome too, but this form of divination is unknown there. In Praeneste, Jupiter and Juno "still hang by the breasts of the primordial goddess," while "the public Roman religion has never recognized Jupiter as *puer*."[6] I believe that the dispute between Rome and Praeneste surrounding the cult of Fortune and its relation to Jupiter, which Angelo Brelich has analyzed marvelously, can shed light on the entire problem of the Roman relation between *prima* and *summa*, that is, how the Romans solved this problem.

Fortuna is primordial in a more radical sense than both Janus and Saturn. Praeneste's Fortune is not only the firstborn (*primigenia*) but seems to exist before any difference, duality, or order (*kosmos*) that is established among distinct beings. It is a precosmic reality, as its water symbol shows. On the opposite side is Jupiter, who is the sovereign order, the founder (he is there when Rome is founded), legislator, and guarantor of that which is everlasting and that which supports the law (*ius*). Jupiter's voice decisively lays the foundation; "fate is the voice of Jupiter"—"*vox enim Iovis fatum est*," says Servius in Virgil's *Aeneid* (1.10). While Fortune constantly threatens to shake up the newly formed order, rattling its boundaries and distinctions (that is why the introduction of his cult in Rome has plebeian origins: Servius Tullius is its founder!), Jupiter states that what he says is *fatum*, which is to say removed from the unforeseeable. Thus, according to the mythos that founds Rome's strength, it is necessary for Rome that Fortune kneel before Jupiter and that the *primigenia* goddess be subdued dialectically by the latter. Fortune cannot appear to be a preexisting force with respect to Jupiter's *potestas*; this would risk collapsing the *kosmos* or declaring it subject to fate. To assert Rome's power, Fortune must be simply the condition and origin of the cult of Jupiter, that is, of his *fatum*. In Rome's eyes, as Brelich concludes, to maintain an autonomous cult of Fortune would have meant to be "stubborn" with regard to Jupiter's order, personified in the history of Rome.

We can now see an essential element of the formation of Rome's foundation myth, or, more precisely, of what Rome's *summa* consists. If Rome wants to "remember" how it came to be, it is forced to forget Praeneste, the precosmic figure of Fortune. To be able to imagine the foundation of one's own strength, Rome must forget what appears to be a preexisting force with respect to Jupiter's power. If Rome wants to be "sayable" to itself, it cannot remember a *puer* Jupiter who does not speak and does not "say." Jupiter's voice, for Rome, can only be *fatum*. It would be sacrilegious to think of a speechless (*infans*) Jupiter.

But these considerations reveal a "fatal" law: essential to the virtue of memory, essential to the *mythos* of origins, is the faculty of oblivion. There is no memory that is not at the same time forgetfulness. There is no myth-making imagination of the origins that is not at the same time oblivion. To define and narrate a foundation, an original seed, an *arché*, it is necessary to bracket or forget what this narrative threatens to contradict, namely, the powers that question and problematize the "rule." The *mythos* serves more to forget than it does to remember. Only after forgetting Fortune is it possible to proceed to the *summa* of Capitoline Jupiter. The *summa* coincides so little with the *prima* that the former even require, in order to secure foundation, that the latter be forgotten. For the Roman *potestas* to be revealed in all its fullness, it is necessary to get rid of any primordial, precosmic, indistinct power. This is how the Roman bond between religion and law is inevitably formed. On this basis, it is possible to uphold that supranational order of values which inspires and informs the entire history of Rome.[7]

Roman history follows the same "rhythm" of Fortune's assimilation to Jupiter's *fatum* insofar as it manifests a will of integration and fusion: from the foundation of the temple dedicated to the god Asylum ("safe haven"), from the initial welcome extended to everyone—slaves and debtors, murderers and rebels—desired by the twins Romulus and Remus "in such a way that soon the city overflowed with people" (Plutarch), until it turned the city (*urbs*) into world (*orbis*) and a divided *orbis* into a single *urbs*. "Growing" (*augescens*) is the city's "most appropriate name" (*nomen propinquius*).[8] It is Rome's foundational *mythos* that demands that Rome always expand. "I grow, therefore I am" (*augeor ergo sum*). At the same time the *urbs* remembers its own origins insofar as it assimilates, integrates, makes its own, all the displaced and conquered peoples (*peregrinos, hostes, victos*). And it succeeds not because of Fortune, nor thanks to the speechless powers of Chance, but by the explicit, uttered will of Jupiter: *fatum Iovis*.

The *civitas* that always grows is that of the Roman people (*populus Romanus*).[9] The idea of growth, flowering, continuity, and the succession of generations seems implicit in the very etymology of the term *augere*, which is modeled on an ancient Mesopotamian stem.[10] The city flourishes if the people flourish (*"aucta civitate . . . populo aucto,"* Pomponius Atticus). And the people cannot flourish, cannot guarantee, through their own growth that of the city unless they are sovereign, that is to say, if they do not hold the fundamental *auctoritas*, in short, if the republic (*res publica*) is not a thing of the people (*res populi*).[11] Here is how the foundational myth, the story of the origin, is *arché* insofar as it is a living foundation, a first and immanent cause, and a principle that guides and always governs the growth of the city. This myth tells how *romanus* is not the expression of a specific ethnic group, a stationary root, but a will of ageless, unlimited growth.

But how can one make sense of such a "demon"? How can we imagine such growth? Is a legal and political order conceivable that is also not localized, that is, an order (*Ordnung*) without a place (*Ortung*)? The *urbs* must not disappear when it becomes *orbis*, universal empire. If the *urbs* were to grow old, the very foundation of the empire would end. An abstract empire without roots, and without a myth of its own roots, can be an idea, but it cannot be a political reality endowed with genuine *auctoritas*. Conversely, if Roman law were to be localized in a fixed, determined form, it could not create order in the *orbis*, which is to say it could not sustain the enlargement of the *urbs*.

We need, therefore, to think of a legal localization that is not synonymous for setting in a determinate place.[12] Place (*Ortung*) will have to be the same as law (*ius*). The firm ground (*terra firma*) of the order (*Ordnung*) is the same thing as the will to grow continuously, which the myth establishes, the law states and commands, and history personifies. This is indeed a difficult arrangement (*improbus labor*), but it is the *opus* of Rome: this is the task, and here is the work to be done (*hoc opus, hic labor est*).

Nevertheless, the Roman miracle cannot last forever. As the *urbs* is undone in its universal becoming—in its becoming *orbis* and in the unfolding of its will to grow—the terms, the laws and customs (*nomoi*) of all those cities that it encounters are assimilated to its law. They are integrated to the fate of the *urbs* so that in the end, because of an inevitable logic, Rome will have to pull up its own roots. That passage in Symmachus's *Relatio tertia* on the "affair" over the Victory altar has an epochal, symbolic meaning. In it, the high representative of the pagan party speaks of tolerance and peace for his gods and almost inadvertently uses the term "old" (*senectus*) when referring to Rome. In fact, it is Rome itself that speaks like this: "Excellent princes, fathers of the country, respect my years . . . I want to understand the value of the new rituals that are being instituted, however, it is too late, and possibly offensive, to make amends for someone who is old" (*sera tamen et contumeliosa est emendatio senectutis*).[13] Rome is old! What catastrophe of fate has Jupiter spoken! How can an old organism, in fact, continue to grow? How can the inhabitants of a city, forced now to plead for their own salvation, with no recourse except to fall back on their own memories, which have by now been reduced to a religion of the elderly (*religio veterum*), grow? How can the *urbs* flourish and be extended from generation to generation? The *mythos*, which is the original word of the *civitas augescens*, has been eradicated.

That is to say: for such a *mythos* still to bear fruit, it must be moved. To remain effective and virtuous, the *mythos* cannot continue to demand that it be located in the former Rome. Rome is always the mother, but she is sterile and miserable by now (*vere misera mater*). She is mother, and therefore she must be saved. But to be saved, Rome must be relocated; it must be transferred somewhere else. Such a move cannot be a mere physical and geographic translation because Rome's roots were never only earthly. Rome's *mythos*, its original "word," will never be saved by linking it exclusively to a specific place. The true, authentic translation (*translatio*) is that of the Roman *urbs-orbis* to the Christian *urbs-orbis*, that is, from the harmony of the emperors (*concordia Augustorum*) to the harmony of the Apostles (*concordia Apostolorum*), from the Roman *populus* to the Christian citizens of the city to come (*cives futuri*).[14]

In short, between Symmachus, the "old patrician," and Bishop Ambrose, the latter is the true Roman! He is the one who wants Rome to expand and to continue as mother. He is the one who is most faithful to the *mythos* of the origins, a *mythos* that forces the city to assimilate, integrate, and prevail over other traditions, customs, and languages. Symmachus the pagan (from the village, *pagus*!), Ambrose the citizen (*civis, civitas*!). Rome can be transformed into the City of Christianity because Rome, from its beginnings onward, was "the" growing city, *civitas augescens*. It is Rome's fate, which is to say, Jupiter's fate (*fatum Iovis*), that dictates the forms of the transfer of power (*translatio imperii*) from one to the other.

Yet, reflected in the mirror of Christianity, which is to say in the words of the Fathers (Augustine, Orosius), Rome also reveals another element that has always been a part of its ever-growing nature: the misery of endless wars, the curse of never being at peace. The drive always to grow, always to be capable of growth, to transform what the heart desires most, which is leisure (*otium*), into a desperate kind of nostalgia, as if there were no hope of not moving forward. Rome will never be able to stop its advance and remain at peace. Even if Rome were to return to itself, it would only discover the reason for its compulsion to move forward. The profound nostalgia for the home that is nowhere to be found describes monumental Roman poetry, just as the awareness that the city's destiny is inscribed in the "Cainite," fratricide myth of the origin of the *urbs* is found there as well: "It is so: bitter fates drive the Romans and / the crime of a fraternal murder, / ever since the blood of blameless Remus flowed / into the earth from his descendants."[15] Harsh and ruthless is Jupiter's fate. The word of the highest undeniably makes Rome victorious, but it also makes all its victories mournful (*tristi*). We note that the incomparable poet of the mournful victory (*victoria tristis*) is also the greatest poet of Rome, Virgil.

The same energy that sustains and nourishes the power of Rome is the one that eventually ends by breaking it. Rome is destined to become "delirious," literally "to stray away" (*delirare*) from the terms of its foundation. No longer a city, it will have to move beyond any seat (*sedes*). No simple transfer will satisfy its original desire to become world, that is, to be transformed into a universal Empire. With every new place, the homeless longing (*eros aoikos*) will burn again, generating conflicts, wars, grief, and, then too, nostalgia, despair, and eventually dreadful old age (*misera senectus*). Is just such a Roman fate in store for Western, European politics? One would think so, moving from the city to the state's "icy monsters" (Nietzsche), to the cosmopolis, which is the complete oblivion of the "home" (*oikos*). Such historical development (in the etymological sense of *Geschichte*, of what is originally "sent to us")—wouldn't even be conceivable if there hadn't been a Rome, if there hadn't been the fate that compelled Rome to expand. The pilgrim city (*civitas peregrina*) appears to be the revelation and not the negation of the *civitas augescens*. The city is unable to expand continuously if it remains fixed in its own center. To become universal, such a city must leave the center behind and become a pilgrim. The growing city reveals its own truth precisely by abandoning itself. This is what the preaching of the Fathers had after all repeated: "Such is the law of God: that everything that begins must also end."[16] The particular *mythos* of Rome could least of all prevent her decline as it asserted the necessity of becoming *orbis*. Expressed philosophically, and returning to some of my initial considerations, we might say that no foundation myth expresses with greater energy the idea of *arché* as origin of a process, of a becoming, and of nonstop growth. No myth represents the oblivion of the *arché* as precosmic beginning more powerfully than that of Rome. The Roman myth only has eyes for the source, which is to say the primordial will that asserts itself and produces. The Roman myth is the one that speaks of the origin of powers that make history.

This myth, however, has no power with respect to the end of the *civitas*. Since it is only a myth of origin, it also carries fatally within itself the words of decadence and death. As it is also a divine law, everything that has an origin must come to an end. The myth of Rome has no truck for the face of Janus, for that face is not turned to move ahead. Instead, as we might say, the face of Janus is turned in the direction of Fortune. Thus, the excellent, the maximum, the highest, belong inexorably to time, to voracious Kronos. The highest things, the *summa*, are, in fact, within the process of time: moments of its movement, which is even more reason that the *civitas* that embodies them is nothing but a moment. Rome does not conceive the *prima* except to "plunge them" into the *summa*.

Rome makes drastic and perhaps irreversible the forgetfulness of the beginning as pure beginning, which is invisible (*adelon*) and in no way destined to be represented or revealed. Janus has two faces, but neither of them looks at or remembers the immemorial. The myth of Rome is founded on the oblivion of the immemorial and, therefore, on the idea of the beginning as mere "first moment." Yet this idea of beginning, which forgets the origin (*arché*) as invisible (*adelon*) and boundless (*apeiron*), sustains our entire conception of history.

All this is already implied in the sentence "the most essential part of anything is its beginning" (*potissima pars principium est*). It says that the life-giving energy, and, still more, the creative energy, is part of the beginning and therefore already set out, just as all the parts are: they are nothing but a moment. Nevertheless, how can a part be a beginning? Obviously, only as first moment or as cause of a process. Yet the first moment of a process will never be the Beginning. Every cause is in its turn effect. Only the immemorial, whose power is primordial, is truly principle in every part and every moment. As such, the immemorial is also undefinable and indeterminable. No part of the movement will have a memory of it (not even the most important one, the *potissima*, which is precisely its origin). Yet everything derives from the immemorial. From the boundless (*apeiron*), everything comes into existence, that is, every cosmos and every law. Out of the Invisible (*adelon*) everything that is manifested must be manifested. Out of concealment (*lethe*) everything that is unconcealed, every truth (*aletheia*), is produced. Only the power of this pre-power, only the order (*kosmos*) of this pre-cosmos, can last eternally. This is exactly what the myth of Rome had to forget.

8

DIGRESSIONS ON EMPIRE AND THE THREE ROMES

THE FORM OF EMPIRE TODAY

The term "empire" comes up frequently in discussions on globalization, though it might appear to be a bit too rich in "aura" to be used analytically.[1] Nonetheless, the term does meet a specific need: it grasps the cultural and political meaning of how globalization actually works without reducing it by distinguishing its technical and economic mechanisms. It also at a minimum allows us to pose the question: is the political truly destined to become utterly immanent to the laws of techno-economic development? Is the convergence between the two dimensions going to become final in the perfect "monarchy" of the second? Is the world of the future going to be fully monarchic, if it is not already? The term "empire" does not just evoke similar tendencies from the past but presumes that the decline of the modern state form is irreversible and that its territorially determined sovereignty as well as international law (as the product of agreements and interstate deals) has been weakened. But the term "empire" also assumes that these processes cannot have as outcome a World State regardless of configuration because the state form refers back to a dialectic of representation, that is, to a relation between government and public opinion already overcome by the hegemonic powers of globalization, which again are technical, economic, and financial. Nor could empire agree to a planetary order of great spaces,[2] since those spaces would necessarily constitute antagonistic polarities and so be in contradiction to the motivations of those globalizing powers. Empire could be configured, instead, as a kind of world governance precisely because it rejects every traditional political representation and, therefore, every establishment of autonomous places of the political. Empire's dominion is the informal one of the widespread subordination of the parts to the whole, that is, of the perfect "shaping" (*in-formazione*) of the parts operated by the single language of the whole. And in the logic of world governance, even local realities, reproduced as artifice of the whole, that is, of the global, can be properly compensated for or quieted. A rhetoric of the local is entirely compatible with empire, whether we have in mind the "spiritual one" of technology or the American one—or, still more realistically, a relatively unstable blend of the two.

I believe, however, that those who prophesize empire are impatient. Is Kant's confederation really only a rational-Masonic utopia? Is the federalist perspective capable of expressing only vague functional-organizational reforms within the logic of the old state? Are the great spaces only precarious areas of the market, entirely internal to the affirmation of the global and therefore unlikely to be confused with civilization or with culture? Is the decline of the states so clearly describable, much like how a stone rolls along an inclined plane, or is the state still able to be of value as the center of decisions with respect to the form of globalization? In short, is a politics of states still available to us?

We can only, I'm afraid to say, attempt to "correspond" metaphorically to such questions by limiting the purview of the question. To test the very sense of the term "empire" appears, then, in this context, to be most important. "Empire" refers directly to the Roman idea of empire. But, with regard to that idea, what do we want really to emphasize and retain as fundamental? Or, what in the Roman idea of empire appears to us at odds with respect to the imperial tendencies of today? What do we think of ourselves, and what kind of mythology are we creating, when we speak of empire today compared to what the Romans themselves "generations after generations thought of themselves?"[3] The past is never dead, as it is clear from the terms that we are forced to use; we always struggle with them to understand our age better. Today it is even more crucial to fight that past that marks our civilization, survives in our idea of law, and is inexorably connected to the idea of Christianity. Our age seems to be headed in one direction: the Greek term *hegemonia* and its corresponding Latin term, *imperium*, reflect this tendency. *Hegemón* is the leader, the prince. Since he "marches forward," he guides, and by guiding he explains the course; in other words, he sets out the path to follow. Since he knows how to prepare the path, and since he is the guide, the leader holds actual *hegemonia*. For this reason, he is allowed to push his own people forward, urging them in the direction that he has prepared. One is an *imperator* for his capacity to "prepare" (*in-parare*) a future and to force his followers to make it a reality (according to the Semitic etymology proposed by Semerano: imperator from *in-duper-ator*, where *duper* is closer to *dabar*, a term that means to exhort, to order).[4]

The present situation is that of a hegemony that has reabsorbed in itself any figure of *hegemon* or *imperator*: a Hegemony of the Word, the empire of an impersonal *dabar* that resounds in the form of an absolute commandment, on pain of being thrown out of the commonwealth of those who respect "human rights." But both in the Greek and Latin terms the reference to a place, a "capital," of hegemony remains unavoidable, as well as reference to a person who embodies it, or to a political head, though nonetheless made of people, that is, a "collective prince," who can clearly be represented. This doesn't seem to be case here, unless we wish to reduce the "complex" of globalization to the equivalence Empire=USA (and to interpret American power as imperialistic, in the traditional sense). Furthermore, the Roman meaning of *imperium-imperator* retains a certain sense of exceptionality, which is expressed best in at least two classical *loci*. In the first, *imperator* is the leader himself, and his role is clearly distinguished from that of the high-ranking officer (*legatus*) to whom is entrusted a specific function and who is supposed to obey a specific task (isn't it true that our administrators and parliamentarians are *legati*; that is, are they not our "delegates"?): "The functions of a lieutenant-general are one thing, those of a commander-in-chief another; the former does what he is commanded to do, the latter must freely deliberate on what matters most."[5] The imperator must deliberate and must decide on the whole; the *legatus* must adhere to what has been decided and so must adhere to the Norm, that is, to the command (*praescriptum*), by carrying it out or by supervising it so that it may come to be.

The imperator clearly appears superior to the norm since he produces it by taking into account the entire situation (a whole that in principle escapes the attention of the *legatus*). This is the sense of the second *locus*: every time the *potestas* grows, the power of the laws diminishes. As we have already said, empire must be avoided (*nec utendum imperio*) when we take action by means of the law (Tacitus, *Annales* 3.59). Yet there are situations in which the acquired legal norms must be subverted, and the prince who "administers" the law must leave his place to the imperator, that is, to the one who holds the *imperium*, so that the latter may dictate new ways. The imperator is constituent power and, therefore, does not act according to the given norms but instead prepares new ones. However, he operates necessarily by means of lieutenants; his will cannot be actualized immediately. The two spheres are inseparable and at the same time absolutely distinct. Well then, doesn't such an idea of empire clash with the current situation in which empire seems to manifest itself as the abstract dominion of absolutely rational norms, of an all-reaching *logos*, excluding in principle the intrusion of the political exception and decision? Isn't the empire of today expressed in the imperative of the universal depoliticization of every relation, namely its reduction to a technically assessable exchange? The regulative idea of the transformation of the political into the economic contrasts metaphysically with the ideas of *hegemonia* and *imperium*. In empire today, in other words, everybody acts as lieutenants (*legati*) with respect to an imperator who does not function anymore as "part" but as a natural and presumed totality.

Still, as soon as we make the effort to understand techno-economic globalization as a political destiny beyond the state, we realize that the strength of the metaphor connecting globalization to the Roman imperial idea is a long way from running out of steam. The idea of *imperium* as a state (*status*) capable of putting an end to the drama of political decision is also a Roman idea. The ecumenical character of the empire is a guarantee for Virgil that the age of the "execrable war" (*bellum nefandum*) could be at an end. The institution of empire is the creation of a sovereign order and much less of a fixed political sovereignty. "Empire without end" (*imperium sine fine*) means two things: first, that the ventures conducted by Roman political and military power have already reached the ends of the earth, that is, of the *orbis* (and therefore there are no more limits); and, second, that the life of the empire, its duration, is no longer threatened by breakups and exceptions. Italy, "a land that teems with empire" ("*gravida imperiis*," *Aeneid* 4.229) has finally produced its real domain: it is manifested as destiny, supported by political action, and certainly not the result of the latter. Empire today, we might say, claims to present itself exactly in this form.

Nonetheless, the empire on which nations stand (by which they are shaped, in-formed, and guided according to destiny and reason) is also the power that "tame[s] the proud" (*Aeneid* 6.851). The expression "*debellare su-*

perbos" implies, literally, the necessity of war and also, therefore, of a leader capable of confronting the emergency with a free hand (*libere*, as Caesar says), unconstrained by those norms that work precisely in normal situations. But who are the "proud" today? No longer the enemies (*hostes*) of the ancient "execrable war" of that creative vortex who seized the virgin Camilla, Euryalus, Turnus, and Nisus (Dante, *Inferno* 1.106–107), tragic figures of destiny whose lesson finally appears to us as obvious.[6] The proud are those who today refuse the empire, unreasonably; they are, therefore, the enemies of the peace that empire alone can guarantee. They are those who still want to divide what has been finally put together and to sow disharmony where harmony was achieved. The war against them, therefore, is not the war of a political power against another but of "peace" itself against the principle of division and heresy. Seen from this perspective, once again, the Roman metaphor appears perfectly suitable for illustrating the imperial tendencies of our era.

GROWING AND RENEWAL

This tentative approach, which leads to more radical distinctions, which in turn shed light on new analogies, expresses our struggle with the past and our search for the identity of the present moment. To develop this "play" in all its potential, however, it is not enough to reflect on the idea of empire in the same way that it was elaborated in imperial times, which is to say based on its mature ideology. Rather, we have to understand its origins and genesis, and this takes us back to the very origin (*origo*) of the Roman *civitas*, to that *origo* which always counts as the most important part (*potissima pars*), that is, as the beginning (*arché*), in every sense, of an organism.[7] The words of Sallust and Livy will suffice to make my meaning clear. "A dispersed multitude of different habits" (*multitudo diversa atque vaga*) gave life to the Roman *civitas*. It's incredible remembering (*incredibile memoratu*) how people with diverse lineages, languages, habits, and traditions were able to come together within the same walls (*in una moenia convenere*) and build a city. What is responsible for this miracle? The *civitas* is built on the strength of a unity of intentions, common interest, and common purpose (*concordia civitas facta erat*). The *civitas* is also the product of political action sustained by the idea of harmony (Sallust, *De coniuratione Catilinae* 6.1–2). Only through laws, by dictating *iura*, was Romulus able to unify one people out of that dispersed multitude (*coalescere in populi unius corpus*). The obedience to the law makes the citizen, not land, nor blood, nor religion.[8] A citizen is whoever accepts the artifice of the law and takes refuge in it, even "a promiscuous crowd of freemen and slaves" (*sine discrimine liber an servus esset*). This was precisely the first sign of the incipient power of the Roman *civitas* (Livy, *Ab Urbe condita* 1.8).

A pact (*foedus*) founds Roman power, a common feeling (*concordia*), which does not begin in any identity of tribe (*genos*) but is rather expressed in the strength of the law, in the sacredness of the *iura*. The documenting linguistic data confirm "the composite nature of the Roman population," the wide influence of both Greeks and Etruscans, just as the Curia, the "pivot element" of the political institutions of archaic Rome, testifies how in it blood relations and ethnic distinctions had no weight.[9] We are at the antipodes of the Greek *polis*, and this original opposition illuminates the entire history of the idea of empire. On one hand, the value of autochthony; on the other, "aborigines . . . without laws" ("*aborigenes . . . sine legibus*," Sallust, *De coniuratione Catilinae* 6.1–2) and the Trojans (the heirs of sacred Troy!), who come together harmoniously in their city. On one hand, the Greek "union of hearts" (*homonoia*) as conservation of preexisting equilibriums, as custody of the organic structure of the *polis*; on the other, *concordia* as process, as a dynamic through which "different hearts" (*cordia*) are welcomed and privileges and rights are extended progressively to new people (Momigliano, *Storia e storiografia*, 272). On one hand, the great fear with which the entire Greek culture (*paideia*) looks at the growth of the *polis*; on the other, the Roman *civitas* as growing city (*civitas augescens*) that exists in virtue of its capacity to incorporate new people and new territories and that could not even survive if it did not tend to the empire without end (*imperium sine fine*).[10]

The idea of the city that grows is therefore key to the myth of universal empire. It is not a plant that grows from a land and from one blood; thanks to its rootlessness, the Roman *civitas* is destined from its birth (*ab origine*) always to grow. Nothing can stop it. By excluding any presumed purity in its origins (*potissima pars!*), Rome will be able to "comprehend," assimilate, and transform every people and every land, to be ecumenical (*orbis*), and to become for everyone a safe haven (*asylum*).

To grow is to be transformed. To grow always implies knowing how to be transformed in relation to new events and the occasions that arise because of them. That does not mean, however, that one has merely to adjust, for that would not characterize a *civitas* that grows, thanks to its capacity to assimilate and integrate. In fact, new events and occasions govern the *civitas*. To be transformed means, therefore, to rejuvenate. Rome's eternity does not imply a static capacity to continue in time but the harsh effort to renew itself constantly. The *civitas augescens* needs endless *renovatio*. The idea of empire stands on the city's effort to abide not despite but thanks to its eternal renewal. Nothing new (*novum*), therefore, ought to be judged badly as alien (*alienum*) but, on the contrary, as a potentially positive energy for the growth of the power of the *civitas*. And the Roman *civitas* knows how to learn even from its most mortal enemies, as Toynbee shows in his great book on Hannibal.[11]

In the same way, just as no border of lineage or blood can hinder the empire of the Roman *civitas*, neither can one specific religious form capture its essence. Civil religion (*religio civilis*) means that all the citizens on whose harmony the *civitas* originates and is founded must recognize themselves as members of this community, belong to its future destiny, and assert the power of Rome as their own supreme good. In no way can civil religion be compared to state religion. The cult of Rome guarantees full rights to any other form of cult or religion.[12] Moreover, besides their own gods the Romans also worshipped the gods of the vanquished peoples (*numina victa*), as Minucius Felix reminds us. It would be an unacceptable sin of pride to equate the victory over an enemy people to the decline, or, worse, to the end, of its gods. The vanquished gods, instead, will have new life in Rome. Given hospitality in Rome, they will receive those honors that they clearly did not receive from those who were defeated. Nothing more than this attests to the universal power of Rome: the presence of so many guest gods and not one exiled! "Evoked by their cities of origins, they will all partake, in the end, to the eternal *Renovatio* of the *Urbs*."[13] An absolutely pluralistic polytheism, at least until the post-Constantinian age. Undoubtedly, the idea of a state religion results from the political success of Christianity.

The entirely Roman notion of *populus*, founded on the principles and the idea of harmony we just explained, is based as the "reunion of a multitude united on the basis of consensus for the laws and the common good" ("*unita iuris consensus et utilitatis communione,*" Cicero, *De re publica* 1.39). The *civitas augescens* broadens progressively the right to citizenship, until with the edict of Antoninus (the *Constitutio Antonina*) it encompasses almost all the free inhabitants within the borders of the empire.[14] Now Rome has become an *orbis*, and the semantic wealth of its name persists even in the language of the new Islamic civilization, which for centuries was hegemonic in the Mediterranean: the territories of the ancient empire are still called *Rum*, and *Rum* is the name of the territory of the Ottoman Empire, which was once Roman.[15] The great Ibn Battuta calls *Rum* the land that once was of the Romans and now belongs to Islam. In short, Rome continues to be the name of the lands where the *cives romani* once lived.

ROME, BYZANTIUM, MOSCOW

Why "evoke" this idea of empire today? Does globalization, perhaps, produce harmony (*concordia*), extend rights, and increase citizenship entirely on the political bases of agreement to the laws (*iura*)?[16] Is there room in the contemporary meeting of civilizations for "giving hospitality" to the gods from whichever land they come and to make them their own? Does the unstoppable convergence of economic and political systems rely, perhaps, on the idea of an original pact (*foedus*), or do federal perspectives only appear as mere recommendations from a functional engineering that is part of planetary governance? And would the re-presentation of the principal ideas of the Roman Empire (*imperium populi romani*) be realistic, there where globalization cannot be simply reduced to a people, to the politico-military power of a *civitas* that continues to be "this" city even after it becomes *orbis*? Does it make sense to continue using the imperial metaphor to characterize a political form of the process of globalization that is at odds with its current form? Can we undertake this so as to be able to point to a possible political alternative excluded by the latter yet which the latter does not have the power to deny (given that its political outcome cannot be overlooked, and also because any idea of empire, even the modern one, always reminds us of the Roman Empire)?[17]

With these questions in mind, let's continue our brief inquiry. Clearly, the coincidence of eternity and renewal (*aeternitas et renovatio*) in the idea of the growing city also implies Rome's mobility. Rome does not simply expand but moves to where its citizens live. Since Rome perennially renews itself, and since it is constantly moving on to better things (*transire ad meliora*), even transferring the seat of the empire will be part of its origins and initial possibilities. Because Rome doesn't have a fixed root and because it is *mobilis*, transfer (*translatio*) is one of the forms of its being in perennial transition. In so doing, Rome remains faithful to the origin because the origin, as we have seen, has the character of *civitas augescens*. The transfer, however, also expresses the supreme danger, which is the most threatening side (*facies*) of the process of transfer (*transire*), especially as it makes evident how the continuous growth of the city cannot be trimmed but must proceed via interruptions, jumps, and the repositioning of its power. We are here at the core of our comparison: the Roman idea of empire must also be expressed in that of *translatio imperii*, which, incidentally, Christianity understood very well when it applied this perspective to the Catholic Church. Yet such *translatio* creates problems for the unity of the imperium.[18] If the institutional structure (mythologies included) rules out the possibility of *translatio*, the empire will not be able to pursue the harmony, growth, and renewal that characterizes the Roman *civitas*. The consistent and radical pursuit of these ends is a political decision that no origin can guarantee. It is open, therefore, to the risk of upsetting the balance of its previous organism. To be sure, such a political decision will destroy the image of destiny or of nature that the original *civitas* offered. A centered empire, and one that is immobile, will never be "without end," will never enjoy eternal renewal. It will simply be just *rule*. How can an empire organized according to places, specific territories, and great spaces avoid being transformed—and, in the end, undone—by the logic of states? Can the *auctoritas* of the *civitas augescens* always produce new individualities, new forms of power, and so extend its power to constantly new subjects and increase the *auctoritas* by dividing it? The history of Rome's *translatio imperii* dramatically documents this question, one that is still "fatal" for us today. A careful consideration of the issue may lead to some preliminary conclusions.

The founding of Constantinople is still seen completely from the perspective of renewal (*renovatio*). Rome cannot be divided, but it can be strengthened by creating its own sister (*Roma soror*).[19] The rearticulation of power does not eliminate the monarchic principle but instead obeys the reality of the *orbis*. Chronologically, Constantinople is a second Rome, but not as value. The reason is that Constantinople takes part fully in that "most important part" (*potissima pars*) that is the origin of the *civitas*, which, since its foundation, does not enjoy any of the traits of the Greek polis.[20] Even Constantinople's ecumenism maintains many of the traits of Roman polytheism. The Roman custom (*mos*) is confused with Christian rituals but is not suppressed at all. "Whoever is God in Heaven" (*quicquid est divinitatis in sede caelesti*) is still evoked to protect the city, so that all the subjects of the empire can live together in peace and well-being ("*placatum et propitium possit existere,*" Edict of Milan, A.D. 313). Certainly, the time in which the city functioned as a safe haven (*asylum*) of men and gods is long past, but those times of a rigid state religion are yet to come.

Constantinople will always be Roman, and the Byzantines will always call themselves Romans and not Latins. Yet the monarchy of the two Romes will soon show its own weakness. As we have seen, the *civitas augescens*, once it has reached its imperial phase, means in turn the *translatio imperii*, but this dynamic erodes the cultural and political form of the *civitas*. If we want to understand the power provided by the Roman imperial perspective, it is crucial to see that among the factors leading to the schism between the two Romes, the two compete precisely in the name of the *civitas augescens*. To be sure, Rome now presents itself in terms of Christian evangelization and ecumenism, but the restless heart (*inquietum cor*) of the pilgrim city (*civitas peregrinans*) could not beat as strongly as it does if it were not and did not recognize itself as the heir of the Roman city.

In Toynbee's view, the conversion of the prince of Kiev and the foundation of the Christian *Rus* are two fatal dates for universal history. Together, they illustrate the division between the two Romes and also, with the transfer (*transire*) of the idea of Rome to a new, immense space, Rome's inexhaustible capacity to expand and renew itself. The prince of Kiev immediately recognizes Byzantium's jurisdiction, but just as immediately, he sees himself as the new Constantine. He is not simply a follower but a leader, *auctor*, Augustus, beginner and founder of a new Rome essentially connected to its Roman origin. When Russia was first baptized, the Roman vision was established with messianic and eschatological tones. The third Rome is the "worker of the eleventh hour" (Matt. 20:12), the last who will be first. The last Rome regains the power of origins; it is *arché*. Russia is called on to save the idea of Rome, which the schism seemed to have killed, and this meant that the new Rome was to defend orthodoxy forcefully. We shall see how this dual objective, held to be completely natural at the beginning, will emerge in all its problematic character in the sixteenth and seventeenth centuries.

Of course, the image of Moscow as the Third Rome is established as the real and proper foundational myth only after Constantinople falls. Moscow was fully recognized by the Orthodox Church and not resisted by the Roman Church for its political dimension, not even when the bishop of Moscow declared Ivan III the new Caesar, Czar, Constantine of the new Constantinople, and Russia the only orthodox land. A century later, the process was repeated with Ivan the Terrible (though the Russian term *grosny* also evokes the idea of authority and majesty, *auctoritas* and *maiestas*) and with the constitution of the patriarchy of Moscow imperial city. Ivan IV rises as the emperor of the Christian orthodox of the entire *universe* and ruthlessly concentrates in himself all political power, thereby subjugating to that power the fate of the church. In this last *translatio*, the figure of the Roman imperial monarchy takes on, in short, the traits of the most rigid autocracy.

To understand these events, whose importance for European history is impossible to underestimate, it isn't enough just to remember, again with Toynbee, how the survival of *Rus* was constantly threatened from East and West, caught as it was between two fires, between the assaults coming from the immense Asian plains and from those European "hungry wolves" (as Byzantium had learned to call the Franks and the Latins before collapsing under the blows of the Ottomans). The full integration of church and state, in a perspective that remains essentially foreign to the political theology of Western Europe (and that is the true foundation of the very idea of the totalitarian state), originates in Byzantium or, better, in an interpretation of the tragedy of the Second Rome that would find the reasons for its disintegration in the weakness of the *imperium*, in the breaking down of feudal political power (seen as source of every corruption), and in the emperor's loss of his role as supreme guardian of the orthodoxy.[21] That is to say, Russian autocracy ought to be interpreted both politically, within the perspective of the Third Rome, and eschatologically, a point I have already alluded to.

How does such a transfer maintain the idea of empire founded on the growing city? In Russia, the element of resistance with respect to other powers, of containment and defense (also utilizing languages, techniques, and the institutions that come from them, as is the case with Peter the Great and that occurs yet again in the twentieth century), has precedence with respect to the energy devoted to expansion. Essentially, autocracy contradicts that *concordia* dynamically understood as the extension of rights, whose idea did not disappear in the imperial age. The Byzantine "symphony" between church and state (*sacerdotium et imperium*) is replaced by a fundamentally different conception, one that subordinates the church to the demands of concentrating political power. The Third Rome, in reality, claims to be the last one, the place in which the *civitas augescens* is made complete. This place, however, can only be its end and not where it is renewed. The last Rome is no longer Rome. The empire that wants to continue, to remain stable and secure, to defend its own orthodoxy, immune from other people and other gods, is no longer an empire in the Roman sense of the word. Yet the relation rests precisely in such a contrast: the idea of *translatio* is constitutively put "in doubt." On one hand and in light of its original meaning, *translatio* can be expressed as the mobility of Rome, as its capacity to distribute its own power without diminishing it and, indeed, in so doing, strengthening its power. On the other hand, it can also signify its simple recollocation and a new spatial determination. The Roman *concordia*, one that is always produced through conflict, is forever the result of agreements and political understandings. It survives because *concordia* is able to renew itself and because it cannot be reconciled to an autocratic conception of empire. Yet Rome's "arrested development" within the confines of a state (which may be the expression of any imperialistic aim) is a possibility that always inheres in the idea of *translatio*.

Vladimir Solovyov's theological and political utopia can be read—much like the utopias of Nicolai Berdyaev and Mikhail Bulgakov, all of whom were wrestling with the apocalypse—as a call to *Rus* to return in the true wake of Rome. Rome is the immutable center, but Roman does not mean Latin![22] The center is the tireless author of modifications and translations of power, of its organization and extension to new places and subjects. A center unable to move outside itself generates schism. The consensus (*concordia*) promulgated is universal coercion, the same rope (*corda*) for all. The Roman center of which Solovyov speaks is instead one of universal paternity. It lives only in the autonomous life of sons, those who could never be limited to autocracy if they would only recognize their common origin, if they would recognize themselves in that communal city (*civitas communis*). Such a communal city does not belong to anyone, that is, to any ethnic group, culture, religious creed, but shapes (in-forms) the life of all. Only insofar as Rome radiates the communal city and is welcoming will it not wither and freeze or crumble into separate states, states that reject the empire of the people (*imperium populi*) the more they are imperialistic.

The unity of the empire as the harmony of sovereign members. Within this frame, Russia is not a third and last Rome but rather an energy that promotes Russia as renewal, bridge, mobile hinge, place, and border, against which the East and the West are called on to "transgress" reciprocally: this is how the "unifying vocation" of the great Russians between the nineteenth and twentieth centuries expresses itself. Their vision rejects any pan-Slavism, any nationalist imperialism, and any form of autocracy. On the contrary, their desire develops and transforms precisely this Roman inheritance.[23] This vision of *Rus*, that is, this Russian eschatology, is indispensable for a Europe that does not intend to define itself as only Western, a Europe that wants to be *civitas augescens* beyond any *religio civilis* and thus to be a *civitas* that grows and that is open to becoming a pilgrim (*augescens et peregrinans*). Russia is perhaps the place where this perspective was most betrayed, and for this reason, perhaps, Russia may begin again to renew itself with greater strength from this position. Certainly, a Europe without Russia can in no way "remember" itself and so in no way have a foundation and, with it, a future.

THE NECESSARY TWILIGHT

In what terms can we speak today of a form of empire? Clearly, the form of empire is presently in decline: that of separate state organisms and imperialist nationalisms, of international right as the product of state sovereignty territorially determined. In no way does this process have empire as its end. Its direction seems to be the exact opposite with respect to that idea of empire of which we have spoken to this point. If anything, the progressive convergence of economic and political systems and the disintegration of different cultures is a case of imperialism and not empire. A pact (*foedus*) among subjects that are already reduced to One, previously integrated, would be simply the victors dictating the terms to the defeated. Only a pact born of effort and desire, of universal individualities, is able establish an idea of empire as the empire of the people. Indeed, this situation does not describe in any way the reality of the Roman Empire. Yet it persists in the *possibility* of Roman Empire; it remains faithful to the Roman idea to the extent that it intends to take it up again.

According to the Roman idea, in no way is it "imperial" to conceive of the new as alien (*novum* as *alienum*). Instead, we have today the radical inability to offer hospitality to other gods—where the term "to offer hospitality" does not connote relativism, nor empty indifference, but rather friendship (*amicitia*), recognition of the necessity of the other in the construction of our identity, and the recognition that only thanks to the energy that emanates from this *amicitia* is the city able to grow.[24] Today we have the paganism of a secularized civil religion without having any of the polytheistic pluralism of Rome. The perfect *religio civilis*, in fact, is the "American religion," perfectly incapable of any *pietas* with respect to other religions.[25] The vanquished gods (*numina victa*), in the literal sense of the term, flow into the "center" as empty simulacra, while on the outside they continue to be fought against with no quarter given. The United States is not a "normal" imperialistic power. Nevertheless, it will never be able to revitalize the Roman imperial idea.

But not even an omniglobal and integrating "network" can do so. That right to citizenship, which universal *concordia* requires, is entirely indifferent to the "net." To be connected to the network does not in any way entail being a *cives*, which is to say those whose consent produces the *civitas* and those on whose consent the legitimacy of the law is founded. In the network, equality can be thought in terms absolutely separated from freedom. The structural ideology of the network constitutes itself as a techno-administrative mechanism. Its ideology is to present its own undeniable hierarchical order as nothing other than the natural result of that mechanism, removed of any political significance—which is metaphysically in contrast to the utterly political myth of the *civitas augescens* and its empire. However, the universality, that is, the true ecumenical character of the network (of which American politics must be considered just a part, albeit a major one), remains necessarily open to the demand for the extension of rights without ends (*sine fine*), for the affirmation of individualities that conceive the network as their own universality and, therefore, as a universal pact that the individual demands in order to be universal. Within the framework of the present decline of the separate states and their supranational organisms, such a possibility of universality is hard to imagine, but this is not the case with the network, which is only apparently technological. The ecumenical dimension that the network embraces makes it possible to think of a pact as the politico-institutional realization of an actual *concordia* in which the will of everyone to have a friendship (*philia*) with the other is present. While remaining a foreigner, the other too can have a "radiating" effect.

Presently, globalization seems to proceed by excluding every polarity. The universality of the network, instead, is entirely conceivable as a pluralism of relations between places, and between places and cultural "great spaces," as a communication of vital experiences. The idea of *renovatio* is entrenched in this communicative context. In a simply hierarchical network (and therefore centered on hegemonic knots), there are no actual new events that take place but rather only new products, those manifestations of the unique *logos* that no *novum* will be able to transform and that must remain immune from any break-in of the new. This same network, however, is thinkable as upside down, that is, as a space-time in which polarities are re-created (*renovatio*) and that take on, in all forms of their relations, a universal value: cultural and religious polarities, polarities between political systems, polarities that can finally move beyond the logic friend-enemy, as they live together, joined in the totality of the network. In this federation, the interest and will of everyone are expressed.

But which political subject today is able to contaminate the form of globalization with this idea of empire? Possibly, only a Europe capable of drawing creatively from its own origin of mobility, a Europe that sees its own growth as assimilation and reception of energy and its own power as the power of the rights it promotes and the subjects that benefit from them. For such a Europe to emerge, *this* Europe must reach its twilight.[26] To be more than just "West," Europe must fully accept its "twilight" destiny. The twilight of the Europe of separate states; the twilight of Europe that has learned to "metaphorize" Rome only in an absolute, autocratic, or imperialistic sense; of that Europe that today regards its own Orient as land to be annexed, its own Mediterranean as essentially *alienum*—the twilight of this Europe is now required, especially if we want to think of Europe as actively and subjectively engaged in a new form of globalization. One cannot say if and how this twilight can become reality, but it is certainly possible to think it, as it forms an analogy, in the strongest sense of the term, with a sense of our European past, which, however misunderstood, betrayed and forgotten, still lives in our history.

POST SCRIPTUM: AFTER SEPTEMBER 11

We can't imagine a more dramatic confirmation of the contradictions that the very idea of a universal empire faces today and that I tried to express at the end of the preceding essay. How are we to relate to the apocalyptic dimension of the events we have lived through recently? During these last months, after the turning point that was September 11, it seems to me that no comment, no analysis, has been able to match its far-reaching implications. Even the wisest and most judicious words seem unable to express the sense of telluric insecurity that radiates from it and envelops everything.

There is no doubt that the attack at the heart of the supposed empire has demonstrated the unbelievable cultural as well as technical unpreparedness of its entire intelligence apparatus. Undoubtedly, the organizational level of the attack makes us think of the strongest, most widespread, and deep-rooted complicity at the level of foreign nations. Moreover, this also makes credible the necessity of a traditional military response . . . There is no doubt that no army of spies will ever be able to prevent men ready to die, who are well organized and well financed, from bringing destruction to the very heart of the metropolis. The processes of globalization that generate one single world market, world crime organizations, and the new terrorism are the same and perhaps inseparable . . . Without a doubt, war has changed both in substance and in form. The last one that was fought in a traditional way was perhaps the one between Israel and the Arab countries in 1973. We have lived with its disastrous effects ever since. An interstate war does not resolve anything. Punitive expeditions end up only increasing the ranks of terrorists. To believe that one can reduce the war to the level of police actions is, on the other hand, a laughable utopia. Reasons that are more serious can be found. No peace treaty is possible without a resolution to the Palestine-Israel issue. Certainly, the economic disparity between North and South continues to be fertile ground for every conflict. Certainly, the macroscopic economic and social injustices "naturally" tend to be represented in ideological or ideological-religious terms, with regard to various cultures and civilizations. Certainly, the reform of supranational organizations, starting with the United Nations, which is utterly hindered by principles of equality and unanimity, appears urgent, and the same goes for defining a European Union foreign and defense policy.

And the list could go on.

Nonetheless, discussions such as these or thousands like them introduce the need for a truly political conversion. I shall try to characterize it by proceeding by negation. What ended once and for all with September 11? The belle époque of globalization, as the sociologist Aldo Bonomi aptly has put it. A short season, indeed. The dream of a techno-administrative path to universal well-being and an almost automatic mobilization of all consciences and all cultures in the direction of the victorious models of the West didn't last long. A decade—from the collapse of the so-called real socialism—marked by the revival in grand style of a secularized sense of Providence, cheap liberalism, and ideological hangovers caused by the decline of politics or even the end of history. Now we know (everyone now knows, from the antiglobalization movement to the neo–free traders, at least those endowed with reason) that globalization, in order to exist, has to be controlled politically, that no destiny can assure its success, that no new Order of the Earth will be born spontaneously from the planetary Westernization of economic forms and systems. Recently, we confused the growing and rapid convergence of the latter with the idea of globalization. We learned painfully that we are dealing with very distinct dimensions. And then what? What lies ahead is uncharted: *hic sunt leones*. To assert that depoliticization was a bad policy does not mean building a better one; to recognize that the neutralization of the conflicts by way of techno-economic solutions results in their multiplication does not entail knowing how to resolve them.

Still proceeding by negation, we know for certain that we will not be able to reinstate the former politics founded on the relation between sovereign states. The era of opposing hegemonic wills, of fighting states, is over, that much is clear, with the apparent victory of one of them, of one of their species anyway. Never, however, as in this case is the old saying "woe to the vanquished!" (*vae victis!*) more appropriately changed to "woe to the victors!" (*vae victoribus!*). Here we grasp the fundamental issue: can a state, in the intrinsic limits of its nature, have a truly world empire? Or must the tragic imperialistic season conclude with the ending of the era of absolute state power? Is it conceivable that the world can be conquered by a system of absolutely deterritorialized powers, by a supersociety that dominates the financial resources and the media, and of which the national political leaderships are more and more either a direct expression or a dependent variable? Is it conceivable to govern globalization by eradicating any difference of place and culture or, at the most, by simply tolerating it? The "realists" reply that no one believes in globalization as a peaceful unification; globalization proceeds by tearing and breaking. The end of the era that began with the Yalta Conference appears to have made this outcome inevitable. A relative equilibrium was possible but only through terror. Today's globalization, rather, is by its nature permanent restlessness, contradiction, and conflict. Yet our "realists" are quick to add that we are dealing only with local conflicts that do not seriously threaten the present system of power, the "empire."

Didn't September 11 wake them up from their dogmatic sleep? Is it true, then, that no great power, no new state power can assert itself against globalization but global terrorism? And this terrorism has its roots in those processes of fragmentation and contradictions that the global order reproduces. The new terrorism thinks locally and works globally. The effects of its global operations can bring about, if prolonged in time, the dislocation and the destabilization of the economic order with the greatest and most dramatic social and political consequences. A true political realism, therefore, would make sure to do everything possible to overcome those local conflicts in order to eliminate the contradictions. Nothing is more vacuously utopian than to believe such contradictions to be inevitable and to pretend at the same time that the Westernization of the world is guaranteed.

Where are we headed? The questions that I asked, metaphorically, at the end of my essay now return, questions I could have never imagined would have been so quickly translated "politically" (*in politicis*). Does the telluric insecurity of today intensify the idea and, consequently, the search for a supreme authority? Mind you, this authority can also be understood pluralistically. Great imperial ideas are not ruled by a simplistic reduction to one (*reductio ad unum*) but through the subsumption of all organisms to the common good, embodied necessarily in a shared authority. We have lived and relived over the last few years all kinds of pale, secularized versions of these great ideas. How many times have we appealed to the Great Arbiter, the one able to transcend the sovereignty of the single states—states dominated by special interests! Doesn't it seem natural to the majority that a monarch, being ontologically free from any interest or special need, ought to be the first defender of each state's subjects? This perspective (which to be coherent ought to assert as well that the authority of the empire comes from God) was invoked frequently and indirectly during the most recent conflicts. Are we going to have, then, a Fourth Rome? Or can we meet this idea head on (an idea that ought to be explained in all its radicalism, without simulation and hypocrisy) with the one suggested in my essay: of a globalization built around great spaces and authentic cultural polarities? I believe that either the new Order of the Earth will try to be authentically federative or that the apocalyptic scenario, which some of the greatest political realists of the twentieth century outlined a decade ago, will become inevitable: a single great power, a single empire (which today would be that supersociety of which we spoke), immersed in a multitude of local conflicts, a natural humus of desperate and global terrorism.

The real confrontation, it seems to me, moves today between these two positions. Both have to come to terms (or ought to come to terms) seriously with the insecurity and anguish that all of us feel and that become more unbearable each and every day. But only the federative option (*pensiero federativo*) seems to be able to express an actual search for peace, "on the peace of faith" (*de pace fidei*), and not only a temporary agreement concocted between inevitable wars.[27] To me this seems to be the highest and most urgent theoretical and political work today: a federative thinking capable of measuring itself against the processes of globalization in all its aspects. Not a vague "ought-to-be" but an "ought-to-be" that is alive in real movements. The need for justice is not a dream, as the "realists" maintain, but a fact of historical reality, and not to acknowledge it is first of all a political error. An ethics of responsibility entirely exempt from "non-negotiable" convictions has never existed and will never exist. To reduce everything, as we are doing today, outside of the usual rhetoric, to a clash between powerful wills, to relations of force, is just nonsense. The years we are living are decisive, and the authentic decision is one between that idea of empire and universal and global federalism.

Great spaces and cultural identities: these two dimensions are not identical, but they do intersect. To face the foremost problem today, namely our relation to Islam, it's clear that we are dealing with a large political, cultural, and religious space and with a time that is intertwined at every point with the West. Is it realistic to imagine that such a space and time, one that is irreducibly plural, can be forced to "enter" into the space and time of the West? If our relation to Islam is based on the assumption that modernization is equivalent to Westernization and that a movement of Islamic reform must be conceived necessarily as a declaration of faith in "our" progress (by which we mean a pragmatic and rationalistic attitude as well as the separation between politics and religion), these very same political factors that have caused today's conflict will only be consolidated further.

We ought instead to be working on the differences that constitute the history of Islamic civilization so that it not surrender its entire representation to fundamentalisms and extremisms that, at their base, express more an utterly political and secularized will to power than they do a loyalty to a religious tradition. That is, we need to work through distinctions, using them to build strategies and alliances and not simply occasional agreements of interest as is being done now. We need to see in the *sunnah* (the "path") and the journey of the *shariah* (the "law") the sign of a loyalty that renews itself. The vision of a sacred and unalterable *shariah* does not use up by any means all the senses of Islam. On the contrary. The history of Islam demonstrates how its capacity to evolve varies depending upon the community in question. Certainly, the origin they share is common and unique, but it is also "perfect," precisely because it includes all its own diverse interpretations. The Text is absolutely normative, but from the text we are called on to derive analogically the sense of our actions and the norms to regulate our lives. It would be desirable if the West did not forget that, on the basis of just this analogical tradition, Moslem society was for centuries more given to the encounter with the other, to accept cultural "amalgams," more mobile internally in its classes and ranks than European societies were. The idea of Islam as the cult of the very abstract One, absolutely negative with respect to the particular, absorbing and erasing every individuality, is a Western philosophical idea. It is built on the basis of pure prejudice—even though from this idea does not derive, necessarily, a negative judgment of Islamic civilization. Think of Hegel's words: "Never has enthusiasm, as such, performed greater deeds."[28]

We are paying for centuries of misunderstandings attributable essentially to reciprocal ignorance, which exchanges and trade relations have not been enough to heal. And God only knows how such ignorance can have dramatic repercussions in concrete political and diplomatic action. The history of American diplomacy in the last half-century is witness to that. In fact, American diplomacy was essentially based on the following principle: our absolute, irreducible enemy is Soviet communism. As long as this enemy cannot not be "converted," any other position (including, needless to say, dictators of every kind, brutal fascists, etc.) was seen as either tolerable or, in the end, capable of being integrated. Indeed, this is how Islamic societies were treated: as societies that in the end would end up being ruled by entirely Westernized leaderships or, at the least, with strictly Western methods and thus easily enrolled in the defense of "our" interests. Despite those who claim that theology and philosophy are merely an ornament, we have here a momentous theological and philosophical error that was probably responsible for misguiding American foreign policy right up until the end of the Cold War and then beyond! Europe should have made its presence felt; it should have expressed a historical memory that, instead, it completely lost. On one hand, Europe should have remembered the essential European-Western character of "real communism" (by no means Asian!); on the other, it should have called the United States' attention to an analysis of Islamic societies, the challenges evident in them, the contradictory positions that were being expressed—in short, the urgent need to abandon the suicidal vision of "one" Islam, entirely ordained in every respect to be subordinated and integrated in the strategies and interests of the West.

The next few years—I fear that we won't have to wait too long—will show us how much European blindness and powerlessness will weigh on our own future. We can already see how they have contributed to the strengthening of fundamentalist positions in Moslem communities, including what amounts to a masterpiece: the Islamization of the struggle of the Palestinian people (the Arab people with the greatest presence of Christians and with the strongest tradition of lay politics). It has reached such a point that now, without the slightest peep, and even in very large sectors of Islamic communities, one accepts that jihad involves cruel attacks on innocents, with acts of terrorism carried out through suicide—which is totally foreign to any Islamic tradition and to any possible and imaginable interpretation of the Law. The radical exclusion of any form of cruelty and the absolute obligation to spare women, the old, children, the sick, and religious people from the conditions of war (unless they themselves had taken a personal part in it) defines the idea of jihad in its military sense. This because it is well known (or it ought to be) that the essential meaning of the term is purely religious: "forcing oneself on the way to God" to overcome personal weaknesses and appetites. Terrorism today can feign a religious foundation only to the extent to which Western politics and culture have been unable to understand the various Islams and to find a dialogue within them.

As Gilles Kepel has shown, this is how, on the ruins of Westernizing nationalisms and the failed policies of development and overcoming tremendous internal inequalities, we have witnessed the expansion of a fundamentalist Islamism that is capable of using religion unscrupulously as a weapon of identity and of mobilization.[29] In confronting the absolute enemy, communism, the West "craftily" gave birth to this Islamism, exploiting it for that war in Afghanistan, which probably provided the mortal blow to Russian power. At the end of that conflict, the diaspora of Afghan war-riors has affected the entire West. In those years, and together with the Afghan veterans (that is, until a few years ago!), some of the most cruel opponents of the moderate Arab states were welcome guests in New York and London. With all the evidence, this is the true, primary objective of the new terrorism: to undermine these regimes, to replace their political lead-ership, and to control the great resources of raw materials that those coun-tries have at their disposal and that are fundamental to the survival of the Western economy. Certainly, the American strategy, followed somewhat passively by Europe, did nothing to prevent such an outcome or even to understand its possibility.

We return, thus, to the overall problem that I had wanted to highlight metaphorically in my essay. On one hand, is it possible to develop an impe-rial policy in the absence of such a staggering lack of comprehension "from within" of the players involved, of the discourses of each one, of the "long wave" of cultural and religious traditions? Certainly not. On the other hand, doesn't understanding these factors lead to a perspective that rejects every imperial policy? The need to work through differences, and through clear distinctions, by refusing simplifications and one-dimensional images, even those held by one's opponents, leads logically, I believe, to an international policy and law built on that idea of great spaces and cultural identities that are federated among themselves, in the full recognition of the autonomy of everyone. If the West fails to move in such a direction, I fear that it will once again make true Robert Musil's ominous saying: "I would sooner believe that it was the Devil who constructed the European world, and that God has decided to let His rival show what he can do."[30]

9

MORE ON THE IDEA OF EMPIRE

There can be no doubt that the most important mark of the era that World War II opened and that was conclusively confirmed with the collapse of the USSR (much more so than with the hegemony of the United States) is the crisis of sovereignty understood in territorial terms. "Crisis" does not mean the end of sovereignty, and no one is able to predict how long this age will resist. Even less predictable today is the political form that will follow the great baroque figure of the modern state—probably it will not be a form in the traditional sense of the word. What is certain is that today it is nearly impossible to conceive of land, sea, and aerial spaces as "irradiations" of state politics and their will to power or conceive of global order as the result of their regulative capacities. The state will also last a little while longer, but it won't be a regulative power any longer. Will the state still be called on to exercise its functions of containment? To put off the more painful and radical consequences of the processes already underway? We have here, in all its urgency, the problem of the *katechon*.[1] Will political forms see their own "curbing" functions slowly reduced by the disruptive assault of technological progress, in its most radical and universal sense? Public intervention in democratic countries immediately after World War II can already be read as a rather simple manifestation of the *katechon*. The state comes to an end as an autonomous will to power, but, at the same time, it takes on the essential bureaucratic and administrative functions of control, policing, and regulation, functions that nonetheless derive their meaning from the global system and are located within a network of interests and strategies that completely transcend the national scene. The *katechon*-state certainly knows the immanent risks in such a "transcending" turn, but there is no way for the state to oppose it, and for reasons that have to do with the state's origin and nature. The process of depoliticization, in fact, is inscribed in the state's very DNA, no less than the regulative idea of a universal hegemony, which, by resolving every conflict, also silences the motivations of the political. States therefore that originate in the European Law (*ius publicum europaeum*) are all Western: the expression of a virtual space that does not allow for autonomy, a space that only allows the unlimited expansion of the West. In such a space, boundaries can only be signaled by open doors.

Does this mean that we have to speak of the political unreality of the states, as the most insightful contemporary interpreter of Hegel, Alexandre Kojève, did in 1945?[2] No, but we have to be careful not to confuse regulatory power with organizing power. All Western states, in the laws they express and in the agreements, treatises, and conventions to which they give life, must be understood as only a "dependent variable" of a comprehensive system of power whereby the distinction between economic interest and political power loses all actual value. Does this mean in turn the mere subordination of the state form to other disciplines? No, but its limited sovereignty cannot be in any way the source of political contradiction. Among the "three" (market, state, community), there is no identity but, for the moment, an occasional interweaving of conflict and cooperation. However, this in no way means that among them we do not find well-defined hierarchies and differentials of energy. The tendency of the era toward global unity will never be expressed as a reduction to One (*ad Unum*) but rather will be articulated in a "chaotic holism," as Geminello Alvi puts it, especially because global unity is based on the constant reproduction of differences and imbalances.[3] The problem consists in analyzing whether these imbalances can eventually evolve into a polyarchic pluralism. And nothing at this point makes one think it likely. The hegemonic politico-economic system does not goosestep as one. Rather, it is highly articulated. It is a complex language whose containment functions are likely to collide with those of expansion. The "natural" interests of the business community, aiming to expand the markets and restrict the competition, demand regulatory interventions that cannot "represent" them immediately. The more innovative functions in the field of research live in the hyperspace of the freedom of information that does not coincide at all with the dominant oligopolistic interests.[4] All these asymmetries and the many others ought to be understood thoroughly (regardless of any apologia or indictment for what has been called the "single paradigm").[5] The incontrovertible fact remains that these different factors (although they express an order, that is, a hierarchy) act according to a sense, even a vocation, I would say. The global world calls to them. The empire without end (*imperium sine fine*), at least in the territorial sense of whose "goodness" they must all persuade or be persuaded ("*compelle intrari!*"), forms their common horizon.[6]

What do I understand by this? That the contradiction, that is, the sway of the negative on which the future of international relations depends, does not lie between the idea of the "global era" and some point of resistance with respect to it or lie with some difficulty within its unfolding. The contradiction is to be found entirely within the idea itself, that is, between the two opposing ideas of the global era, without simulation, timidity, and irenic-reconciliatory exercises with the world of yesterday.

Here it is "worthwhile to think about" (I am invoking Heidegger loosely) the essay of Kojève's I quoted above. Not the concrete results of its discourse but instead its philosophy. If the global era is the age of the eradication of the *nomos* and of the order without place (*Ordnung ohne Ortung*), and if it still enjoys a political configuration, by which I mean the present occasional interdependence between supranational organisms and authorities endowed with technological competence, state politics, politics directly developed by economic power, state legislation, market law (*lex mercatoria*), and ghosts of international law; if they all take on progressively the form of political global institutions—then these will not be produced as a logical development out of the state form.[7]

The politics beyond the state has become the problem of our era, and the answer may well be that there is no politics beyond the state but only "weak governance" of the factors authentically decisive in the distribution of power, in the hierarchical ordering of space, and in legislative activity. (In this regard, one does not usually pay sufficient attention to how strong we assume a world governed technologically and administratively would be; we are speaking precisely of an inexorable destiny of depoliticization.) In any case, we do know that beyond the state there is no World State waiting for us, whether the form be authoritarian, centralized, or federal. The state will continue, as long as it is a territorially determined energy, even though its policies may be imperial. Its sovereignty will never be transformed in abstract power; it will always be conditioned by traditions, interests, and historically concrete languages. The expression "World State" ought not to be confused with the idea of a state capable, under the right circumstances, to develop, unique among all states, a politics that has a truly planetary scale. However strong, this state will always be a dependent variable of the system we have described. It will be able to do "everything"—but not what is essential, namely, to establish and guide a new global order guaranteed by global institutions. From the crisis of the states to global order, there is a hiatus, a leap, which is not answered by dreaming up imaginary bridges. Rather it occurs by "changing minds": by reasoning, that is, according to a political perspective that is truly *other*.

Does the idea of empire provide at least a working hypothesis for such a project? It was Kojève's hypothesis, which was entirely different with respect to Jünger's World State, even if it came about under the same conditions.[8] If destiny has a global order in store for us, it will not be statelike or poststate (unless chronologically), nor will it be the automatic outcome of the planetary affirmation of market laws (even the most passionate adherents seem to have abandoned this old belle époque utopia). It will be supranational in the precise sense of the term; that is, it will include nations and peoples (*nationes et gentes*) rather than states. It will take the lead in deconstructing the artificial identifies of states, and it will seek its own political legitimization precisely on those subjects, organisms, and communities whose power the state has always considered byproducts. By being supranational, this global order relates constantly to nations, and its order is more fixed than that of the state. But its place (*Ortung*) is not territorial. The nations and people that compose it are moving cultural energies, and as they are in relation, they are not entities that can be rigidly classified. An idea of empire as a supranational political order, as the dynamic expression of the pact (*foedus*) among nations that make it up, contrast completely and obviously with the rule of One, with the assertion of a single *logos*. On one hand, we know that the logic of the states cannot but end up in the submission to the rule of One. On the other hand, if we proceed in the deconstruction of the state, even moving toward a genuinely federal perspective (and not toward fragmentation into microstates), we will only perform a work of containment, a delaying function, if not openly reactionary.[9]

Similarly, it is clear that empire, if it is conceived as a supranational organism (or, better, transnational) and is formed by nations capable, by tradition and history, of giving life to a coherent organism of treaties (*foedera*), this empire will never be able to assert itself as a *universal* empire. It will always be a great space, but it will be fixed as *political* form. This concept of empire transposed in the planetary dimension dissolves in the emptiest utopia, while the World State can still appear a realistic option (but only if determined on the basis of the will to power of a historically defined state). In itself, the World State is a political figure doomed to fail. The universal empire (if by empire we understand what we described) expresses, rather, only the purest ideology of depoliticization, that is, the resolution of all conflicts in a *societas* of all nations. To be sure, the world can become *one* system, or perhaps it is already, but the world will never be *one* society. Realistically, therefore, the problem of global political institutions can be faced only in the dimension of great transnational spaces. "Global," in an abstract universal key, can only mean the affirmation of techno-administrative logics that are dependent on economic-financial powers and freed of any problem of political legitimacy.

In any case, the great imperial forms have always maintained a very clear sense of their own limitations, even at the height of their universal claims. Empire without end (*imperium sine fine*) indicates the time and life of Rome, yet it coexists with the awareness and the care for frontiers (*limes*). Rome does not want to repeat the dream of Alexander. Even more immanent is the limit in the medieval idea of empire, which develops in the tension between two dominions (*duo ministeria*), between religious *fides* and *fides* to the emperor. While Byzantium throughout its entire history sought to overcome this tension, the Christian empire lives off the impossible equilibrium between the authorities who claim legitimacy to transfer power from the Greeks to the Germans (*translatio imperii Graecis in Germanos*). And it is deeply significant that in such a struggle, political authority insists on recognizing the power of the different nations. The Christian empire, we could say somewhat anachronistically, does not oppose the nations' autonomy; rather, it aims to prevent their metamorphosis into states. The church, for its part, while opposing any attempt at a "territorial church" and insisting on its universal essence, seizes upon every process of fragmentation of the imperial organism as an opportunity to strengthen its own autonomy and authority. The paradoxical character of this situation prevents any absolutist solution, both in the Caesarian-papist sense and in that of universal political empire.

In this context, it becomes all the more important to meditate on the "Roman metaphor" by combining, if possible, memory, realism, and imagination.[10] For all of its history, Rome remained faithful to an idea of the city as energy, as a creative force (*civitas augescens*), that is, as something metaphysically in opposition to the "static" sense of state. Even the imperial *orbis* did not have any foundation without the living memory of this "most important" origin (*origo: potissima pars!*): the individuality of the *urbs*. This city is not the Hellenic *polis*, which even in its more cosmopolitan moments failed to overcome its ethnoracial roots and give life with the other *poleis* to stable relations. Rome is from the moment it is born (*ab origine*) a safe haven for absolutely distinct peoples; it stands on its ability to renew the harmony (*concordia*) among the peoples and the groups who live in it. An utterly political concept of citizenship dominates its history. Thus the *orbis*, on the model of the *urbs*, is understood as plurality of *civitates, nationes, gentes*, whose individuality is acknowledged in the concreteness of their own traditions and federated in the Roman commune according to different and specific modalities.[11] Did this federalist effort of assimilation and integration fail?[12] Is the shared Roman fatherland (*Roma communis patria*) nothing more than an ideology? This does not diminish in any way the fact that Rome was also experienced as a politically effective regulative idea, without which we could not account for the expansion of its citizenship, the absence of any form of real state religion, and not even the techniques of administration that for centuries supported the empire, where various cities continued to enjoy the greatest autonomy in deciding on their own issues. Certainly, Rome is "convinced" that it is predestined to rule the world (to "tame the proud," *debellare superbos*) and that its wars, therefore, are "just" (even though in Virgil this adjective never appears!).[13] But the order Rome pursues is not by any means the one that results from the elimination of differences or not even from the imposition of a cultural model.

Rome does not think of itself as the center. Instead, all the realities that gradually come to form the Roman *orbis* become the center. The pact (*foedus*), which constitutes the only means to overcome war and establish a regime of friendship and hospitality (*amicitia et hospitium*), somehow has a retroactive value. Those who belong, even if defeated, are transformed into winners (in the words of Aeneas, *Aeneid* 12.190, Latins and Trojans are "both nations, undefeated,"—*ambae invictas gentes*—if they are capable of *foedus*) and partake of every right (above all the right, precisely, to preserve their own identity). To be sure, and let's repeat this, such an imperial idea is threatened by monarchic tendencies that become more and more aggressive with the passing of time. And yet the *principatus*, even when it seems more inclined to forget radically its republican origins, never dares to present itself as superior to the law (*legibus solutus*), as *the* Authority. It would never dare dictate its own will to all the organisms of the empire, on the basis of the monarch's certainty that the salvation of the *orbis* depends on his decisions.

Is such an imperial space so structured conceivable today? Is it thinkable on the basis of not merely conventional agreements and deals between identities rich in historical-cultural meaning? An empire that exists on its differences? Is it conceivable that such differences can produce, according to their own principles (*iuxta propria principia*), a true pact (*foedus*), which is to say that between them a degree of trust (*fidelitas*) can exist that does not enslave one at the expense of another? We have already seen how this idea will not work in a context of a world state or a universal-planetary empire. A world state is conceivable only as the imperialistic assertion of a state. In its turn, the universal empire is conceivable only as the product of the global eradication of any cultural difference, as "emancipation" of the world-system from any nation, people, and city. Yet can the "Roman metaphor" actually work? Can one repeat the "exercise" Machiavelli conducted on the first ten books of Livy?!

First of all, a question must be answered: after the Battle of Actium, that is, after the collapse of the Berlin Wall, after the American victory in the Great Civil War of the West, did the United States follow that imperial policy that Rome pursued (perhaps in vain)? Whoever claims that the politics of the future is possible only in the dimension of empire has the duty to formulate the question honestly. How does the United States interpret its mission today? In the sense of *auctoritas* that founds new global institutions? What emerges, rather, is a clear will to limit to the utmost the authority and the autonomy of the existing few. Or, rather, American politics reveals in this regard an obvious and typical asymmetry: to keep the political supranational organisms weak and strengthen (nominally) the techno-economic ones. This does not result only from reasons of expediency, since it is clear, in the latter case, that the United States' political weight is unquestionable. What is expressed here is a concept of globalization and of the new world order. American politics presupposes that the latter can only originate from the complete integration of the different areas of the planet into a single techno-economic space. In this vision all the world is a periphery, more or less close to the "city on the hill," to be "healed" by good example, if possible— as we hope—or by direct intervention (*"compelle intrari!"*).[14]

The regulative idea of such a political culture, therefore, is not imperialistic, nor does it tend toward the creation of a world state. Rather it moves to the formation of a universal empire as a unique system whose peace is guaranteed by the military force of the United States and its true allies. Such an idea suffers, therefore, the resistance it will inevitably produce: the dramatic contradictions originating from its "imperial" superopposition.[15] Therefore, the unique system does not claim at all, according to the pacifist universalism of certain technocracies, that world order can be spontaneously produced by automatisms and laws of techno-economic supremacy. Yet it most certainly does reduce the function of the political to essentially maintaining the peace of the system (which naturally entails the full assent of a culture, a mindset—a *forma mentis*—and a hierarchy of values).

The United States believes—and they could not do otherwise given their history—that the new *nomos* of the earth is the result of the universal achievement of technology and the ubiquitous projection of their own economic-military system. They will never expand their own domain territorially as Rome did, and they will never create a universal citizenship. They will never build a peace founded on the reciprocal foundation of the *foedus*. Will they be able to maintain the peace for the West on their own conditions? Technically, that's most likely. But at what social cost? At what level of protection of civil rights? With what backsliding in terms of economic and financial power, including the push toward oligopoly even in the most innovative sectors of the net economy? No one knows; *hic sunt leones*. But no one can seriously exclude the possibility that the American imperial logic, which is absolutely not comparable to the classical logics, may develop in an "infinite just war" protected by an ideology of "humanitarian intolerance."[16] The politics of this empire would be transformed by necessity, then, into a government of perennial emergency.

Before giving in to this perspective as it if were our destiny, or reacting to it by returning to the ancient womb of the state, or by devoting oneself to the bad Masonic and Enlightenment utopias of planetary federations (that is of the society of all nations), let's at least imagine the possibility of a globalization organized by concrete polarities and by determined historical and cultural individualities as well as by the large spaces that acknowledge one another thanks to shared memory or, at least, by common destinations. Has today's globalization already destroyed such a possibility, or, worse, will the idea of these empires give way to a "clash of civilizations"? Honestly, the clash of civilizations is made possible precisely for the opposite reason, namely, that contemporary globalization exacts a unique and indifferent time-space and only conceives of place as the point where interests, investments, and wars fortuitously land. Only a policy that knows that its own partiality cannot be surmounted and knows also how to put such partiality to use at the level required by our global era, which is to say, beyond any nationalistic nostalgia—only such a policy can form the foundation for an understanding between culture and civilization. Similarly, the local can never be saved in a globalization that proceeds in the sense of an abstract, universal homogenization. The metaphor of the global simply mystifies the fact that the local is being transformed into a mere product of the global. The individuality of place maintains its meaning only within the sphere of great spaces, concretely and historically defined, of which we speak, just as they did in the Roman idea of empire.

Without imperial polyarchy, there is no "place," just as there is no possibility for a *nomos* of the earth that is different from the universal affirmation of a market law (*lex mercatoria*), one defended by military power and predicated in the name of laws that no international jurisdiction sets out and safeguards. A new, real international law, capable of moving beyond that eclectic defense of civil rights at the service of every political meddling or military intervention (which today seems to have taken the place of the old law founded on interstate agreements) will only come about thanks to a pact (*foedus*) between the concrete universalities of the great imperial spaces. If this is utopia, how more truly utopian is that of an international law abstracted from any actual global institution and bound to the nonending and stressful search for a universal authority that will affirm human rights?

The idea of a polyarchic, polycentric globalization, whether realistic or not, seems today to be the only political meaning capable of giving a "soul," as the saying goes, to the European Union. How else can we interpret the effort of constructing the unity of *nationes, gentes, civitates* of Europe that doesn't lead to universal depoliticization? Can Europe give itself a political task—if it wants political union—other than that of demonstrating the practicability, on a planetary scale, of the idea of coexistence, of a *foedus* among great cultural spaces thought of as autonomous and necessary? Without such a perspective, there is only the transformation of Europe into an Atlantic peninsula, a myopic strategy for the United States itself. In fact, we know that American policy will always need allies, allies capable of making clear to America its limitations and the risks of America's imperial exposure and not simply obedient subjects. However, Europe cannot survive, not even in its present, precarious state, not even as an important area of exchange and significant market, if it is incapable of any autonomous, far-reaching political and cultural strategy.

Europe needs to recognize that in the current situation it cannot elaborate an imperial policy in the sense that we have often set out here. Only a perfectly balanced Europe between the Atlantic world, the Mediterranean, and the "great Russian land" is able to do that. A Europe that is centered on a presumed Franco-Carolingian axis will end up, thanks to the inexorable law of unintended consequences, as an appendage of the Anglo-Saxon powers. Such a consideration has nothing to do with unrealistic anti-Atlanticism. Once again, it's a question of knowing whether or not we want Europe to be a "great space" (Schmitt) capable of its own political initiative. If this is the meaning of the European Union, then it will be achieved only if Europe becomes a plural space, one able to nurture in itself the very plurality of the West. To be the heir, indeed, of the three Romes, of the "transfers of power" that have marked European history, in vital dialogue and conflict with other Mediterranean civilizations.[17] No other European space is able to balance, in the construction of political unity, the cultural, technological, and military power of Great Britain in its own indissoluble *foedus* (which will always be a priority with respect to any other alliance) with the great American island and its victorious "European heresy." Here is where we differ from Kojève. A Latin empire is impossible. Impossible and, indeed, portending of new conflicts with Germany and Eastern Europe. The "European empire" will be, if it comes to pass, the ambiguous power formed from the agreement between its always contrasting voices. Common voices, precisely, because of their centuries of tension and conjoined finally, by means of these very tensions, in reciprocal recognition.[18]

However, if this perspective is to be politically effective, it will have to answer the following question: who are the subjects that want such a Europe? What constituent forces can become its subject? Will such a Europe be the outcome of the labor of some "separate intelligence"? A "happy" mix of powerful economic interests, of cosmopolitan enlightenment fortuitously allied to Catholic universalism, and of disenchanted realism grown on the political collapse of the continental powers after a century of unprecedented civil wars have brought us here. An extraordinary result, but the next steps won't happen in the same way and by the same means. The great European space of which we spoke will be, if it will be, the work of European citizens, of social movements for a European political citizenship richer than those national ones and that provide an exemplary model of the new global order.[19]

The European subject is dramatically missing today, and ideologies or sermons will not bring it back. First, what will is political effort that aims at defining new and higher forms of citizenship and solidarity beyond the national context. This is precisely what is not happening now: the conservative opposition (absolutely bipartisan) to European political union is constantly nourished by the asymmetry among national constitutions (which impose redistributive criteria within a universal vision of the state's obligation, in order to guarantee the enjoyment of specific rights) and the inspiring principles of European treatises, which are absolutely formal in this respect (very vague principles of "cohesion," "well-balanced and endurable development," etc.). The philosophy underpinning treatises has not moved one step beyond the classical liberal stance that guarantees justice and security for the citizen with respect to the state. There is no positive formula for a social European citizenship. There is no definition of the positive traits of the relation between the citizen and the union nor of the bond between citizens and the union regardless of nationality and residence.[20]

European citizens do not take part directly in any decision of the union. Therefore, they don't form a society (unlike every other federal country in which there is a direct relationship between the citizens of the single states and the central government). Without a European society, however, there is no political union. And such a society can only be built by demonstrating that at the level of community one can enrich, intensify, and implement the rights of citizenship.

Here the Roman metaphor comes back forcefully. The construction of a double tier of citizenship, in which the more universal one does not eliminate national specificities (but increases and more effectively safeguards the rights that have matured in them), is essentially a Roman idea.[21] A European citizenship that does not require a European People and a European Nation but instead a federative society of people and nations is a Roman

one. These two ideas, namely, a citizenship foreign to any ethnic-racial prejudice, founded on a political *concordia*, and an idea of *concordia* that does
not regard all conflicts as only destructive (but on the contrary is regener-
ated and renewed precisely by conflict), are "constituent energies" of the
European political union that can only move ahead if we remember the
Roman root from which they come.

Without such a European identity, in a Europe where the sovereignty of
the people is not practiced on a continental scale and where *nationes, civitates, gentes* are still prisoners of the national states, in a Europe incapable
of representing its own plural community, reduced to its techno-economic
dimension (the economic unity, to be sure, remains the *conditio sine qua
non*) and to only one of its geopolitical dimensions (the Atlantic one)—it is
impossible to balance the physiological tendencies of the American imperial policy, with its century-long "soliloquizing." It will be equally impossible to think the construction of a global order founded on that "law of
plurality" which Hannah Arendt defined as (or did she hope for?) the Law
of the Earth.

10

EMPIRE AND *KATECHON*: A QUESTION OF POLITICAL THEOLOGY (FROM PAUL, 2 THESSALONIANS 2)

As we saw earlier, an empire is such when the sense of *auctoritas* is strictly joined to that of state. No empire is simply conservative. The "city" it wants to edify is either growing (*augescens*), or it is not. It is *urbs* only insofar as it aims at becoming *orbis*. However, the empire form also wants to continue without end (*sine fine*), but not artificially, nor conventionally, as the "mortal god," the state form. Its own strength consists in this paradox: to be that energy which develops "always-beyond" (all empires have always expressed this aspiration) and, at the same time (*in uno*), to be able to guarantee stability and security: energy that perfectly persists in its unending growth. In short, we could say that the temporality proper to the form of empire is the epoch. The will to power of empire is expressed in epoch making. *Epoché* means suspension, stopping, motionless delay. Time no longer moves from moment to moment (*movimentum*), and in empire time takes on its exact form. The movement of time appears to be realized in the epoch that the empire brands with its own character. Hence, it is understood that this *epoché* puts an end also to the properly skeptical *epoché* that consists of doubt, uncertainty, and insecurity. The epoch of the empire silences, finally, the one understood as the suspension of judgment, the provisional and precarious search for a stable ground on which to build our dwellings. The solid Cartesian cogito, "I think," replies at last to the *dubito*, "I doubt."

But the term "epoch" cannot be separated etymologically from the other, the *katechein*, to which Carl Schmitt forcefully drew our attention. More or less from his work of the 1930s and then with more intensity with the 1950 *Nomos of the Earth* on, *katechein* is at the center of discussions on political theology, which is to say, on the relation between, on one hand, the tradition and dogma of the Christian Middle Ages and, on the other, that of modern secularization.[1] *To katechon*, neuter, and *ho katechon*, masculine, derive from *katechein*, which means: to detain, to contain, to slow down, and that which slows down or he or she who slows down. To be epoch making means being able to detain or contain all that dissolves the supremacy of the ruling spiritual-political form. We could differentiate between the power that truly stops the energies that aim at dissolving a given order and those that limit themselves to keeping them at bay or containing them. But it is clear that both dimensions intersect.

The empire has to do with *katechein* just as any form of earthly power does. Any law, any jurisdiction expresses a *katechontic* subjectivity. The term, as we know, originates in Paul's Second Letter to the Thessalonians (unlike the first letter, this letter is possibly apocryphal but comes certainly from Paul's inner circle and is representative of his thinking). The context is the eschatological tone of 1 Thessalonians 5:2, Matthew 23:36–43, Apocalypse 16:15, and other texts of ancient Christian literature such as, especially, Didaché 16:1–8. The community Paul is addressing is upset because of a letter that had been sent to them, which clearly spoke of the imminent coming (*parousia*) of Jesus Christ, that is, the end of the time of waiting. As that letter was wrongly attributed to him, Paul meets their impatience and outlines the moments of apocalyptic time (2 Thess. 2:3–12). To be sure, time is short: the time we live is eschatological; that is, it is the last time. But, within the spasm of its instant, the following still must occur: first the Man of lawlessness or iniquity (*anomia*) has to be revealed, that is, the Son of perdition (*apoleia*), the one who, as Man and as Son, is the perfect Adversary (*antikeimenos*) of Jesus, the Son of God. This apocalypse of *anomia*, however, is now held back by something (*to katechon*) that prevents it from being revealed in all its fullness. The *antikeimenos* already "acts"; it is already "at work" (*energeitai*); it already demonstrates its devastating energy. But its timing (*kairos*) has not yet arrived, that is, the time of its supreme fullness has not come yet. In order to be realized, he who holds it back (*ho katechon*) must be eliminated. Then the final struggle will take place: the confrontation (*duellum*), without any further mediation or delay, between the Son of Perdition and the Son of Salvation, until the former is annihilated by the Spirit that comes from the mouth of the Lord.

Therefore, one needs to be patient, in the image of God who suffers and awaits (*patibilis et patiens*), in the certain hope that everything will end with the victory of those who during the time of tribulation were able to stand in the faith in the Truth, while those who have instead believed the lie of the Wicked have been annihilated. Yet the Spirit of the Lord will come (*parousia*) only when the *kairos* of the *antikeimenos* is perfect. Paul, turning to the Thessalonians as if they knew what or whom he is referring to, writes how the adversary is held back, delayed, and contained by another force. Between the use of the neuter (*to*) and the masculine (*ho*) no contradiction will be found. The same goes for the adversary. They are incarnated spiritual powers that have a real, certain presence. Exactly like the *logos*, they become flesh and live historically.

Who or what is the *katechon*? How does the *katechon* work, and what value should we attributed to it? In *De civitate Dei*, Augustine admits to his essential ignorance, but he is well aware of the long exegetical tradition on the topic. The reference to this figure remains quite vague in Irenaeus, who in *Adversus haereseos* is the first to quote 2 Thessalonians, as well as in Hippolytus's *Commentary on Daniel*. In the succession of empires that the Lord has willed, the power of Rome to create an epoch is greater than any other, but Rome too will collapse, and the empire will be divided in ten kingdoms (Rev. 17). Its unity is only an "ape," that is, a parody of the universalism of true faith, just as the multiethnic unity of its army is false and artificial. To be sure, in these authors the image of Rome "holds up," but not with respect to the adversary. On the contrary, the image appears to correspond to the event of the latter's affirmation. The empire "prophesies" the apocalypse of lawlessness (*anomia*) rather than keeping it at bay.

Tertullian's *Apologeticum* offers a different vision. In the famous passage in which Tertullian claims for Christians the virtue of invoking God for the well-being of the emperors (*pro salute imperatorum*), he also claims to know that

the terrible catastrophe imminent on the world-universe and the same end of our age (*saeculum*) . . . will be delayed (*retardari*) until the passing of the Roman Empire. Since we don't want to go through this experience (*nolimus experiri*), we pray that it may be deferred (*differiri*) and, in so doing (with our prayers) we favor the duration of Rome.

It is entirely beside the point to read Tertullian's passage as a tactic so as to avoid persecution or so not to incite Roman anger. Here the reference seems to be rather to Paul's Letter to the Romans 13. Christians know that emperors, as any political authority, receive their powers from God, and, therefore, they too invoke the emperors' salvation. Caesar is "put in power by our God" (*a nostro Deo constitutus*). Legal order and the law do not save one from sin but contain it. As long as sin is held in abeyance in them and by them, while their power continues, the apocalypse of the adversary, together with "horrible suffering," will be deferred and delayed.

Is the cosmic-eschatological role of the *katechon* therefore positive? Does such a role coincide with Rome's, the imperial form par excellence? Tertullian's words may be understood to say that the law of the empire is opposed to the spreading of the *anomia* embodied by the adversary and that the empire's mission is implicitly allied to that of the church (*ekklesia*). This conclusion would project onto the *katechon* the shadow of the political theology of the fourth and fifth centuries (Eusebius, partly Orosius, but not Augustine!). This is what Carl Schmitt has in mind. In Paul and in ancient Christian literature, the idea of the Old Testament that the political power is willed by God still has value, but the *katechontic* duty of the earthly sovereign does not express any intention to reject the claims of the adversary and the coming of his apocalypse. The empires follow one after another in the form of the beasts of Daniel's prophecy, and this is how they are introduced, in particular, in John's Revelation.

We could claim that the universalism of the empire represents a "providential" factor for the preaching of the Word to the city and the world (*urbi et orbi*), but, by its own nature, the empire is powerless against the fate of the age, which cannot but move quickly toward the precipitous hour (*kairos*) of the *antikeimenos*. This is clear as well in Tertullian: it is not the power of the empire that restrains but rather the prayers of Christians. In this sense, we ought to understand the words of the apologists Aristides and Justin (*Apologia* 1.16–45). The true katechontic power is the Christian seed, and all empires work unaware that they soon will be annihilated. Even those authors who are inclined to see the *katechon* in the empire admit that the latter's work is only effective when combined with the power of prayer or, as

John Chrysostom says in *Homelia* 4, the grace of the Spirit. In fact, what really holds back the *katechon* is the invocation to the Lord to grant us *more time* so that a greater number of people can be converted or so that the Gospel can be preached to all peoples. These, at least, are Theodore of Mopsuestia's and Theodoret of Cyrus's views when commenting on Paul's Second Letter to the Thessalonians. They were disputing openly with other interpretations that alluded to the Roman Empire.

Yet the meaning of *katechon* varies radically according to how we understand the anomy of the adversary. If anomy and perdition (*apoleia*) correspond to a total absence of the law, anarchy, and destruction, then the *katechon* in its being law and sovereignty (albeit in a worldly sense) sits opposite the adversary. If anomy and perdition imply a completely different spiritual-eschatological sense, then once again the *katechon* will have to be conceived (within the framework of the succession of empires) as a moment of the terrible history leading to the affirmation of the Ungodly. Doesn't empire also entail war and destruction? Did Rome ever close the doors of the temple of Janus? Yet the law of the *katechon* is also law that is capable of moderating, containing, and governing. Is not the final anomy also a *nomos*? Who, after all, is the *antikeimenos*? Within the context of Paul's letters and of John's Revelation there can be no doubt: he is the body formed by the *antichrists*. They give life to a community and do not come only from "outside"; they do not assail the *Civitas Dei* from outside. Rather they come "from us" even though not being "of us" (1 John 2:18). Augustine takes up the theme even more dramatically in his *Tractatus on John's Letter* and in *De doctrina christiana*. There are in the church, mixed within it, those who are of the body of Satan. Many have already exited the body, but many are still inside and have not left (*intus sunt, non exierunt*). "Do we dare say it": let everyone ask himself if he or she does not belong to their ranks. The *antikeimenos* does not express vague anarchic expectations. He is radically the opposite of the *nomos* of love (*agape*). In him, the *nomos* of the Antichrist is represented. His argument (*ratio*) consists in denying that Jesus is the Christ and the Savior. In denying that he is the Savior, the *antikeimenos* denies the very possibility of salvation. And it is against such a salvation, the one that comes from Christ, that he represents the spirit of perdition (*apoleia*). No generic anomy, no generic destruction, even less atheistic "discourses" are present. The reason why the Antichrist is *apoleia* is because he essentially means to destroy the faith that Jesus is the Christ, that is, the faith in salvation. The spreading of the despair about faith (*desperatio de fide*) constitutes his mission, which is exactly the opposite of what ought to be the mission of the church.

If that's so, then how can the empire claim to be the *katechon* in the exact sense of expressing an opposition, whether conscious or not, to the adversary? The sign of the Roman Empire is also antichristic. Its law can contain the dissolution of political and social ties but only in the name of its own, autonomous power. The empire contains the wounded, sinful nature (*natura vulnerata*), ready to commit evil for its own duration. Its only aim is the preservation of its own energy; it could not even manage to be "accompanied" by the prayers of the saints. In fact, these prayers presuppose their own greater power with respect to the power of the empire, which explains why they do not intend them to be confused with other prayers. They claim these to be only idolatry and superstition. Their very same manifestation intends to show, implicitly, the weakness of the empire, together with that of the many idols in its temples, with respect to the patience and well-founded hope of the Christians.

Even in the militant church operating in the secular world (in the *saeculum*) we can find antichrists. But the empire's very essence is antichristic. If we are concerned here with an authentic hegemonic will to "make epoch," then the empire can only portray itself as savior; it can only represent its own ideas as that of the Age, as a whole. Any religious creed, therefore, will have to be joined to this idea: every *religio* must be *civilis* as well. Caesar and God cannot proceed separately, even less in the sense—one that appears clearly in all the ancient exegesis—in which Caesar belongs to the techno-bureaucratic administrative offices, without any power over mind and soul. The imperial form cannot tolerate any eschatological reservations about itself.

If this is the case, then empire contains within itself the rampant spirit of the Antichrist, as much as it presents itself as legitimate violence against any anarchic aspiration. Its law punishes sin (without ever succeeding in overcoming it). It withholds or stops, for a moment, the violence of the Antichrist but keeps within itself the very seed of the adversary and its opposition to the *nomos* of the truth and love. It wins over all law and any measure of justice based on exchange and retribution. If the empire is *katechon*, it is so in both senses. However, it also expresses the will to allow the energy of the adversary to last as long as possible, by delaying its fullest manifestation, since this moment is destined to coincide with the empire's own annihilation. By willing itself *sine fine*, the empire also wills *sine fine* the energy of the *antikeimenos*, that is the energy of the Antichrists. Such an order is impossible to maintain. The contradiction between the Son of Perdition and the Son of Salvation, namely between *apoleia* (properly understood as will to destroy the christological symbol) and salvation (*soteria*), will never be settled once and for all. It is a conflict (*polemos*) that cannot be resolved in an armistice or a peace. It leads necessarily to the final confrontation (*duellum*) as an eschatological and insurmountable image of the relation friend-enemy.

On one hand, far from making political authority sacred, the recognition that political authority is willed by God reduces political authority to a product of sinful nature (*natura vulnerata*), dictating boundaries that no imperial sovereignty can ever accept. Boundaries, on the other hand, are also meant to be swept away by the fury of the Antichrist, of the antichrists. In fact, the idea that earthly sovereignty can represent a power from above capable of stopping and deferring the apocalypse of the adversary originates in the political thought of the post-Napoleonic Restoration, which in its turn was essentially Eusebian. Carl Schmitt draws from that school of thought and especially from Donoso Cortés, whom Jacob Taubes rightly called an apocalyptic of the Restoration.[2] But this perspective is possible only (it is worth repeating it) by reducing the anomy of the apocalyptic texts to a near synonym of political anarchy. The *antikeimenos*, on the contrary, rises above any power (or even of what is called God or is worshipped as God) to install himself in the temple of God, in order to show himself as the only God. That is, he demands hierarchy, order, and worship.

In this sense, clearly the empire plays a part. Its part is to "contain" the adversary. In its will to duration, the empire also attempts to hold back and slow down the energies that constitute the body of the adversary, for it knows that their explosion will also spell the end of empire. At the same time, the empire preserves in itself the Adversary's vehemence, feeding on it to meet its own appetite for power (*libido dominandi*). It will also inevitably prefigure, even if in "contained" form, the will to show itself as God, destined to be revealed only in the moment (*kairos*) the adversary rises. The latter puts an end to the form of the empire but at the same time fulfils it by showing its true colors.

For all these reasons, neither can the empire be sublated in katechontic power, nor can katechontic power be easily assimilated to a "weak" form of sovereignty, as we have assumed at first glance. A simply administrative-distributive *katechon* is not able to withhold or delay anything.[3] An authentic empire, however, precisely in its most strident opposition to any anarchy from below and precisely by claiming for itself genuine *auctoritas* inevitably participates in that same antichristic energy that will eventually undo it. An empire cannot be defined within the confines of the *katechon* because of the productive energy that characterizes its demon and because of the claim of its own autonomy with respect to any ideas, values, or higher-ordered powers. The empire's autonomy cannot be entirely curbed, as in the end the impetus of the anomy that the *antikeimenos* encompasses appears to be beyond any containment.

But if the empire is not reducible to *katechon*, what kind of compromise can be reached between its form and the church? Or, more generally, between its "epoch" and the spiritual power that claims to represent (in its form, in its symbol, in its cults) the totality of the age and to know its ultimate objective? It would seem that the only compromise available is between the church and those who work in slowing down the adversary with the aim of providing people with more time to be converted to the Truth. If the epoch-making trait of political sovereignty is manifested with this purpose in mind, then complicity with the preaching of the *verbum* is possible. Yet, as we saw, it is impossible to establish such intent in political action. Once we see the inevitability of the political order, we have to assert its *auctoritas*, which will ultimately involve, in one form or another, a conflict with the spiritual authorities. Finally, if we wish to *unite* the two dimensions, then we need to anticipate, in this moment exactly, how powerful the adversary is, as it is precisely this "unity" that Satan suggested to Jesus.

Undoubtedly, even the empire holds back. Even its form, although made up of wars, suffering, and impositions, contains, "holds-in-form," impulses, appetites, and instincts that will run rampant but only in the anomy. In fact, in the anomy they are the law, the precise reverse of Christ's new order (*mandatum novum*). But only one power seems katechontic in this respect, and that is the one that prays so that the end time will last long enough so that as many as possible pay attention to the voice crying in the desert. Therefore, the *katechon* is the church and only the church. To carry this out means to continue in the secular world and to ask to be permitted to continue. It entails believing fiercely that in the course of time salvation is possible and, more generally, that some relation between time and salvation holds. As a result, it entails the search for compromises with earthly powers. No katechontic power can truly assert that its kingdom is not of this earth and that, therefore, it has nothing to do with the Prince of this world, the one who already displays his energy (*energeitai*).

Among the forms of political sovereignty, empire is the only one that seems able to "contain" the *antikeimenos*. In reality, however, empire is most on the side of the *antikeimenos*. The church may well believe that its prayers are effective, but only at the price of assuming that the church itself will last forever. When will the end of universal conversion come? In pursuing it, doesn't the church wind up forgetting to preach precisely the *end of time* in the coming (*parousia*) of the Lord? Or better still, forgetting that the end of time is *now* for those who believe and that *now* what is needed is to decide for the Truth? This forgetting means, in fact, the withdrawal (*secessio*) from the very act of faith: the loss of faith.

The eschatological picture is thus complete. Against weak, worldly powers, divided among each other and each other internally and incapable of producing order and safety, the power of empires asserts itself. That power will last insofar as it will ape (*simia*) the universalism of the faith in Christ. For this reason, such a power must come into conflict with the authority that claims to be purely spiritual and the "chosen" place where the Spirit represents itself. In such a conflict, the spiritual authority will have to contain within itself, in all the senses of the term, the energy of the *antikeimenos*. As much as the church opposes the adversary, the church preserves it; as much as the church keeps the adversary at bay, the church guarantees its existence. The church itself denounces this contradiction and accelerates the fall of the empire, but, at the same time, the church has to safeguard the adversary by waiting patiently. The church is called on to hold out to the end. It longs for the apocalypse and is afraid, at the same time, that in the *parousia* the Lord will not find faith on earth. Therefore, the church prays for time, but time can give nothing except to the sovereignties of the world. In its incarnate form, the church, therefore, has no choice but to form compromises with these worldly powers. And the history of such a search always places faith, the foundation of our hope, necessarily in doubt.

Only the "logical" evolution of the great politico-theological forms of the empire and the church can destroy the power of the *katechon*. The *katechon* has been understood as an ensemble of figures immanent to these forms, church and empire. These figures are the ones, within the empire, that check its lust for power (*libido dominandi*). They are the ones in any political sovereignty that define the sovereignty's limits, with the purpose of strengthening its structure and extending its duration. They are those within the church that keep the antichrists in check so that the latter will not go fill the ranks of the *antikeimenos*. Therefore, they implicitly pray that the apocalypse may not be and that the waiting for the *parousia* will become interminable. When in fact will all people listen?

This explains the reason why a long exegetic tradition intimately joins the fate of the empire and the church. Even in the *Glossa ordinaria*, which is fundamental for the history of medieval exegesis (though not only), this tradition finds its expression.[4] The time (*kairos*) of the Antichrist will have as its first sign defection (*defectio*) from the empire: "individual" powers will shatter its organism, but the unity of the church will remain. The second sign consists in the crisis of the church itself. Yet both the forms of political sovereignty as well as the historical, religious, and even political symbol of the church will continue. The real withdrawal (*discessio*) that announces the apocalypse of the anomy will first be that of the earthly sovereign and then of the church: *discessio* from the faith in the possibility of salvation. For the political sovereign, it will be the withdrawal from faith in a political order endowed with sense and productive of sense. For the church, it will be the withdrawal from the belief that man is "capable of God" (*capax Dei*) and, therefore, from faith in the very Word of Jesus. The *antikeimenos* is nothing but the Apostate. But the Apostate only triumphs, in the end, thanks to the apostasy of the powers that ought to have contained it. The *logos* of apostasy becomes life and real history in the Apostate.

The katechontic powers present a conservative face (*facies*) that in the end is revealed as deceitful. These powers, in fact, do the work of the apostasy. Thanks to the law of unintended consequences, whether the *katechon* asserts the autonomy of political sovereignty against the passions of the multitude or invokes the deferment of the Final Judgment in order to prepare the multitude better for it, the katechontic energy contains the seed of apostasy within itself. All conservative energy belonging to the *saeculum* will in the end be revealed as an accomplice of the Wicked. The idea that conservative energies can hold back, if not stop, the anomy is the result of two errors. The first consists in not being able to grasp the internal dialectic of anomy (and in not distinguishing the *stasis*, the "civil war" between the political and the spiritual dimensions). The second consists in believing the sign of the Antichrist to be simply anarchic. It is rather the case that, before Judgment, that which is of the Antichrist will be a kingdom, but it will no longer be founded on established sovereignties, that is, on a well-grounded *nomos*, on the "measure" that empire and church represented in the highest way. It will instead be based on the withdrawal or defection (*secessio* or *defectio*) of every order excepting that of the individual will to power, for as long as possible. It will be the kingdom of the apostasy, which the Wicked will make pacific, as it overcomes the "tyranny of values." In truth, however, it will be indifferent to any value that is not quantifiable or exchangeable. It will be the eternal return of crisis, of endemic conflict. Furthermore, any nostalgia for the katechontic powers will only appear as will to powerlessness.

If the wombs of the ancient churches, to paraphrase Max Weber, seem no longer capable and welcoming, those of the state sovereignties are even less so. Yet no new empire can fill the void left by their loss of power. Rather, as Kojève already pointed out at the time in which he saw the European civil war of the twentieth century come to an end, there will be competition, and there will be shorter and shorter and more unforeseeable crises in important political and economic spaces that are no longer homogeneous and institutionally stable.[5] The idea of empire refers to powerful subjectivities and to a political dominance that no longer exists. The new global space (no longer "spatial" at all) fundamentally has many heads and is marked by an endemic conflict among impersonal powers that no longer express any value. The idea that such conflict could have an outcome other than that of its own perpetuation is as senseless as the nostalgia for empire. Only theologically can one state (or believe) that the kingdom of the apostasy will come to an end. It will not be the multitudes from within, however, that produce such an end and that decree it (as many believed that the working class, the product of capitalism, would "justly" put an end to the prehistory of humanity by overcoming and eliminating the bourgeois father). The multitudes are just as far from the angels of the apocalypse as the actual states are far from Hobbes's "mortal god," and just as far as the great political and economic spaces of today are far from the Roman Empire.

Addenda

11

THE EUROPE OF MARÍA ZAMBRANO

We who ask questions ("*nos interrogantes*," according to St. Augustine) are the inhabitants of Europe. We are those who question every tradition and every value and who question the mystery that is at the center of our own faiths.[1] Here, in Europe, even the pilgrim asks questions, indeed never ceases to ask, as he or she makes their way to the Place. Here even the theologian wants to be the one who discovers the truth (*inventor veritatis*). Without Ulysses there wouldn't be a Europe, declares María Zambrano.[2] Ulysses is not the one who suffers adventures and the consequences in his journey home (*nostos*); he is the one who questions and seemingly looks for them. He is the one who learns from his adventures and their consequences. For Ulysses, every experience becomes a problem, and every encounter sets in motion the questioning once again. For him, there is no "given" that is not converted immediately into an exercise for the mind, into a passion for thinking.

Zambrano places Europe under the sign of Ulysses, but from here she also begins her own journey. A European journey if there ever was one: it is Mediterranean and European, and it is a journey through perfectly circumscribed islands, in the bosom of the "primordial" sea, just as clearings in the forest (*claros del bosque*) open up in the sea of vegetation.[3] A journey led by a word that demands clarity and transparency but whose measure is also the sign of the distances that bring together and apart languages, traditions, and gods of this space—of the Mediterranean world. Place, yes— for without a place it would be impossible to go on—but a multiverse place (*luogo multiverso*), a place that shapes possibilities more than establishes realities, a place that in its incessant metamorphoses remains itself. Europe will end when Europe ceases to be in motion (*cesserà di passare*), when its present form no longer has the strength to come to an end.[4]

But what is the status, so to speak, of this questioning? What are the principles regulating its form? This is the problem that anchors María Zambrano's entire work and that finds its most complete expression, it seems to me, in *El hombre y lo divino*.[5] The status of such questioning is paradoxical. On one hand, it certainly refers to a form of initiation. There cannot be a questioning without a "voice from the abyss" (*voz abismática*) that calls. One assumes, therefore, a voice that "cries" again and again, as well as a listening and an ability to listen. On the other hand, it is clear that we would never question if we had not lost our intimacy with that voice or if we knew how to listen perfectly to it. The questioning testifies, then, to a lost intimacy precisely with what nonetheless calls. Therefore, Europe is the space in which one ceaselessly questions the gods and from whence the gods withdraw. In questioning, the greatest intimacy is equivalent to absence, the presence to exile. European philosophy is the conscience of such a destiny: its interrogation turns to the divine when the presence of the gods is lost. At the center of its heart is the absence of what is questioned. Such an original loss accompanies every step and every word of European philosophy.

It is with Diotima's eyes, with *theoría*, that Zambrano analyzes European philosophy, but the language of philosophy is the same as Europe's language.[6] The word, the measure of the word that questions the absent Being, becomes Being itself. It is the "inversion" of Being that, according to Zambrano, Parmenides inaugurates. The Being that is "all full," immobile, laying in itself, without birth or death; the Being that is "nothing of life," that is proper to the *logos*, is inverted in the only Being that requires that it be— and life, the world of its appearances, presences, opinions, is reduced to nonbeing. A systematic and chilling doubt embraces every presence; all immediacy is turned back. The "separation from the initial or natural conditions of life that never ceases to increase," which Valéry sees as the trait of the Mediterranean people,[7] is for Zambrano the product of questioning or, better, of the philosophical questioning that transforms what is the trace of an absence (the questioning word) in the only reality given to us or in the only means allowed us to relate to reality. The insight is extraordinary; so is *l'esprit de finesse*, with which Zambrano follows not history but the being in doubt (*diaporein*), namely, the development from aporia to aporia, of European philosophical questioning. Her care in illuminating its undeclared premises and inevitable consequences is extraordinary as well.

Philosophy truly loves that absent Presence—that Presence which, in the questioning and for the questioning, shows itself to be absent. Philosophy, like Ulysses, really wants to reconnect fully with that Reality, truly wants to reintegrate the original moment of harmony. It can only want it by means of the *logos*, the weapon of the *logos*. It can only desire it by interrogating the Absent Being in order to compel it to a new presence in the *logos*. It can only want it by *comprehending* it, by turning Reality into a concept, and therefore we have *logos* once more.

Philosophy, at least until the modern era, can have no truck with absence. To overcome absence, to remove it, philosophy questions it. Absence, therefore, is sacrificed in order to find the missing harmony, the lost communion. Interrogation, by its very nature, can never leave the Absent alone. The *logos* of philosophy requires that Absence move to Presence, that it be represented and become idea. The questioning, then, originates in an Absence and is at the same time violence against it. It is the claim, the *hybris*, that Absence can be overcome by means of the *logos* and in the *logos*.

Philosophy cannot make do with the absence of the Absent. Philosophy scrutinizes it in order to make the absence of the Absent its own. Either philosophy sacrifices the Absent in the concept, or it despairs that it has failed and, therefore, negates any meaning to its own attempt, to its own examination. Either philosophy kills the absence of the Absent (and therefore what is essential to the Absent), or it kills the very sense of the interrogation. The death of God is the result of philosophy's love of God (*amor Dei*), that is, of its "intellectual" love of God (*amor Dei intellectualis*).

For Zambrano the death of God is also the cipher of the modern, but the genesis that she outlines and the voice with which she speaks are clear and original. The terrible voraciousness of philosophical love (to which she opposes the love object of the Mystic, never to be consumed) is what kills God, after having claimed in every way His full, actual, unveiled presence. The god who dies is the representation known by entire pagan world. Hellas is studded with the graves of gods, but the idea that man can kill Him and that God can die only by the hand of man—this unprecedented idea is Christianity's. If we now combine the love of the *logos*, a love that wants to "invert" any reality and any absence in *logos*, in a path that can only lead, therefore, to the sacrifice of the Absent and the Unknown—the result is Europe, the Europe of our Age, Europe "or" Christianity (*Europa oder Christenheit*). The "inversion" of Being in *logos* that Greek thought carried out was not enough to produce the notion that God could be killed off by means of an interminable philosophical inquiry (*skepsis*). For such "blasphemy" the crucial Event was necessary, namely the Crucifixion.

The modern era gives the name of "freedom" to this idea. Following Ortega y Gasset, Zambrano shows how it is not only a question of freedom but of necessary freedom. The "questioners" who absorb within themselves the object of love can no longer necessarily maintain any relation (*religio*) with it. Questioners, necessarily, are free. A voice no longer guides them in their journey. At this point, questioners are compelled to make "divine" the journey undertaken. That path without destination and that investigation without a critical voice are all that is left. The death of God, according to Zambrano, corresponds to the adoration of History, the most hateful of all idols. Once free of God, one becomes slaves of the idol, and while God was questioned (because His very absence demanded questioning—in fact, faith too was compelled to question, lest it appeared negligent), this idol, History, does not even require questioning since History is already present. History's "things" are already visible, given that no one can reasonably harbor doubts about them.

The "loving questioning" of philosophy produces the death of its own object. Atheistic freedom produces idolatrous beliefs in History and in historical reason as the instrument for interpreting the new god. The European adventure thus seems to proceed via one unintended consequence after another, as if one always had to arrive there where hopes and expectations are challenged. In every gesture, in every intention, it is as if Europe is always looking, in the end, for what arrives in response. Where the questioning subject has apparently reached dry land, in actual fact the subject has only come ashore to a new *aporia*. Any result has much less the taste of a purchase, or a possession, than the taste of the unknown that opens up in front of it.

On this European constant, María Zambrano establishes her idea of the possible response to the idolatrous atheism of the modern. This isn't a question about the "future of Europe." Such a discourse fully belongs to the "historical reason" of the modern,[8] just as the "outlasting" (*infuturante*) attitude belongs to modernity's essence, namely, the relentless invitation to sacrifice to the future, that every instant be sacrificed to the production of the future. Seen from this point of view, the philosophy of praxis is the philosophy of the modern: truth consists in forms of praxis that are capable of producing the future. The place of man is his praxis. The *logos* is expressed— and translated—into action.

And thus, Zambrano writes, any simplicity, any "true nakedness," and any passivity are forgotten.[9] The instant (*in-stans*) is forgotten, the "nowhereness" (*atopia*) of the instant, from which all time is also generated and chronological order is formed—these are forgotten as well. The delay, the stopping is forgotten. Silence is silenced, which was the form in which the Absent spoke to us. Don Quixote is being silenced, who begins a journey guided, precisely, by the nonexistent; Don Quixote, who, in his love for indestructible Absence, constructs his own relations and wants to give life to his own community. That "order of love" (*ordo amoris*, St. Augustine) is silenced, which no possession can destroy since love is not turned into a possession.

This is the Europe that metaphysically runs counter to the figure of the "blessed ones" (*bienaventurados*).[10] They are not the ascetic blessed of ecstasy, they are not strangers to the passions of the soul, and they do not forget the need to act. They feel those passions, simply, with primal force. They act out of necessity; they immediately reverberate with the voice from the abyss (*voz abismática*) that claims them for itself. Moreover, the blessed ones represent perfect individuality. They are that measure of *simple singularity* toward which any being, whether it is aware of it or not, is drawn to and attends, without ever completely being able to reach it. "Blessed" are those who are able to free themselves from any confusion, who can no longer be called other than themselves, and to whom alone their proper names are owed, intangible and irreducible. This explains why they can communicate perfectly. The presence of the individual, his presence here and now, and his action in our midst—all this makes us uneasy and demands a response. All this provokes us. It is a scandal. All these open wounds keep communication flowing. All this exceeds common discourse while it upsets the usual order. But it is word, expression. We could say that only the blessed communicates properly. Only when we come, unexpectedly, into the presence of someone who is perfectly "individual," and therefore unforgettable, do we notice all the power of the expression, the word, the sign, and the sound that they communicate. This is what the blessed alludes to when pointing to the unblemished singularity of his or her experience, to the singularity of the word with which he or she tries to express it. Such singularity is not oriented to the "common," nor to "history," nor to the "general," but rather to the Self of the other who listens and who runs a risk in listening.

The blessed represents a reappraisal, in the spirit of Spanish mysticism, of Plotinus's "sage." Or better, it sheds light on the sage's meaning, its Mediterranean "taste." It is a combination of feeling and metaphysical illumination, an index of that aesthetic fullness that occurs precisely at the height of ecstasy. The happiness of the blessed occurs, gives itself in the instant of the combination (not the confusion) between the height of the immediacy of feeling and the height of the power of the mind. Europe, María Zambrano repeats, has forgotten the name of this happiness and has forgotten it because all of Europe's thought stands on the ground of the oblivion of Being as *event*, having chosen the *history* of Being instead, as the universal and necessary foundation: as supreme Being, substance and nourishment of all the living. Certainly, the thought of the clearings in the forest (*claros del bosque*) meets, even if with quite different tones, Heidegger's Being as *Ereignis*, that is, Being as appropriating event that is never to be converted into object or foundation—because it is pulsation, pure and palpitating presence, elusive life, breath, *pneuma*, breath, and presence that is not externalized. Being that exceeds every being, unlimited gift. This is what we read in the most intense pages of *Claros del bosque*. Plotinus calls *aión* this eternal child (*puer*) of the instant, the eternal, elusive giving of Life in the ungraspable singularity of its beings. All of María Zambrano's intellect and language, "impalpable fire and light of intelligence," is bent on capturing the "flash" of *aión*.

12

WE CANNOT CALL OURSELVES ONLY JUDEO-CHRISTIANS

A Conversation with Jacques Le Goff

Q: The arguments over the European Constitution could really have only resulted in a political compromise. It couldn't have happened differently. But the conflict is bound to continue, as there is no clarity or standard view on how best to confront the shared origins and shared identities. Many politicians and intellectuals continue to wonder if there is such a thing as a European identity. In reading Jacques Le Goff's *The Birth of Europe,* we find evidence to the contrary. On just this theme, Massimo Cacciari has also written widely in of late. Can you tell us, in a few words, what the foundations of European common identity are?[1]

LE GOFF: European identity was constituted in many stages and over a long time. The first stage begins with Greek-Roman culture, which brought us the idea of democracy, the scientific method, the critical method, and the importance of the law. The second stage, which I consider essential, is the medieval one, with the spreading of Judeo-Christian values, the combination of European unity and national diversity. It is the stage of the scholastic and university method, of scholastic philosophy, the birth of the city, and the balance between reason and faith. Later comes the scientific stage of the sixteenth and seventeenth centuries, the eighteenth-century Enlightenment, the French Revolution, romanticism, and the long progress of democracy beginning with the nineteenth century.

CACCIARI: A list of the characteristics that different European nations share wouldn't be of much use. The *form* of their relating seems to me, rather, to constitute their real identity, and this form is conflict (*polemos*): to be recognized and to be distinguished from one another. To be contradicted. The form of European identity is agonistic at its core. This is the form of the Greek archipelago, the form of the Roman *civitas* that founds its greatness on the contradiction between patricians and plebeians; this is the form of Christendom (*respublica Christiana*): two Suns, harmony of opposites (*concordia oppositorum*) as the idea of the catholicity of the Church. The heart of Europe is restless, unsound (*insano*). Those who choose to heal will make it stop.

Q: In the twelfth century, European identity was defined, on one hand, with respect to the Byzantine world and, on the other, with respect to the Islamic world. Do you think that today Europe needs to be defined negatively, distinguishing itself from new Islamic fundamentalism and from the American unilateralism of the Bush administration?

LE GOFF: Obviously, on one hand, today's Europe must differentiate itself from Islamic fundamentalism, on the other hand, from American unilateralism. But to protect itself against terrorism and imperialism, Europe must succeed in maintaining an open identity and not a closed and aggressive one.

CACCIARI: The analogy with the twelfth century makes no sense whatsoever. Europe, then, was defined in competition with (but it was a struggle, an *agon*, as I said earlier!) Islamic civilization, which outclassed Europe in so many areas and not because it was fundamentalist in the sense that we understand today! Today's fundamentalism, as Gilles Kepel and others have reminded us, is historically the product of the nationalization and Westernization of the Islamic peoples between the nineteenth and twentieth centuries. If, and I repeat, if Europe affirms its own identity in the terms I mentioned, intrinsically multilateral, if Europe is able to express its own "I" as inquiry and dialogue, then Europe will be able to play its own role, free with respect to all types of fundamentalism. Can we remember such a time in European history? I could mention one name: St. Francis of Assisi. But is St. Francis still a possibility . . . for us?

Q: Around the year 1000, the shared dream of the pope and the emperor was the entrance of the Slavic world into a united Christianity. Is that still an important theme today?

LE GOFF: The Slavic world became a part of Christianity, effectively and essentially, around the year 1000, and the present expansion of Europe is only the first stage of a return to the medieval expansion, a stage that must be followed by expanding Europe toward Ukraine, Belarus, and, with even more difficulty, though it is necessary, Russia.

CACCIARI: I am currently reading an extraordinary book by Bruno Luiselli, who demonstrates, employing several perspectives, the reciprocal acculturation between the Roman-Christian world and the German and the Celtic world, above all the British and Irish.[2] I don't know if there are similar studies, of a similar quality, on relations between the Western and Slavic worlds, before they became Christian. It's clear that the duty and destiny of Western European civilization have been oriented, since its inception, toward the "East." Europe will bring off this idea when this nostalgia for the East is combined with the other and complementary one, of so much a part of the Slavic culture for the European archipelago, for the Catholic-Mediterranean dimension of Europe.

Q: In your view, who are the men who have contributed the most to the idea of Europe?

LE GOFF: The men who in the Middle Ages explicitly referred to a European unity as their personal dream were Pope Pius II (Enea Silvio Piccolomini) and the Hussite king of Bohemia George of Poděbrady.

CACCIARI: I would like to mention, for my part, those who represented Europe's idea the best, that is, those who have more coherently and tragically pointed out its contradictory nature. On one hand, we have those who wanted to bury the differences, the fanatics of Unity and Order, from the great imperial traditions to the Jacobin ones, in their right-wing and left-wing incarnations. On the other hand, there are the prodigious critics of state worship, of the infernal confusions between *civitas hominis* and *civitas dei*, the federalists, in the most authentic and profound sense of the word—the one that echoes across Giacomo Leopardi's *La ginestra*! Still, we need, realistically, to understand that both sides are Europe. Perhaps for us Europeans democracy only means succeeding from time to time in composing this dissonance.

Q: Le Goff claims that Christianity was an important factor of identity but that the process of European identity had begun earlier and continued even after the secularization of our society. A similar declaration seems to be supported by those who, in drafting the European Constitution, have denied the need to go back to Christian roots only . . .

LE GOFF: The preamble to the European constitution seems to me to have to assert first of all the lay status of the emerging political formation. Once this is established, it can also evoke different ideological and cultural legacies, in particular the Judeo-Christian one.

CACCIARI: What we call secularization is only, in many and decisive areas, the secularization of religious ideas. I can't see any irreparable fractures, and, therefore, the process of European identity (but it is this identity that is precisely a process) can be described according to its own "sense." Let's not fall into any easy historicisms. The sense of a historical process occurs, as Vico teaches us, essentially through the law of unintended consequences and not on the basis of calculations and projects that become reality. In history, we find less teleology than in nature. The problem today isn't about counting how many manifestations or expressions of our culture grow from Christian roots but in analyzing if and how these roots are still "holding up." Then, I believe, it will be clear that such roots are strong only insofar as they are secularized and, essentially, through their reformulation in a key of universalism, philanthropy, and enlightenment. All the great classics of the sociology of religion, from Ernst Troeltsch to Max Scheler, from Émile Durkheim to Max Weber, were engaged in explaining this monumental transformation. Could the European Constitution have been the occasion for reappraising the compromise between Christendom and *Kultur*? Was this Pope Wojtyla's aim? The constituent assembly, to be sure, has abdicated this task. But could it ever have been made a reality?

Q: Many say that Europe suffers from an excess of administrative and economic ties and from a deficit of idealism. Le Goff seems to agree when he writes, "Europe is still to be made and, even, to be thought." What should European politicians and intellectuals do in order to provide impetus to and more breathing space to the idea of the European project?

LE GOFF: Economic identity needs to be balanced by developing a European cultural identity whose historical foundations are wide and deep and that infuse into Europe a dynamism borne by a political will.

CACCIARI: The contradictions undermining the current construction of Europe are clearly at work. No European politician, none of the traditional

European political families, "thinks" Europe, given that to think Europe as an Atlantic appendix or as a Franco-Carolingian axis means not to think Europe at all. Thinking Europe as an occasional crucible of nations or, on the contrary, as a new macrostate, or to conceive of it as a compromise between state interests or, on the contrary, in abstractly utopian terms, as if its traditions, languages, and cultures could ever give shape to a United States of Europe on the American model—all of this makes no difference. There can be no doubt that these contradictions also concern the economic dimension. The fundamental pillar of stability, built up in a different era, collides today with the objective of developing and supporting the activities of education and research. Equally, the obsessive search for EU control of the market appears increasingly ineffective with respect to the irresistible globalization of financial capital. It also seems impotent with respect to conflicts of interests, whose connection to globalization is physiological. Even the economic and administrative construction of Europe needs to be utterly revised. The politicians have to "go back to things": they need to look in the face the radically transformed situation after the Maastricht treaty and redefine the priorities of community action so as to make Europe into an area that develops competitively. Only then we will be able to speak realistically of a European foreign policy and the role of Europe as a great power.

Q: European leadership is being fought over. Do you believe in the need of a leadership to advance the progress of constructing Europe? If so, do you believe that the Franco-German axis can represent this leadership?

LE GOFF: We must combine, which is both difficult and necessary, a degree of power given to every member and at the same time the possibility for a small group of nations, more strongly and more consciously European, to become the pulling force for Europe without ruling it. In this sense, France and Germany play an important role. If Great Britain were to become more European, something that we hope for very strongly, it too would obviously be a part of this European leadership.

CACCIARI: The structure of the European political "families" is simply distressing. Just look at the geography of the Parliament at Strasbourg. You could barely infer from it that the Wall has fallen, that the era of the Yalta Conference is over, and that we are in the twenty-first century. Only a European leadership that radically internalizes the epochal shift, relegating both "right" and "left" to the past as well as state nostalgia alongside with irenic utopias of universal peace, wild laissez-faire and corporative-bureaucratic conservatisms, will be able to push forward a European constituent process. No axis between ancient state powers is capable of leading a similar process. Europe is Middle European as much as it is Mediterranean and Mediterranean as much as Balkan. It is Lisbon as much as it is Budapest and Warsaw. Europe is a "republican" tragedy. It may explode, and it may certainly decline, but it will never be slave to an "axis" for long.

Q: How do you evaluate England's position, which has one foot inside and one outside Europe? What would happen if the Labor Party were to win the referendum on a single monetary system?[3]

LE GOFF: England has to redefine its relation to Europe on the one hand and with the United States on the other. Its privileged relations with the United States must not infringe upon its participation in Europe. The case of the war in Iraq is quite negative in this regard. Another troubling uncertainty comes from the ambiguous attitude of the Labor Party and, above all, of Tony Blair, who turns differently to the United States than he does to Europe.

CACCIARI: Britain's stance goes way back. It is the product of the history and the *ethos* of that country. Great Britain is always going to be on the side of the great Atlantic island, and if, unfortunately, it has to choose between that and Europe, it will never hesitate to choose the former. This isn't going to change with different governments, or with different political majorities. For the same reason, no liberal government will ever come to power in Saudi Arabia. It is important that Great Britain be a full partner in the European Union, but all Europeans have to recognize continually and respect Britain's geopolitical position. Doing so will make it easier on the English government, whether it be with members of the Labor party or the Conservative, to persuade their fellow English citizens to join the euro.

Q: Is your Europeanism shaken by the fact that Europe continues to be divided on basic questions such as peace and war?

LE GOFF: I am aware above all of the great progress made by the European Union and the benefits that have resulted from it. If we put aside the delicate events of the Balkans, which will take a while to stabilize, the whole of Europe has become a place of peace. The development of a European foreign policy and of a European defensive force has to make possible, over the long term, for Europe to have a common position with respect to the existing conflicts in the world.

CACCIARI: It is everyone's Europeanism that is being put to the test. But not just because of the Balkan War, which is absolutely shortsighted and destabilizing and whose wounds and consequences are still difficult to judge. It is Europe as such that is being put to the test. If one understands the plurality of its origins, the complexities of its identity, the tragic character of its history, the idea of a European Union becomes just as necessary as it is difficult. What's going to happen is anyone's guess. This war, as with all those that have occurred ever since the Wall fell, "only" shows that Europe, in order to be Europe, will have to know how to develop its own foreign policy and its own geopolitical strategy. And this will not occur if it doesn't have a force for intervening and a deterrent of its own, that is, its own military capability.

Q: Europe and Orient. Some claim that the new millennium will see the emergence of China and India as new world powers. Do you also believe that America and Europe are destined to decline?

LE GOFF: There is no such a thing as an American and European decline. On the contrary, the theme of decline is an old reactionary refrain inspired in particular by Nazi ideology. The growth of China and India ought to create only new and powerful entities, and globalization has to be oriented toward a balance among America, Europe, the Moslem world, India, China, and Japan in a system of pacific exchange under the aegis of the United Nations and UNESCO. The clash of civilizations is not, fortunately, a likely prospect.

CACCIARI: All political and economic hegemonies, just as they are born, so they die. This is the way things are. On one hand, the European decline is a given fact after the Second World War, where the great European powers did most assuredly commit suicide. The European unity is a monumental project precisely because it is based on the full knowledge of this fact. The recognition that Europe was decisively defeated as the hegemonic area of the planet is at the basis of the idea of the European Union. For the United States, things are quite different. The United States' problems are immense. Economic, financial and political, yet their leadership in all key sectors is indisputable. And we can't see their decline on the horizon any time soon.

Will China grow in harmony with the West? Will a global federation then be possible? I believe that the present Chinese leadership wants to move in this direction, but will it be able to do so? Will "things" go along with plans? There are already conflicts concerning the raw materials market and energy resources, which tell us how difficult an absolutely pacific, peacefully multilateral way will be to reorganizing the planet. Will the new *Nomos* of the earth arise out of innumerable compromises and well-tempered agreements? That's possible. We have to make it happen. But it is also important to keep in mind that the great transformations of the international political equilibriums have never come about only because of good intentions.

NOTES

INTRODUCTION: MASSIMO CACCIARI'S GENEALOGY OF EUROPE

1. "*Man fragt sich, ob die Geschichte nicht gerade eine geistreiche Synthese von zwei nietzscheanischen Begriffen schmiedet, nämlich des guten Europäers und des letzten Menschen. Dies könnte den letzten Europäer ergeben. Wir alle kämpfen darum, nicht zu diesem zu warden.*" Translated from French by Stephan Lackner (Benjamin wrote the letter in French). In Lackner, "'Von einer langen, schwierigen Irrfahrt,'" 67. I am thankful to Massimo Morasso for the reference.

2. The first nineteenth-century continental European who gained a clear sight of the contradiction between humanist legacy and the abyss of the new infinite was Giacomo Leopardi (see *Canti* and *Zibaldone*). Until recently, however, the English-speaking world did not have access to his body of work, and Nietzsche's influence remains unparalleled.

3. For a comprehensive analysis of Cacciari's political philosophy I refer to my introduction in Cacciari's *The Unpolitical: For a Radical Critique of Political Reason* (2009) and my article "The Transcendental Limits of Politics: On Massimo Cacciari's Political Philosophy" (forthcoming in a collection of essays on Italian political theory edited by Antonio Calcagno and published by SUNY Press). Here I will reprise in part my previous paragraph on the first chapter of *Geo-filosofia dell'Europa* (whose English translation, "The Geophilosophy of Europe," is included in *The Unpolitical*). See also Cacciari's "History and Destiny" and my introduction to *Italian Critical Theory*.

4. On the rhetorical construction of the North-South cultural divide and Europe's "rhetorical unconscious," see Dainotto, *Europe (in Theory)*.

5. As an example of Asia's disdain for the sea, we may recall that, as a result of internal power struggles, during the fifteenth century the Chinese empire dismantled its entire fleet, at the same time when the European age of discovery was about to begin. See Diamond, *Guns, Germs, and Steel*, 412.

6. Carl Schmitt addresses directly Paul's 2 Thessalonians in "Beschleuniger wider Willen" (published in 1942, but the theme in Schmitt goes back to 1932). For an overview of Schmitt's numerous references to *katechon*, see Hell, "*Katechon*." See also Massimo Cacciari's *Il potere che frena*, Giorgio Agamben's *State of Exception* and *The Time That Remains*, and Roberto Esposito's *Two* for other interpretations of the *katechon* in current Italian political theory. I am grateful to Renato Giovannoli for his article "Platone e il *katechon*."

7. See John Calvin's *In epistulam Pauli ad Thessalonicenses alteram commentarii* (1550) and De Greef, *The Writings of John Calvin*. An Italian translation of Calvin's passage is included in the appendix to Cacciari's *Il potere che frena*, 216ff.

8. "*Follia dell'Occidente*." I am referring to Emanuele Severino's definition of European nihilism in *Essenza del nichilismo*. Severino traces nihilism back to Plato's "parricide" of Parmenides and the abandonment of Parmenides' absolute distinction between Being and non-Being.

9. See Masi, *Emil Lask*; and Hanson and Kelly, *Michel Henry*.

10. Additional bibliography for this introduction includes Cacciari, "Etica del sapere"; Derrida, *The Other Heading*; Guéhenno, *La fin de la démocratie*; Zambrano, *Persona y democracia*; Prodi, *Un'idea dell'Europa*; Motyl, *Imperial Ends*; Balibar, *We, the People of Europe?*, and Negri, *L'Europa e l'Impero*.

1. THINKING EUROPE

1. The reference is to the Balkan Wars of 1990–1999 and the dissolution of Yugoslavia. [*Editor's note*]

2. The history of European integration is narrated in a critical perspective, from the inside of its techno-structure, in Bino Olivi and Roberto Santaniello, *Storia dell'integrazione europea*. For a thorough historical analysis see Emilio R. Papa, *Storia dell'unificazione europea*; and Valerio Castronovo, *L'avventura dell'unità europea*.

3. Maastricht, The Netherlands, is where the Maastricht Treaty (or Treaty on European Union) that led to the creation of the euro was signed on February 7, 1992. [*Editor's note*]

4. The general structure of the European economic and monetary policy is described in Marco Buti and André Sapir, *La politica economica nell'Unione economica e monetaria europea*.

5. How problematic the federalist perspective is, within the frame of Europe's constitutional issues, appears in the articles included in Sandro Chignola and Giuseppe Duso, eds., *Sui concetti giuridici e politici della costituzione dell'Europa*.

6. "*. . . das Festwerden an der Erdscholle*." G. W. F. Hegel, *Grundlinien der Philosophie des Rechts* (para. 247), 391. I have modified the English translation, "for the

ties of the soil," to match the author's translation. See G. W. F. Hegel, *Elements of the Philosophy of Right*, 268. [*Editor's note*]

7. Gianfranco Miglio's seminal contribution to the theory of the state deals precisely with this crucial question. See his *Le regolarità della politica*.

2. EUROPEANISM

1. The reference is to St. Augustine, "*inquietum est cor nostrum*," *Confessiones*, bk. 1, chap. 1. [*Editor's note*]

2. See Jacques Lévy, *Europe. Une géographie.*

3. Friedrich Nietzsche, *Beyond Good and Evil*, §256.

4. On the history and destiny of the separation between East and West, see the unsurpassed pages of Santo Mazzarino, *Fra oriente e occidente*.

5. "Goodness is described as self-effusive." Thomas Aquinas, *Summa theologica*, "Of Goodness in General," art. 4, reply to objection 2, http://www.ccel.org/ccel/aquinas/summa.html, p. 185. [*Editor's note*]

6. It is a matter of the faith that has sustained the entire recent history of Europe, namely, that Europe could grow without end, keeping and strengthening all the advantages accumulated in the postwar period. This "happy Europe" (*Europa felix*) faces its twilight in the "risk society." See Ulrich Beck and Edgar Grande, *L'Europa cosmopolita*.

7. See Heidrun Friese, Antonio Negri, Peter Wagner, eds., *Europa politica*.

3. TWO GERMAN SPEECHES

1. The speeches were given on November 27, 1999, in Bremen, where the author was awarded the Hannah Arendt Prize, and on March 22, 2000, at the annual Book Fair in Leipzig. [*Editor's note*]

2. Simona Forti, *Vita della mente e tempo della polis*; Roberto Esposito, ed., *La pluralità irrappresentabile*; Alessandro Dal Lago, ed., *Il pensiero plurale di Hannah Arendt*.

3. Simmel's influence is detectable too—a rarely remembered source yet one of crucial importance in twentieth-century German philosophy. It was Simmel who insightfully analyzed the unbridgeable difference between freedom and equality. See Georg Simmel, *Grundfragen der Soziologie*.

4. It is quite clear to me that on these issues and on the philosophy of language, Hannah Arendt has always been faithful to the "stellar friendship" that united her and her first teacher, Martin Heidegger.

5. The prefix "*com*" refers here and elsewhere to the etymology of *communitas* as "*cum+munus*," "*with munus*," where *munus* includes the multiple meaning of "gift," "duty," and "obligation" (hence "appointment," "office," "position"). Com-munity

is therefore a "donation" that comes "*with*" an obligation. See Roberto Esposito, *Communitas*, 4. Esposito refers to Alois Walde and Johann Baptist Hofmann, *Lateinisches etymologisches Wörterbuch*. [*Editor's note*]

6. The author often hyphenates words that include the root "*cor*" (Latin for "heart"), as in "*ri-cor-dare*" ("to remember"), in the sense of "keeping close to one's heart," or "*cor-rispondere*" ("to correspond"), in the sense of a response that has to come from the heart. [*Editor's note*]

7. The quote may have originated with Rafał Leszczyński (1650–1703), palatine of Poznan, Poland, in 1687. It is mentioned in Jean-Jacques Rousseau, *The Social Contract*, bk. 3, sec. 4; and by Thomas Jefferson, who probably read it in Rousseau, in a letter to James Madison dated January 30, 1787. [*Editor's note*]

8. See María Zambrano, "La voz abismática." [*Editor's note*]

9. "*Ein Zeichen sind wir, deutungslos.*" Friedrich Hölderlin, *Mnemosyne, Zweite Fassung* (Mnemosyne, Second Draft, 1803): "We are a sign without meaning." [*Editor's note*]

4. EUROPE OR PHILOSOPHY

1. See Carl Schmitt, *Hamlet or Hecuba*.

2. See my "Names of Place: Border."

3. ". . . *l'uccel di Dio / ne lo stremo d'Europa si ritenne*" ("the bird of God remained near Europe's borders"). Dante Alighieri, *The Divine Comedy, Paradise* 6.5. [*Editor's note*]

4. See Felix Duque, *Los Buenos europeos*.

5. See Peter Sloterdijk, *Weltinnenraum des Kapitals*.

6. ". . . *quella foce stretta / dov'Ercule segnò li suoi riguardi.*" Dante Alighieri, *The Divine Comedy, Inferno* 26.108. [*Editor's note*]

7. See Reinhart Koselleck, *Kritik und Krise*.

8. ". . . *poscia che s'infutura la tua vita*" (". . . your life will long outlast . . ."). Dante Alighieri, *The Divine Comedy, Paradise* 17.98. [*Editor's note*]

9. See Carl Schmitt, *The Nomos of the Earth*.

10. It is the key word for Heidegger from the era of the "world picture." In these pages, we refer constantly to Heidegger's essays "The Question Concerning Technology" and "The Age of World Picture," in *The Question Concerning Technology and Other Essays*, 3–35, 115–154.

11. The most interesting aspect of Biagio de Giovanni's extensive research, *La filosofia e l'Europa moderna*, is to have stressed the importance of philosophy as permanent origin of European history.

12. Hegel refers to Anselm's definition of God as "something greater than can be thought" (*quiddam maius quam cogitari possit*) in Anselm of Canterbury, *Proslogion* 1.112.14–15. [*Editor's note*]

13. See Giacomo Marramao, *Passaggio a Occidente*.

14. Friedrich Nietzsche, fragment 18 from twenty-seven fragments of 1885 intended to supplement Chapter 8 of *Beyond Good and Evil*. [*Editor's note*]

15. I employ the term "program" in Derrida's sense, in his recent contributions to the idea of Europe. See Jacques Derrida, *The Other Heading*. In the pages that follow, I try to combine this term with Hegel's dialectic of *Befriedigung*, understood as joy of coming-closer [*avvicinanza*] and not as reconciliation-synthesis without ulteriority.

16. In short, against the monism of the world-system one should activate the entire energy of Kant's transcendental dialectic!

17. To give freedom because one possesses it presupposes the idea of being omnipotent! Only the omnipotent, Kierkegaard would say, can legitimately presume to be the Liberator.

18. "*Eirene kai asphaleia*," peace and security, according to 1 Thessalonians 5:3, is the "slogan" of the Antichrist!

19. *Philopsychia* ("love of life"), with the negative connotation of an inordinate attachment, is a term introduced by Carlo Michelstaedter in his *Persuasion and Rhetoric* (1910). [*Editor's note*]

20. Isaiah Berlin, *Liberty*, 50.

21. Isaiah Berlin, *The Crooked Timber of Humanity*, 45–46.

5. EUROPE OR CHRISTIANITY

1. The title of this chapter refers to Novalis's *Europa oder Christenheit* (written in 1799 and published posthumously in 1826), a romantic reappraisal of Catholic medieval Europe. Often quoted as an example of anti-Enlightenment, reactionary romanticism, Novalis's essay is remarkable in its appeal to a European cosmopolitanism and unity that would have been lost in the nationalist turn of the nineteenth century. [*Editor's note*]

2. I have developed at length these highly problematic aspects of Christianity in *Dell'Inizio*, 305–357; and in "Filosofia e Teologia."

3. This difference is at the center of the interpretation that Heidegger gives of the origins of Christianity and of Paul in his Freiburg lectures of 1920–1921. See Martin Heidegger, *The Phenomenology of Religious Life*.

4. Friedrich Nietzsche, *The Gay Science* (§125). In an earlier version, the madman is Zarathustra himself.

5. Friedrich Nietzsche, *The Anti-Christ* (§18).

6. Friedrich Nietzsche, *Thus Spoke Zarathustra*, bk. 4, "Retired," 209–212.

7. Karl Löwith, "Hegels Aufhebung der christlichen Religion," in *Vorträge und Anhandlungen*, 59.

8. Ibid., 55. According to Hegel, without this foundation we would by necessity remain subject to the "foreign authority" (*fremde Autorität*) of the simple faith (80).

9. The demonstration of "God as Spirit" is Hegel's philosophy as a whole, and there is no need to give references in this case.

10. Only Alexandre Kojève seems to me to have dealt with this issue with great rigor. His *Introduction to the Reading of Hegel: Lectures on the Phenomenology of the Spirit* is a constant presence throughout this chapter.

11. It is the inevitable consequence of every form of spiritualization or absolutization of the *logos*. This theme is explicit in the work of Adolf von Harnack but is also recurrent in Ernest Troeltsch.

12. On the weight of Marcion's influence (conscious or unconscious) from Luther to philosophy and to contemporary political theology, see Jacob Taubes, *The Political Theology of Paul*. See also note 2 of Chapter 10, below.

13. Marcion of Sinope (ca. 80–ca. 160 A.D.) denied that the God of the Old Testament and the God of the New Testament were one and the same and considered the Old Testament inferior to the new one. Pelagius (ca. 354–ca. 420–440) rejected every idea of predestination and was a strong defender of free will. Augustine accused him of denying the necessity of divine grace. [*Editor's note*]

14. On this issue, important contributions have been collected in Michele Nicoletti and Giorgio Penzo, eds., *Kierkegaard. Filosofia e teologia del paradosso*.

15. See Emanuele Severino, "La fede, il dubbio."

16. See Benedetto Croce, "Perché non possiamo non dirci 'cristiani.'" In this 1942 essay, Croce argues in favor of Christian morality without subscribing to religious faith. [*Editor's note*]

17. It seems to me that Erich Przywara's fundamental work on analogy can be further developed in this direction. See Przywara, *Analogia entis: Metaphysick*.

18. The reference here is to the use and abuse of Ernst Bloch's "principle of hope." See Bloch, *The Principle of Hope*. [*Editor's note*]

19. Paul Natorp, *Über Platos Ideenlehre*. The author refers to the Italian edition, *Logos-Psyche-Eros*, 90. [*Editor's note*]

20. The reference here, as it is easy to understand, is to the problem of the *katechon*, a figure obsessively present in Carl Schmitt's work even if never applied to the Catholic Church. However, if the church, as historical system and administrative apparatus, is the inheritor of the universalism of the Roman Empire, it will also have inherited its "breaking" function. See Chapter 10, below, for a more detailed discussion of the *katechon*.

21. The author relies on the Italian meaning of *tradire* (to betray), whose Latin etymology (*tradere*) means "to carry." [*Editor's note*]

6. WHAT IS EMPIRE?

1. On this respect, Herfried Münkler's *Empires* provides a comprehensive comparative history of the ideas of empire and historical empires.

2. See Alois Dempf's classic *Sacrum imperium*.

3. ". . . to spare defeated peoples, tame the proud" ("*parcere subiectis et debellare superbos*," Virgil, *Aeneid* 6.853). All translations from Virgil are taken from the edition listed in the bibliography. [*Editor's note*]

4. In ancient Rome, the doors of the temple of Janus Bifrons (the two-faced god) were closed only in time of peace. Criticism of the Roman Empire is expressed in Augustine's *The City of God* (*Civitas Dei*) and in Augustine's disciple Paulus Orosius's *History Against the Pagans* (*Historiarum adversum paganos*). Eusebius of Caesarea was in the Emperor Constantine's favor and eulogized him in his *Life of Constantine* (*Vita Constantini*), although the paternity of the work has been disputed. [*Editor's note*]

7. THE MYTH OF THE GROWING CITY

1. See Hans Blumenberg, *Work on Myth*.

2. See Gaius's introduction to his treatise on the Twelve Tables, as it is excerpted in the *Digest*: "When about to embark on a work of interpretation of the ancient laws, I decided that, of necessity, I would first trace my record back to the origins of the city, not because I wished to pad out my commentary but because I am aware that in all matters, the most effectively completed task is the one that creates a consistent whole from all its parts; and assuredly the most essential part of anything is its beginning" (*et certe cuiusque rei potissima pars principium est*). Quoted in Jill Harries, "Lawyers and Citizens from Republic to Empire: Gaius on the Twelve Tables and Antonine Rome," 71. [*Editor's note*] On Gaius's famous passage, see Lelio Lantella's profound philosophical interpretation, "*Potissima pars principium est.*" [*Author's note*]

3. See Georges Dumézil, *Archaic Roman Religion*.

4. Santo Mazzarino, *Dalla monarchia allo stato repubblicano*, 17.

5. On the figures of Romulus and Numa, see Georges Dumézil, *Les dieux souverains des indo-européens*.

6. Angelo Brelich, "Roma e Praeneste," in *Tre variazioni romane sul tema delle origini*, 25, 30–33.

7. See Marta Sordi, "*Universalità* e *aeternitas* di Roma." See also several important contributions on the same theme in Pierangelo Catalano, *Diritto e persona*.

8. See Maria Pia Baccari, "Il concetto giuridico di *civitas augescens*: origine e continuità."

9. See Pierangelo Catalano, *Populus Romanus Quirites*, and "Alcuni sviluppi del concetto giuridico di '*imperium populi Romani.*'"

10. Giovanni Semerano, *Le origini della cultura europea*, vol. 2, tome 2, 524.

11. See Giovanni Lobrano, *Res publica res populi*.

12. Maria Pia Baccari, *Cittadini popoli e comunione nella legislazione dei secoli IV–VI*, 153.

13. In A.D. 384 Symmachus, prefect of the city of Rome, addressed a letter known as *Relation 3* (*Relatio tertia*) to the emperors Valentinian, Theodosius, and Arcadius, requesting that the Altar of Victory be restored to the Senate House. Symmachus argued that the removal of the altar had caused a famine and pleaded for tolerance toward pagan practices and beliefs that by the late fourth century were less and less tolerable to the Christian hierarchy. Ambrose, the bishop of Milan, responded to Valentinian, the emperor in the West, urging him to deny Symmachus's request (Ambrose, *Epistles* 17 and 18). See Fabrizio Canfora, ed., *L'altare della vittoria. Simmaco, Ambrogio.* [*Editor's note*]

14. I have already discussed the notions of *civis futurus* and *civitas peregrina* in my *Geo-filosofia dell'Europa* and *L'Arcipelago*.

15. "*Sic est; acerba fata Romanos agunt/scelusque fraternae necis/ut immerentis fluxit in terram Remi/sacer nepotibus cruor*" (Horace, *Epod* 7.17–20).

16. ". . . *haec Dei lex est: ut omnia orta occidant*" (Caecylius Ciprianus, *Liber ad Demetrianum* 3).

8. DIGRESSIONS ON EMPIRE AND THE THREE ROMES

1. This entire chapter is a debate with Michael Hardt and Antonio Negri's *Empire*. For a review of the American bibliography on the subject, see Rita Di Leo, *Il primato americano*.

2. The theme of "great spaces" inevitably calls to mind the work of Carl Schmitt. Beside *Nomos of the Earth*, see also the essays translated and collected in Carl Schmitt, *L'unità del mondo*; and Ernst Jünger, *Der Gordische Knoten*. The Italian edition, *Il nodo di Gordio. Dialogo su Oriente e Occidente nella storia del mondo*, includes an exchange with Carl Schmitt.

3. ". . . generazione dopo generazione pensarono di se stessi." Attilio Momigliano, *Storia e storiografia antica*, 201.

4. Giovanni Semerano, *Le origini della cultura europea*, vol. 2, tome 2, 433.

5. "*Aliae sunt legati partes atque* [*aliae*] *imperatoris, alter omnia agere ad praescriptum, alter libere ad summam rerum consulere debet*" (Caesar, *Bellum Civile* 3.51).

6. See Francesco Sini, *Bellum nefandum*.

7. See Lelio Lantella, "*Potissima pars principium est.*"

8. See Marta Sordi, "Universalità e *aeternitas* di Roma."

9. Attilio Momigliano, *Storia e storiografia antica*, 183.

10. See Maria Pia Baccari, "Il concetto giuridico di *civitas augescens*: origine e continuitá."

11. See Arnold J. Toynbee, *Hannibal's Legacy*.

12. See Robert Turcan, "Lois romaines, dieux étrangers et 'religion d'État.'"

13. On the figure of *evocatio* (the procedure for drawing a foreign tutelary god to Rome), see Georges Dumézil, *L'oubli de l'homme et l'honneur des dieux*, 135–150. Among Livy's masterpieces, beside Camillus's speech to exorcise the desertion of Rome after the Gaul's fire (see Santo Mazzarino, *Il pensiero storico classico*, 3:44), I would place those pages Livy devotes to the theme of *evocatio* where Camillus is the central figure (5.21–22). Before unleashing the final attack on Veius, the dictator prays to Juno Regina, "who now protects Veius" (*quae nunc Veios colis*), to follow the victors to their city and to appoint her to her new residence. After the city was plundered, "when all the human wealth was already taken out of Veius" and it was time to remove "the gifts of the god and the gods themselves" (*deum dona ipsosque deos*), the attitude of the Romans is no longer that of plunderers but of devotees. Young men clean and purified, in pure white clothing, are given the task of transporting Juno's simulacrum to Rome. They enter the temple with great respect, and before daring to touch the statue one of them says, "Do you want to come to Rome, Juno?" (*Visne Romam ire, Iuno?*). The legend goes, Livy tells us, that a voice answered giving consent.

14. See Pierangelo Catalano, *Populus Romanus Quirites*. See also "Una civitas communis."

15. See Vincenzo Poggi, "*Rum*, dalla prima alla seconda Roma."

16. On the comparative concept of the Roman law (*ius romanum*), see Pierangelo Catalano, *Diritto e persona*; Giovanni Lobrano, *Diritto pubblico romano e costituzionalismi moderni*, and *Res publica res populi*.

17. See Pierangelo Catalano, "Alcuni sviluppi del concetto giuridico di *imperium populi romani*," and "Impero: un concetto dimenticato del diritto pubblico."

18. See Paolo Siniscalco, *Il cammino di Cristo nell'Impero romano*.

19. See Paolo Siniscalco, "Sur Constantinople et sa foundation."

20. See Riccardo Maisano, "La fondazione della nuova Roma nella prospettiva politica e culturale di Temistio."

21. See Ivan il Terribile [Ivan the Terrible], *Un buon governo nel Regno*.

22. See Vladimir S. Solovyov, "Lettera a Strossmayer" (1886), and "L'idea russa" (1888), in *Il problema dell'ecumenismo*. See also Tomáš Špidlik, *L'idea russa*, chap. 4.

23. See Vittorio Strada et al., *Filosofia, religione, letteratura in Russia all'inizio del XX Secolo*, especially the essays by I. A. Vinogradov on Dostoyevsky and Adriano Dell'Asta on Solovyov. See also Roberto Valle, *Dostoevskij politico e i suoi interpreti. L'esodo dall'Occidente*. See also the great synthesis by Nikolaj A. Berdyaev, *Russkaja Ideja. Osnovnye Problemy Russkoj Mysli* (Italian trans.: *L'idea russa. I problemi fondamentali del pensiero russo. 19. e inizio del 20. secolo*).

24. Namely, not the friendship that presupposes the proximity of beings or even the equality between them, or justice, which makes equals unequal. How can

Thomas Aquinas—Simone Weil asks—call himself a Christian by supporting these Aristotelian theses? Is it because "justice has made man and God equal before there could be a union of Love"? (Weil, *Quaderni*, 4:388). For a synthetic but profound treatment of the theme of "political friendship," which I believe to be very important today, see Giorgio Carnevali, *Dell'amicizia politica*.

25. See Harold Bloom, *The American Religion*.

26. I would like to refer here to my *Geo-filosofia dell'Europa* and *L'Arcipelago*.

27. The author refers to Nicholas of Cusa, *De pace fidei* (*On the Peace of Faith*, 1453). [*Editor's note*]

28. G. W. F. Hegel, *Philosophy of History*, part 4, sec. 1, chap. 2, "Mohametanism," 376. [*Editor's note*]

29. See Gilles Kepel, *Jihad: The Trail of Political Islam*. [*Editor's note*]

30. Robert Musil, *The Man Without Qualities*, vol. 2, chap. 121, p. 422.

9. MORE ON THE IDEA OF EMPIRE

1. On the wake of Carl Schmitt and his dialogue with Jacob Taubes, I have stressed the theological and political importance of the Pauline figure of the *katechon* for many years now. Now the theme has become almost fashionable. Beside the many works on the topic, see those published in *Katechonten*. See also Chapter 10, below.

2. See Alexandre Kojève, "L'Empire latin."

3. See Geminello Alvi, *Dell'estremo Occidente*.

4. This is a decisive aspect for the future of the *net economy*, emphasized with great effectiveness by Carlo Formenti in *Mercanti di futuro*.

5. See Angelo Bolaffi and Giacomo Marramao, *Frammento e sistema*.

6. "*Compelle intrari!*" ("Compel people to come in!"). It is the Master's instruction in Jesus' parable of the banquet: "Go out to the highways and hedges and compel people to come in, that my house may be filled" (Luke 14:23). The author refers here, metaphorically, to the debated interpretation of the passage (by Catholics and Protestants alike) that asks secular authorities to coerce people into the teachings of the church. [*Editor's note*]

7. The chaotic interweaving of these jurisdictional forms is by now at the center of the scientific investigation of the more historically minded law makers. I have found especially interesting the contributions by Natalino Irti, *Norma e luoghi*; and Stefano Rodotà, "Diritto, diritti, globalizzazione."

8. See Ernst Jünger, *Der Weltstaat*, which should be read in "divergent agreement" (to quote the title of Jacob Taubes's *Ad Carl Schmitt. Gegenstreibige Fügung*) with Schmitt's idea of the "unity of the world" by "great spaces," already present in his writings of the 1930s, to which, once again in "divergent agreement," Kojève responds in the already quoted essay (*L'Empire latin*). However, Schmitt's

"great spaces" are irremediably invalidated at their root by a nationalist prejudice destined to fail.

9. We would also want to pose at the same time the question of the supranational order (that is, of the new political institutions of the globalized world).

10. To my knowledge, beside intelligent and innovative Romanist scholars such as Pierangelo Catalano and his school, only Rémi Brague, recently, has taken seriously the "Roman metaphor." See his *Europe, la voie romaine*.

11. Arnold J. Toynbee insists particularly on these characteristics of the Roman *polis*. See his *Hellenism*.

12. Santo Mazzarino seems to think so in his *The End of the Ancient World*.

13. See Francesco Sini, *Bellum nefandum*.

14. On the great themes of the frontier, open space, and the center-periphery relation in the most longstanding traits of American politics, the most stimulating research, in my view, is that of William A. Williams. See *The Contours of American History* and *From Colony to Empire*.

15. See Chalmers A. Johnson, *Blowback*.

16. Danilo Zolo has insisted, for a while now, and with particular effectiveness, on the risks of such a drift, at least in his *I signori della pace*.

17. On Europe's Mediterranean mind, see Franco Cassano, *Southern Thought and Other Essays on the Mediterranean*. On the more dramatic aspects of political and economic importance, see Bruno Amoroso, *Europa e Mediterraneo*. For information on the historical reasons of the present catastrophes, see Andrea Riccardi, ed., *Il Mediterraneo nel Novecento*.

18. See Biagio De Giovanni, *L'ambigua potenza dell'Europa*.

19. Many of the essays collected in Heidrun Friese, Antonio Negri, and Peter Wager, eds., *Europa politica*, seem to be "in search of" the European subject.

20. Antonio López Pina has dealt with these issues with great clarity in an important article, "La ciudadanía: presupuesto de una república europea."

21. On the much-debated issue of Roman citizenship see Mario Bretone, *Storia del diritto romano*.

10. EMPIRE AND *KATECHON*: A QUESTION OF POLITICAL THEOLOGY (FROM PAUL, 2 THESSALONIANS 2)

1. For a survey of the question of the *katechon* in Carl Schmitt, see Felix Grossheutschi, *Carl Schmitt und die Lehre vom Katechon*. Important contributions can also be found in *Il Katéchon (2Ts 2, 6–7) e l'Anticristo*; Giovanni Filoramo, ed., *Teologie politiche*; Paolo Bettiolo and Giovanni Filoramo, eds., *Il dio mortale*; and *Katechonten*.

2. Carl Schmitt, "A Pan-European Interpretation of Donoso Cortés." On the relation between Schmitt and the philosophy of Restoration, see the critique of

Taubes and the exchange-dispute between the two "enemies" in Jacob Taubes, *Ad Carl Schmitt. Gegenstreibige Fügung*. Taubes, however, gives an entirely misleading Marcionite image of Paul as a radical nihilist with respect to worldly powers.

3. This is the focus of the dispute between Carl Schmitt and Alexandre Kojève (with Taubes as one of the great and, at the time, one of the few interlocutors of the jurist). See "Der Briefwechsel Kojève-Schmitt," in *Schmittiana*. For Kojève see in particular *La Notion de l'autorité*.

4. *Glossa ordinaria* is the standard commentary on the Scriptures in the Carolingian period. [*Editor's note*]

5. See Alexandre Kojève, "L'Empire latin."

11. THE EUROPE OF MARÍA ZAMBRANO

1. This lecture was given at the conclusion of the International Symposium of Studies on María Zambrano, held in Malaga, Spain, on November 4, 1994.

2. See Antonio Colinas, "Sobre la iniciación. Conversación con María Zambrano."

3. María Zambrano, *Claros del bosque*. The meaning of "*claros*" in Zambrano's work has been explained as the interweaving of evidence and latency, clearing and maze.

4. This idea is at the center of my *Geo-filosofia dell'Europa*.

5. In my view, this work, together with *El sueño creador* (first edited by Elena Croce, published in Rome in 1960 and then republished in Mexico in 1965), is the fundamental philosophical work of María Zambrano. My argument, in the pages that follow, is based on the theses contained in this work.

6. See María Zambrano, "Diotima (fragmentos)."

7. Paul Valéry, "Inspirations méditerranéennes," 1096.

8. The term "historical reason" refers to *Critica della ragione storica* (*Critique of Historical Reason*), the Italian translation of Wilhelm Dilthey's *Das Wesen der Philosophie*. [*Editor's note*]

9. We ought to explain, at this point, the dense network of relations that connects Zambrano's work to the mysticism of the *Siglo de Oro*. See at least María Zambrano, "San Juan de la Cruz. De la 'noche oscura' a la màs clara mistica," in *Senderos*. Zambrano's *De la Aurora* is perhaps the work where her closeness to the "flash" of the mystic word-expression freed from the necessity of discourse and misunderstanding is most intense.

10. *Los bienaventurados* is the title of Zambrano's last book.

12. WE CANNOT CALL OURSELVES ONLY JUDEO-CHRISTIANS: A CONVERSATION WITH JACQUES LE GOFF

1. The interview was conducted and edited by Vittorio Borelli with the help of Lidia Fornasiero. The reference is to Jacques Le Goff, *The Birth of Europe*. [*Editor's note*]

2. Bruno Luiselli, *La formazione della cultura europea occidentale*.

3. That was an issue at the time the interview was conducted (2004). Great Britain has not joined the eurozone. [*Editor's note*]

WORKS CITED

Agamben, Giorgio. 1993. *The Coming Community*. Trans. Michael Hardt. Minneapolis: University of Minnesota Press.

———. 2005. *State of Exception*. Trans. Kevin Attell. Chicago: University of Chicago Press.

———. 2005. *The Time That Remains: A Commentary on the Letter to the Romans*. Trans. Patricia Dailey. Stanford, Calif.: Stanford University Press.

Alighieri, Dante. 1982–1984. *The Divine Comedy*. Trans. Allen Mandelbaum. New York: Bantam.

Alvi, Geminello. 1993. *Dell'estremo Occidente. Il secolo americano in Europa: Storie economiche 1916–1933*. Florence: Nardi.

Amoroso, Bruno. 2000. *Europa e Mediterraneo. Le sfide del futuro*. Bari: Dedalo.

Aquinas, St. Thomas. *Summa theologica by Saint Thomas Aquinas*. http://www.ccel .org/ccel/aquinas/summa.html.

Arendt, Hannah. 1958. *The Human Condition*. Chicago: University of Chicago Press.

Asimov, Isaac. 1951. *Foundation*. New York: Bantam.

———. 1952. *Foundation and Empire*. New York: Bantam.

———. 1953. *Second Foundation*. New York: Bantam.

Baccari, Maria Pia. 1995. "Il concetto giuridico di *civitas augescens*: origine e continuità." *Studia et documenta Historiae et Iuris* 41: 759–788.

———. 1996. *Cittadini popoli e comunione nella legislazione dei secoli IV–VI*. Turin: Giappichelli.

Badiou, Alain. 2005. *Metapolitics*. Trans. Joseph Barker. New York: Verso.

Balibar, Étienne. 2003. *We, the People of Europe? Reflections on Transnational Citizenship*. Trans. James Swenson. Princeton, N.J.: Princeton University Press.

Barker, Ernest, George Clark, and Paul Vaucher, eds. 1954. *The European Inheritance*. 3 vols. Oxford: Clarendon.

Beck, Ulrich, and Edgar Grande. 2006. *L'Europa cosmopolita. Società e politica nella seconda modernità*. Rome: Carocci.

Berdjaev, Nikolaj Aleksandrovic. 1971. *Russkaja Ideja. Osnovnye Problemy Russkoj Mysli*. Paris: YMCA.

———. 1992. *L'idea russa. I problemi fondamentali del pensiero russo. 19. e inizio del 20. secolo*. Trans. Cinzia del Lotto. Milan: Mursia.

Berlin, Isaiah. 1990. *The Crooked Timber of Humanity*. Ed. Henry Hardy. Princeton, N.J.: Princeton University Press.

———. 2002. *Liberty. Incorporating Four Essays on Liberty*. Ed. Henry Hardy. Oxford: Oxford University Press.

Bettiolo, Paolo, and Giovanni Filoramo, eds. 2002. *Il dio mortale. Teologie politiche tra antico e contemporaneo*. Brescia: Morcelliana.

Bloch, Ernst. 1995. *The Principle of Hope*. 3 vols. Trans. Neville Plaice and Stephen Plaice. Cambridge, Mass.: The MIT Press.

Bloom, Harold. 1992. *The American Religion: The Emergence of the Post-Christian Nation*. New York: Simon & Schuster.

Blumenberg, Hans, 1988. *Work on Myth*. Trans. Robert M. Wallace. Cambridge, Mass.: The MIT Press.

Bolaffi, Angelo, and Giacomo Marramao. 2001. *Frammento e sistema. Il conflitto-mondo da Sarajevo a Manhattan*. Rome: Donzelli.

Brague, Rémi. 1999. *Europe, la voie romaine*. 2nd rev. and exp. ed. Paris: Gallimard.

Braudel, Fernand. 1972–1973. *The Mediterranean and the Mediterranean World in the Age of Philip II*. Trans. Siân Reynolds. London: Collins.

Brelich, Angelo. 1955. *Tre variazioni romane sul tema delle origini*. Rome: Edizioni dell'Ateneo.

Bretone, Mario. 1987. *Storia del diritto romano*. Rome-Bari: Laterza.

Buti, Marco, and André Sapir. 1999. *La politica economica nell'Unione economica e monetaria europea. Uno studio della commissione europea*. Bologna: Il Mulino.

Cacciari, Massimo. 1995. "Filosofia e teologia." In *La Filosofia*, ed. Paolo Rossi, 2:365–421. Turin: Utet.

———. 1997. *L'Arcipelago*. Milan: Adelphi.

———. 1997. "Etica del sapere." *MicroMega—Almanacco di Filosofia '97*: 67–72.

———. 2003. *Geo-filosofia dell'Europa*. 2nd rev. ed. Milan: Adelphi.

———. 2007. "Names of Place: Border." In *Contemporary Italian Philosophy: Crossing the Borders of Ethics, Politics, and Religion*, ed. Silvia Benso and Brian Schroeder, trans. Silvia Benso, 277–283. Albany, N.Y.: SUNY Press.

———. 2009. *The Unpolitical: On the Radical Critique of Political Reason*. Ed. Alessandro Carrera, trans. Massimo Verdicchio. New York: Fordham University Press.

——. 2011. "History and Destiny." Trans. Thomas Behr. In *Italian Critical Theory* (Monographic Issue). *Annali d'Italianistica* 29: 59–67.

——. 2011. *Dell'inizio*. 2nd rev. ed. Milan: Adelphi.

——. 2013. *Il potere che frena. Saggio di teologia politica*. Milan: Adelphi.

Canfora, Fabrizio, ed. 1991. *L'altare della vittoria. Simmaco, Ambrogio*. With a note by Luciano Canfora. Palermo: Sellerio.

Carnevali, Giorgio. 2001. *Dell'amicizia politica. Tra teoria e storia*. Rome-Bari: Laterza.

Carrera, Alessandro, ed. 2011. *Italian Critical Theory* (Monographic Issue). *Annali d'Italianistica* 29.

Cassano, Franco. 2011. *Southern Thought and Other Essays on the Mediterranean*. Ed. and trans. Norma Bouchard and Valerio Ferme. New York: Fordham University Press.

Castronovo, Valerio. 2004. *L'avventura dell'unità uropea. Una sfida con la storia e il futuro*. Turin: Einaudi.

Catalano, Pierangelo. 1974. *Populus Romanus Quirites*. Turin: Giappichelli.

——. 1984. "Alcuni sviluppi del concetto giuridico di '*imperium populi Romani.*'" In *Popoli e spazio romano tra diritto e profezia. III Seminario internazionale di studi storici. Da Roma alla Terza Roma*, 649–668. Naples: Edizioni Scientifiche Italiane.

——. 1990. *Diritto e persona. Studi su origine e attualità del sistema romano*. Turin: Giappichelli.

——. 1995. "*Una civitas communis.*" *Studia et documenta Historiae et Iuris* 41: 65–80.

——. 2000. "Impero: un concetto dimenticato del diritto pubblico." In *Cristianità ed Europa. Miscellanea in onore di Luigi Prosdocimi*, ed. Cesare Alzati, 125–140. Rome: Herder.

Chignola, Sandro, and Giuseppe Duso. 2005. *Sui concetti giuridici e politici della costituzione dell'Europa*. Milan: Franco Angeli.

Colinas, Antonio. 1986. "Sobre la iniciación. Conversación con María Zambrano." *Cuadernos del Norte* 38: 65–80.

Croce, Benedetto. 1945. "Perché non possiamo non dirci 'cristiani.'" In *Discorsi di varia filosofia*, 1:11–27. Bari: Laterza.

Dainotto, Roberto M. 2007. *Europe (in Theory)*. Durham, N.C.: Duke University Press.

Dal Lago, Alessandro, ed. 1990. *Il pensiero plurale di Hannah Arendt. Testi e contributi di Hannah Arendt et al.* (Monographic Issue). *aut-aut* 239–240.

De Giovanni, Biagio. 2002. *L'ambigua potenza dell'Europa*. Naples: Guida.

——. 2004. *La filosofia e l'Europa moderna*. Bologna: il Mulino.

De Greef, Wulfert, ed. 2008. *The Writings of John Calvin: An Introductory Guide*. Expanded ed. Louisville, Ky.: Westminster John Knox.

Deleuze, Gilles, and Félix Guattari. 1987. *A Thousand Plateaus: Capitalism and Schizophrenia*. Trans. Brian Massumi et al. Minneapolis: University of Minnesota Press.

Dempf, Alois. 1929. *Sacrum imperium. Geschichts-und Staatsphilosophie des Mittelalters und der politischen Renaissance*. Munich-Berlin: Oldenberg.

Derrida, Jacques. 1992. *The Other Heading: Reflections on Today's Europe*. Trans. Pascale-Anne Brault and Michael B. Naas. Bloomington: Indiana University Press.

———. 2006. *Politics of Friendship*. Trans. George Collins. New York: Verso.

Diamond, Jared. 2006. *Guns, Germs, and Steel: The Fates of Human Societies*. 2nd rev. ed. New York: Norton.

Di Leo, Rita. 2000. *Il primato americano. Il punto di vista degli Stati Uniti dopo la caduta del muro di Berlino*. Bologna: il Mulino.

Dilthey, Wilhelm. 1914. *Das Wesen der Philosophie*. In *Gesammelte Schriften*. Leipzig-Berlin: Teubner. [*Critica della ragione storica*, trans. Pietro Rossi. Turin: Einaudi, 1954].

Dumézil, Georges. 1970. *Archaic Roman Religion with an Appendix on the Religion of the Etruscans*. Trans. Philip Krapp, foreword by Mircea Eliade. Chicago: University of Chicago Press.

———. 1977. *Les dieux souverains des indo-européens*. Paris. Gallimard.

———. 1985. *L'oubli de l'homme et l'honneur des dieux et autres essais*. Paris: Gallimard.

Duque, Felix, 2003. *Los buenos europeos. Hacia una filosofia de la Europa contemporánea*. Oviedo: Nobel.

Esposito, Roberto, ed. 1987. *La pluralità irrappresentabile. Il pensiero politico di Hannah Arendt*. Urbino: Quattro Venti.

———. 2010. *Communitas: The Origin and Destiny of Community*. Trans. Timothy Campbell. Stanford, Calif.: Stanford University Press.

———. 2015. *Two: The Machine of Political Theology and the Place of Thought*. Trans. Zakiya Hanafi. New York: Fordham University Press.

Filoramo, Giovanni, ed. 2005. *Teologie politiche. Modelli a confronto*. Brescia: Morcelliana.

Formenti, Carlo. 2002. *Mercanti di futuro. Utopia e crisi della net economy*. Turin: Einaudi.

Forti, Simona. 1994. *Vita della mente e tempo della polis. Hannah Arendt tra filosofia e politica*. Milan: Angeli.

Friese, Heidrun, Antonio Negri, and Peter Wagner, eds. 2002. *Europa politica. Ragioni di una necessità*. Rome: Manifestolibri.

Galli, Carlo. 2010. *Political Spaces and Global War*. Ed. Adam Sitze. Trans. Elizabeth Fay. Minneapolis: University of Minnesota Press.

Giovannoli, Renato. 2005. "Il *katechon* e la successione delle costituzioni politiche in Platone (*Repubblica* VIII–IX)." *Rivista di ascetica e mistica* (Florence, Convento San Marco) 30, no. 4: 751–772.

Gossheutschi, Felix. 1996. *Carl Schmitt und die Lehre von Katechon*. Berlin: Duncker und Humblot.

Guéhenno, Jean-Marie. 1993. *La fin de la démocratie*. Paris: Flammarion.

Hanson, Jeffrey, and Michael R. Kelly, eds. 2014. *Michel Henry: The Affects of Thought*. London: Bloomsbury.

Hardt, Michael, and Antonio Negri. 2000. *Empire*. Cambridge, Mass.: Harvard University Press.

Harries, Jill. 2014. "Lawyers and Citizens from Republic to Empire: Gaius on the Twelve Tables and Antonine Rome." In *The City in the Classical and Post-Classical World: Changing Contexts of Power and Identity*, ed. Claudia Rapp and H. A. Drake, 62–80. New York: Cambridge University Press.

Hegel, G. W. F. 1899. *Philosophy of History*. Trans J. Sibree. Prefaces by Charles Engel and J. Sibree. New York: Colonial. Repr. Kitchener, Ont.: Batoche, 2001.

———. 1970. *Grundlinien der Philosophie des Rechts*. In *Werke in zwanzig Bänden*, bd. 7. Frankfurt am Main: Suhrkamp.

———. 1991. *Elements of the Philosophy of Right*. Ed. Allen V. Wood. Trans. H. B. Nisbet. Cambridge: Cambridge University Press.

Heidegger, Martin. 1977. *The Question Concerning Technology and Other Essays*. Trans. William Lovitt. New York: Harper & Row.

———. 2004. *The Phenomenology of Religious Life*. Trans. Matthias Fritsch and Jennifer Anna Gosetti-Ferencei. Bloomington: Indiana University Press.

Hell, Julia. 2009. "*Katechon:* Carl Schmitt's Imperial Theology and the Ruins of the Future." *Germanic Review* 84, no. 4: 283–326.

Irti, Natalino. 2001. *Norma e luoghi. Problemi di geo-diritto*. Rome-Bari: Laterza.

Ivan il Terribile (Ivan the Terrible). 2000. *Un buon governo nel Regno. Il carteggio con Andrej Kurbskij*. Trans. Pia Pera. With an essay by J. S. Lur'e. Milan: Adelphi.

Johnson, Chalmers A. 2001. *Blowback: The Cost and Consequences of American Empire*. New York: Holt.

Jünger, Ernst. 1953. *Der Gordische Knot*. Frankfurt am Main: Klostermann.

———. 1960. *Der Weltstaat. Organismus und Organisation*. Stuttgart: Klett.

———. 1987. *Il nodo di Gordio. Dialogo su oriente e occidente nella storia del mondo*. Ed. by Carlo Galli. Trans. Giuseppina Panzieri. Bologna: il Mulino. [This volume includes an exchange with Carl Schmitt.]

[Il] Katéchon (2Ts 2, 6–7) e l'Anticristo. Teologia e politica di fronte al mistero dell'anomia. 2009. (Monographic Issue). *Politica e religione*.

Katechonten. 2001. (Monographic Issue). *Tumult* 25.

Kepel, Gilles. 2003. *Jihad: The Trail of Political Islam*. Trans. Anthony F. Roberts. Cambridge, Mass.: Belknap Press of Harvard University Press.

Kojève, Alexandre. 1969. *Introduction to the Reading of Hegel: Lectures on the Phenomenology of the Spirit*. Comp. Raymond Queneau. Ed. Allan Bloom. Trans. James H. Nichols. Ithaca, N.Y.: Cornell University Press.

———. 1990. "L'Empire latin. Esquisse d'une doctrine de la politique français." *La règle du jeu* 1, no. 1: 7–25.

———. 2004. *La Notion de l'autorité* (1942). Ed. François Terré. Paris: Gallimard.

Koselleck, Reinhardt. 1959. *Kritik und Krise. Ein Beitrag zur Pathogenese der bürgerlichen Welt*. Freiburg-München: Karl Alber.

Lackner, Stephan. "'Von einer langen, schwierigen Irrfahrt': Aus unveröffentlichten Briefen Walter Benjamins." *Neue Deutsche Hefte* 26, no. 161, H. 1 (1979): 48–69.

Lantella, Lelio. 1983. "*Potissima pars principium est.*" In *Studi in onore di Cesare Sanfilippo*, ed. Facoltà di Giurisprudenza dell'Università di Catania, 4:283–304. Milan: Giuffrè.

Le Goff, Jacques. 2005. *The Birth of Europe*. Trans. Janet Lloyd. Oxford: Blackwell.

Leopardi, Giacomo. 2010. *Canti*. Trans. Jonathan Galassi. New York: Farrar, Straus & Giroux.

———. *Zibaldone*. 2013. Ed. Franco D'Intino and Michael Caesar. Trans. Kathleen Baldwin et al. New York: Farrar, Straus & Giroux.

Lévy, Jacques. 1997. *Europe. Une géographie*. Paris: Hachette.

Llull, Ramon. 1994. *The Book of the Gentile and the Three Wise Men* (abridged). In *Doctor Illuminatus: A Ramon Llull Reader*, ed. Anthony Bonner, 73–172. Princeton, N.J.: Princeton University Press.

Lobrano, Giovanni. 1989. *Diritto pubblico romano e costituzionalismi moderni*. Sassari: Delfino.

———. 1996. *Res publica res populi. La legge e la limitazione del potere*. Turin: Giappichelli.

López Pina, Antonio. 2000. "La ciudadanía: presupuesto de una república europea. Apuntes para una política del Derecho." *Civitas Europa* 5: 95–120.

Löwith, Karl. 1966. *Vorträge und Anhandlungen. Zur Kritik der Christlichen Überlieferung*. Stuttgart: Kohlhammer.

Luiselli, Bruno. 2003. *La formazione della cultura europea occidentale*. Rome: Herder.

Maisano, Riccardo. 1997. "La fondazione della nuova Roma nella prospettiva politica e culturale di Temistio." In *XVII Seminario internazionale di studi storici. Da Roma alla terza Roma*. Rome: [University material; no indication of publisher and pages].

Marramao, Giacomo. 2003. *Passaggio a Occidente. Filosofia e globalizzazione*. Turin: Bollati Boringhieri.

Masi, Felice. 2010. *Emil Lask. Il pathos della forma*. Macerata: Quodlibet, 2010.

Mazzarino, Santo. 1944. *Dalla monarchia allo stato repubblicano. Ricerche di storia romana arcaica*. Catania: Agnini.

———. 1947. *Fra oriente e occidente. Ricerche di storia greca arcaica*. Florence: La Nuova Italia.

———. 1966. *The End of the Ancient World*. Trans. George Holmes. New York: Knopf.

———. 1972. *Il pensiero storico classico*, vol. 3. Bari. Laterza.

———. 1988. *La fine del mondo antico*. Milan: Rizzoli.

Michelstaedter, Carlo. 2004. *Persuasion and Rhetoric*. Trans. Valentino Scott Russell, Cinzia Sartini Blum, and David J. Depew. New Haven, Conn.: Yale University Press.

Miglio, Gianfranco. 1988. *Le regolarità della politica. Scritti scelti, raccolti e pubblicati dagli allievi*. 2 vols. Milan: Giuffrè.

Momigliano, Attilio. 1987. *Storia e storiografia antica*. Bologna: Il Mulino.

Morasso, Massimo. "Il buon europeo e l'ultimo uomo. Sull'idea dell'Europa interiore." *Atelier* 14, no. 53 (March 2009): 8–19.

Motyl, Alexander J. 2001. *Imperial Ends: The Decay, Collapse, and Revival of Empire*. New York: Columbia University Press.

Münkler, Herfried. 2007. *Empires: The Logic of World Domination from Ancient Rome to the United States*. Trans. Patrick Camiller. Cambridge, Mass.: Polity.

Musil, Robert. 1979. *The Man Without Qualities*. Trans. Eithne Wilkins and Ernst Kaiser. London: Picador.

Natorp, Paul. 1914. *Über Platos Ideenlehre*. Berlin: Reuter und Reichard.

———. 1999. *Logos-Psyche-Eros. Metacritica alla dottrina platonica delle idee*. Trans. Vincenzo Cicero. Intro. by Giovanni Reale. Milan: Vita e pensiero.

Negri, Antonio. 2003. *L'Europa e l'impero. Riflessioni sul processo costituente*. Roma: Manifestolibri.

Nicholas of Cusa. 1993. *De pace fidei*. In *Toward a New Council of Florence: "On the peace of faith" and Other Works by Nicolaus of Cusa*, trans. William F. Wertz. Washington, D.C.: Schiller Institute.

Nicoletti, Michele, and Giorgio Penzo. 1999. *Kierkegaard. Filosofia e teologia del paradosso. Atti del convegno tenuto a Trento il 4–6 dicembre 1996*. Brescia: Morcelliana.

Nietzsche, Friedrich. 2001. *The Gay Science*. Ed. Bernard Williams. Trans. Josefine Nauckhoff. Cambridge: Cambridge University Press.

———. 2002. *Beyond Good and Evil: Prelude to a Philosophy of the Future*. Ed. Rolf-Peter Horstmann and Judith Norman. Trans. Judith Norman. Cambridge: Cambridge University Press.

———. 2005. *The Anti-Christ, Ecce Homo, Twilight of the Idols, and Other Writings*. Ed. Aaron Ridley and Judith Norman. Trans. Judith Norman. Cambridge: Cambridge University Press.

———. 2006. *Thus Spoke Zarathustra*. Ed. Adrian Del Caro and Robert B. Pippin. Trans. Adrian Del Caro. Cambridge: Cambridge University Press.

———. "Twenty-Seven Fragments of 1885 Intended to Supplement Chapter VIII of *Beyond Good and Evil*." Trans. J. M. Kennedy. http://www.american-buddha .com/lit.genealogyofmoralsnietzsche.4.htm.

Olivi, Bino, and Roberto Santaniello. 2005. *Storia dell'integrazione europea*. Bologna: Il Mulino.

Origo Gentis Romanae: The Origin of the Roman People (2004). http://www.tertullian .org/fathers/origo_01_trans.htm.

Papa, Emilio R. 2006. *Storia dell'unificazione europea. Dall'idea di Europa al trattato per una nuova costituzione europea*. Milan: Bompiani.

Plutarch, 1870. *A Discourse Concerning Socrates's Daemon (De genio Socratis—Peri tou Sokratous daimoniou)*. In *Plutarch's Morals*, vol. 2, trans. from the Greek by several hands, corrected and rev. by William W. Goodwin. Boston: Little, Brown, & Company.

Poggi, Vincenzo. 1991. "*Rum*, dalla prima alla seconda Roma." *XI Seminario internazionale di studi storici. Da Roma alla Terza Roma*. Rome: [University material; no indication of publisher and pages].

Prodi, Romano. 1999. *Un'idea dell'Europa*. Bologna: Il Mulino.

Przywara, Erich. 1932. *Analogia entis: Metaphysick*. Munich: Kosel.

Riccardi, Andrea. 1994. *Il Mediterraneo nel Novecento. Religioni e Stati*. Cinisello Balsamo: San Paolo.

Rodotà, Stefano. 2000. "Diritto, diritti, globalizzazione." *Rivista giuridica del lavoro* 4: 25–40.

Schmitt, Carl. 1995. "Beschleuniger wider Willen, oder: Problematik der westlichen Hemisphäre" (1942). In *Staat, Grossraum, Nomos. Arbeiten aus den Jahren 1916–1969*, ed. Günter Maschke, 431–436. Berlin: Dunckler und Humblot.

———. 1996. *Roman Catholicism and Political Form* [1923]. Trans. Gary L. Ulmen. Westport, Conn.: Greenwood.

———. 1997. *Land and Sea*. Trans. Simona Draghici. Washington, D.C.: Plutarch.

———. 2002. "A Pan-European Interpretation of Donoso Cortés." *Telos* 125: 100–115.

———. 2003a. *L'unità del mondo*. Ed. Alessandro Campi. Rome: Pellicani.

———. 2003b. *The Nomos of the Earth and the International Law of Jus Publicum Europaeum*. Trans. Gary L. Ulmen. Candor, N.Y.: Telos.

———. 2009. *Hamlet or Hecuba. The Intrusion of the Time Into Play*. Trans. David Pan and Jennifer R. Rust. Candor, N.Y.: Telos.

Schmitt, Carl, and Alexandre Kojève. 1998. "Der Briefwechsel Kojève–Schmitt." Ed. Piet Tomissen. *Schmittiana. Beiträge zu Leben und Werk Carl Schmitts* 6: 100–124.

Semerano, Giovanni. 1994. *Le origini della cultura europea*. Vol. 2: *Dizionari etimo-logici. Basi semitiche delle lingue indoeuropee*. Tome 2: *Dizionario della lingua latina e di voci moderne*. Florence: Olschki.

Severino, Emanuele. 1975. "La fede, il dubbio." In Emanuele Severino et al., *Studi in onore di Gustavo Bontadini*, 2:500–521. Milan: Vita e Pensiero.

———. 1978. *Gli abitatori del tempo. Cristianesimo, marxismo, tecnica*. Rome: Armando.

———. 1982. *Essenza del nichilismo*. 2nd rev. ed. Milan: Adelphi.

Simmel, Georg. 1917. *Grundfragen der Soziologie. Individuum und Gesellschaft*. Berlin-Leipzig: Göschen.

Sini, Francesco. 1991. *Bellum nefandum. Virgilio e il problema del "diritto internazionale antico."* Sassari: Libreria Dessì.

Siniscalco, Paolo. 1987. *Il cammino di Cristo nell'impero romano*. Rome-Bari: Laterza.

———. 1997. "Sur Costantinople et sa foundation". In *XVII Seminario internazionale di studi storici. Da Roma alla Terza Roma*. Rome: [University material; no indication of publisher and pages].

Sloterdijk, Peter, 2004. *Weltinnenraum des Kapitals. Die Letzte Kugel*. Frankfurt am Main: Suhrkamp.

Solovyov, Vladimir S. 1973. *Il problema dell'ecumenismo*. Ed. by Centro Studi Russia Cristiana. Trans. Pietro Modesto. Milan: Jaca Book.

Sordi, Marta. 1996. "*Universalità* e *aeternitas* di Roma." In *XVI Seminario internazionale di studi storici. Da Roma alla Terza Roma*. Rome: [University material; no indication of publisher or pages].

Špidlik, Tomáš. 1995. *L'idea russa: un'altra visione dell'uomo*. Rome: Lipa.

Strada, Vittorio, et al. 1993. *Filosofia, religione, letteratura in Russia all'inizio del XX secolo. Atti del convegno 3–4 luglio 1989*. Naples: Guida.

Taubes, Jacob. 1987. *Ad Carl Schmitt. Gegenstreibige Fügung*. Berlin: Merve.

———. 2004. *The Political Theology of Paul*. Ed. Aleida Assmann et al. Trans. Dana Hollander. Stanford, Calif.: Stanford University Press.

Tocqueville, Alexis de. 1955. *The Old Régime and the French Revolution*. Trans. Stuart Gilbert. New York: Doubleday.

Toynbee, Arnold J. 1959. *Hellenism: The History of a Civilization*. Oxford: Oxford University Press.

———. 1965. *Hannibal's Legacy: The Hannibalic War's Effects on Roman Life*. Oxford: Oxford University Press.

Turcan, Robert. 1991. "Lois romaines, dieux étrangers et 'religion d'Etat.'" In *XI Seminario internazionale di studi storici. Da Roma alla terza Roma*. Rome: [University material; no indication of publisher and pages].

Valéry, Paul. 1957. "Inspiration méditerranénnes." In *Variété, Oeuvres*, ed. Jean Hytier, 1:1096. Paris.

Valle, Roberto. 1990. *Dostoevskij politico e i suoi interpreti. L'esodo dall'Occidente.* Intro. Vittorio Strada. Rome: Archivio Guido Izzi.

Virgil. 1971. *Aeneid.* Trans. Allen Mandelbaum. Berkeley: University of California Press.

Walde, Alois, and Johann Baptist Hofmann. 1938–1956. *Lateinisches etymologisches Wörterbuch.* Heidelberg: Winter.

Weil, Simone. 1993. *Quaderni,* vol. 4. Ed. Giancarlo Gaeta. Milan: Adelphi.

Williams, William A. 2011. *The Contours of American History* (1961). 2nd ed. with an intro. by Greg Grandin. New York: Verso.

———. 1972. *From Colony to Empire: Essays in the History of American Foreign Relations.* New York: Wiley.

Zambrano, María. 1955. *El hombre y lo divino.* Buenos Aires: Fondo de cultura económica. Repr. Madrid: Siruela, 1991.

———. 1956. "Diotima (fragmentos)." *Botteghe oscure* 8, no. 16. Also in María Zambrano. *Hacia un saber sobre el alma.* Madrid: Alianza Tres, 1987.

———. 1965. *El sueño creador. Los sueños, el soñar y la creación por la palabra.* Veracruz, Mexico: Universidad Veracruzana, Facultad de Filosofía, Letras y Ciencias.

———. 1977. *Claros del bosque.* Barcelona: Seix Barral.

———. 1986. *De la Aurora.* Madrid: Turner.

———. 1986. *Senderos.* Barcelona: Anthropos.

———. 1986. "La voz abismática." *Diario* 16, no. 7: 3–8.

———. 1990. *Los Bienaventurados.* Madrid: Siruela.

———. 1996. *Persona y democracia. La historia sacrificial* (1958). Madrid: Siruela.

Zolo, Danilo. 1998. *I signori della pace. Una critica del globalismo giuridico.* Rome: Carocci.

INDEX OF NAMES

Accarino, Bruno, 49
Adorno, Theodor W., 66
Aeschylus, 8, 45,
Agamben, Giorgio, 20, 174, 187
Alexander the Great, 9, 45, 137
Alighieri, Dante, 12, 55, 58, 59, 115, 176, 187
Alvi, Geminello, 134, 182, 187
Ambrose, St., 107, 180
Amoroso, Bruno, 183, 187
Anselm of Canterbury, St., 61, 176
Aquinas, St. Thomas, 17, 66, 175, 182, 187
Arendt, Hannah, 13, 16, 49–53, 144, 175, 187, 189, 190
Aristides of Athens, 148
Aristotle, 8, 17, 45, 102
Asimov, Isaac, 2, 187
Augustine, St., 10, 11, 17, 89, 100, 102, 107, 147, 149, 159, 163, 175, 178, 179

Baccari, Maria Pia, 179, 180, 187
Bacon, Francis, 15
Badiou, Alain, 22, 24, 187
Balibar, Étienne, 16, 174, 187
Barker, Ernest, 3, 187
Bataille, Georges, 19
Battuta, Ibn, 118
Beck, Ulrich, 175, 188
Benjamin, Walter, 1, 67, 173, 192
Berdyaev, Nicolai, 122, 181
Berlin, Isaiah, 68, 177, 188
Bettiolo, Paolo, 183, 188
Blair, Tony, 170
Bloch, Ernst, 178, 188
Bloom, Harold, 182, 188
Blumenberg, Hans, 179, 188
Bodei, Remo, 49
Bolaffi, Angelo, 182, 188

Bonomi, Aldo, 126
Borelli, Vittorio, ix, 185
Brague, Rémi, 183, 188
Brelich, Angelo, 104, 179, 188
Bretone, Mario, 183, 188
Bulgakov, Mikhail, 122
Bush, George W., 166
Buti, Marco, 174, 188

Caesar, Julius, 99, 115, 121, 137, 148, 150, 180
Camus, Albert, 16
Canetti, Elias, 19
Canfora, Fabrizio, 180, 189
Canfora, Luciano, 189
Carnevali, Giorgio, 182, 189
Cassano, Franco, 183, 189
Castronovo, Valerio, 174, 189
Catalano, Pierangelo, 179, 181, 183, 189
Char, René, 18
Charlemagne, 15
Chignola, Sandro, 174, 189
Cicero, Marcus Tullius, 10, 117
Ciprianus (Caecylius Ciprianus), 180
Clark, George, 187
Colinas, Antonio, 184, 189
Columbus, Christopher, 48
Cortés, Donoso Juan, 151, 183, 194
Croce, Benedetto, 22, 178, 189
Croce, Elena, 184

Dainotto, Roberto M., 173, 189
Dal Lago, Alessandro, 49, 175, 189
De Giovanni, Biagio, 176, 183, 189
De Greef, Wulfert, 174, 189
Deleuze, Gilles, 6, 190
Dell'Asta, Adriano, 181
Dempf, Aloys, 179, 190

Derrida, Jacques, 16, 20, 174, 177, 190
Diamond, Jared, 173, 190
Di Leo, Rita, 180, 190
Dilthey, Wilhelm, 184, 190
Dostoyevsky (Dostoevsky), Fyodor, 19,
    181, 196
Dumézil, George, 102, 179, 181, 190
Duque, Felix, 176, 190
Durkheim, Émile, 168
Duso, Giuseppe, 174, 189

Eckhart, Meister Johann, 61
Erasmus of Rotterdam, Desiderius, 59
Esposito, Roberto, 49, 174, 175, 176, 190
Eusebius, 100, 148, 179

Feuerbach, Ludwig, 20
Filoramo, Giovanni, 183, 188, 190
Flores d'Arcais, Paolo, 49
Formenti, Carlo, 182, 190
Fornasiero, Lidia, 185
Forti, Simona, 49, 175, 190
Francis of Assisi, St., 166
Freud, Sigmund, 3
Friese, Heidrun, 175, 183, 190

Gaius, 179, 191
Galli, Carlo, 49, 190, 191
Gentile, Giovanni, 61
George of Poděbrady, King, 167
Giovannoli, Renato, 174, 191
Gorgias, 45
Gossheutschi, Felix, 191
Grande, Edgar, 175, 188
Guattari, Félix, 6, 190
Guéhenno, Jean-Marie, 174, 191

Habermas, Jürgen, 15
Hanson, Jeffrey, 174, 191
Hardt, Michael, 25, 180, 191
Harnack, Adolf von, 178
Harries, Jill, 179, 191
Hegel, Georg Wilhelm Friedrich, 9, 16, 18,
    22, 23, 42, 51, 59, 61, 63, 71–79, 82, 83, 103,
    130, 134, 174–78, 182, 191, 192
Heidegger, Martin, 16, 54, 61, 67, 135, 164,
    175–77, 191
Hell, Julia, 174, 191
Henry, Michel, 20, 174, 191
Heraclitus, 56
Hobbes, Thomas, 12, 155
Hofmann, Johan Baptist, 176, 196
Hölderlin, Friedrich, 18, 176
Horace, 180
Husserl, Edmund, 16, 17, 61

Illuminati, Augusto, 49
Irti, Natalino, 182, 191
Ivan III, 121
Ivan the Terrible (Ivan IV Vasil'evič), 121,
    181, 191

Jefferson, Thomas, 176
Joaquim de Fiore, 75
John, St., 149
John Chrysostom, 149
John of Patmos, 148, 149
Johnson, Chalmers A., 183, 191
Jung, Carl Gustav, 3
Jünger, Ernst, 27, 59, 180, 182, 191

Kant, Immanuel, 17, 61, 112, 177, 198
Kelly, Michael R. 174, 191
Kepel, Gilles, 131, 166, 182, 192
Kierkegaard, Søren, 72, 82, 177, 178, 193
Kojève, Alexandre, 27, 28, 51, 134, 135, 136,
    142, 155, 178, 182, 184, 189, 194
Koselleck, Rheinhardt, 176, 192

Lackner, Stephan, 1, 173, 192
Lamprocles, 29
Lantella, Lelio, 179, 180, 192
Lask, Emil, 20, 174, 193
Le Goff, Jacques, 16, 165–71, 185, 192
Leopardi, Giacomo, 12, 19, 167, 173, 192
Leszczyński, Rafał, 176
Lévy, Jacques, 175, 192
Livy, Titus, 115, 116, 139, 181
Llull, Ramon, 13, 17, 55, 192
Lobrano, Giovanni, 179, 181, 192
López Pina, Antonio, 183, 192
Löwith, Karl, 177, 192
Lucretius, 55
Luiselli, Bruno, 185, 192

Machiavelli, Niccolò, 8, 46, 59, 139, 197
Madison, James, 176
Maisano, Riccardo, 181, 192
Marcion of Sinope, 22, 74, 84, 178, 184
Marramao, Giacomo, 177, 182, 188, 192
Marx, Karl, 9, 24, 61, 72
Masi, Felice, 174, 193
Matthew, St., 69, 146
Mazzarino, Santo, 7, 175, 181, 183, 193
Michelstaedter, Carlo, 177, 193
Miglio, Gianfranco, 175, 193
Minucius Felix, Marcus, 117
Momigliano, Attilio, 116, 180, 193
Morasso, Massimo, 173, 193
Moses, 56
Motyl, Alexander J., 174, 193

Münkler, Herfried, 178, 193
Musil, Robert, 132, 182, 193

Napoleon, 15, 151
Natorp, Paul, 88, 178, 193
Negri, Antonio, 16, 24, 25, 28, 174, 175, 180, 183, 190, 191, 193
Nicholas of Cusa, 13, 14, 17, 61, 182, 193
Nicoletti Michele, 193
Nietzsche, Friedrich, 1, 4, 17, 12, 16–19, 21, 38, 45, 56, 61, 63, 70–72, 85, 108, 173, 175, 177, 193, 194
Novalis, 177

Obama, Barack H., 28
Olivi, Bino, 174, 194
Origen, 18
Orosius, 100, 107, 148
Ortega y Gasset, José, 16, 162

Papa, Emilio R., 174, 194
Parmenides, 8, 160, 174
Paul, St., 10, 11, 22, 24, 59, 74, 145–49, 174, 177–79, 182–84, 195
Pausanias, 29
Penzo, Giorgio, 178, 193
Pelagius, 178
Peter the Great, 121
Pius II, Pope (Enea Silvio Piccolomini), 167
Plato, 8, 9, 21, 45, 48, 55, 61
Plotinus, 164
Plutarch, 29, 105, 194
Poggi, Vincenzo, 181, 194
Pomponius Atticus, 106
Prodi, Romano, 194
Przywara, Erich, 178, 194

Reich, Wilhelm, 3
Riccardi, Andrea, 183, 194
Rodotà, Stefano, 182, 194
Rousseau, Jean-Jacques, 176

Sallust (Gaius Sallustius Crispus), 115, 116
Santaniello, Roberto, 174, 194
Sapir, André, 174, 188
Sartre, Jean-Paul, 16
Savarino, Luca, 49
Scheler, Max, 168
Schmitt, Carl, 6, 8, 11
Semerano, Giovanni, 113, 179, 180, 195

Servius Tullius, 104
Severino, Emanuele, 13, 16, 22, 174, 178, 195
Simmel, Georg, 175, 195
Simmias, 29
Siniscalco, Paolo, 181, 195
Sloterdijk, Peter, 176, 195
Socrates, 8, 29, 31, 194
Solovyov, Vladimir, 122, 181, 195
Sordi, Marta, 179, 180, 195
Spengler, Oswald, 16
Špidlik, Tomáš, 181, 195
Spinoza, Baruch, 9, 17
Strada, Vittorio, 181, 195, 196
Symmachus, 106, 107, 180

Tacitus, x, 113
Taubes, Jacob, 151, 178, 182, 184, 195
Tertullian, Quintus Septimius Florens, 147, 148, 194
Theodore of Mopsuestia, 149
Theodoret of Cyrus, 149
Thomas, St. See Aquinas, St. Thomas
Thucydides, 9
Tocqueville, Alexis de, 15, 19, 27, 38, 51, 195
Tomissen, Piet, 194
Toynbee, Arnold J., 117, 120, 121, 180, 183, 195
Troeltsch, Ernst, 117, 120, 121, 180, 183, 195
Turcan, Robert, 180, 195

Valéry, Paul, 16, 160, 184, 195
Valle, Roberto, 181, 196
Varro, Marcus Terentius, 102
Vaucher, Paul, 187
Vico, Giovanni Battista, 46, 168
Vinogradov, I. A., 181
Virgil, 97, 104, 108, 114, 138, 179, 195, 196
Volpi, Franco, 49

Wagner, Peter, 175, 190
Walde, Alois, 176, 196
Weber, Max, 155, 168
Weil, Simone, 16, 27, 49, 182, 196
Williams, William A., 183, 196
Wojtyla, Karol (Pope John Paul II), 168

Zambrano, María, 16, 17, 20, 54, 60, 159–64, 176, 184, 189, 196
Žižek, Slavoj, 16
Zolo, Danilo, 183, 196

COMMONALITIES

Timothy C. Campbell, series editor

Roberto Esposito, *Terms of the Political: Community, Immunity, Biopolitics.*
Translated by Rhiannon Noel Welch. Introduction by Vanessa Lemm.

Maurizio Ferraris, *Documentality: Why It Is Necessary to Leave Traces.*
Translated by Richard Davies.

Dimitris Vardoulakis, *Sovereignty and Its Other: Toward the Dejustification of Violence.*

Anne Emmanuelle Berger, *The Queer Turn in Feminism: Identities, Sexualities, and the Theater of Gender.* Translated by Catherine Porter.

James D. Lilley, *Common Things: Romance and the Aesthetics of Belonging in Atlantic Modernity.*

Jean-Luc Nancy, *Identity: Fragments, Frankness.* Translated by François Raffoul.

Miguel Vatter, *Between Form and Event: Machiavelli's Theory of Political Freedom.*

Miguel Vatter, *The Republic of the Living: Biopolitics and the Critique of Civil Society.*

Maurizio Ferraris, *Where Are You? An Ontology of the Cell Phone.*
Translated by Sarah De Sanctis.

Irving Goh, *The Reject: Community, Politics, and Religion after the Subject.*

Kevin Attell, *Giorgio Agamben: Beyond the Threshold of Deconstruction.*

J. Hillis Miller, *Communities in Fiction.*

Remo Bodei, *The Life of Things, the Love of Things.* Translated by Murtha Baca.

Gabriela Basterra, *The Subject of Freedom: Kant, Levinas*.

Roberto Esposito, *Categories of the Impolitical*. Translated by Connal Parsley.

Roberto Esposito, *Two: The Machine of Political Theology and the Place of Thought*. Translated by Zakiya Hanafi.

Akiba Lerner, *Redemptive Hope: From the Age of Enlightenment to the Age of Obama*.

Massimo Cacciari, *Europe and Empire: On the Political Forms of Globalization*. Edited by Alessandro Carrera, Translated by Massimo Verdicchio.

Adriana Cavarero and Angelo Scola, *Thou Shalt Not Kill: A Political and Theological Dialogue*. Translated by Margaret Adams Groesbeck and Adam Sitze.

Emanuele Coccia, *Sensible Life: A Micro-ontology of the Image*. Translated by Scott Alan Stuart, Introduction by Kevin Attell.

www.ingramcontent.com/pod-product-compliance
Lightning Source LLC
Chambersburg PA
CBHW032135020426
42334CB00016B/1176